EASY PIANO

W9-BXG-278

THE BEST BROADWAY SONGS EVER

(800) 876-9777
10075 SW Beav-Hills Hwy (503) 641-5691
733 SW 10th (503) 228-6659
12334 SE Division (503) 760-6881

HAL•LEONARD®
CORPORATION
7777 W. BLUEMOUND RD. P.O. BOX 13819 MILWAUKEE, WI 53213

ISBN 0-7935-0734-0

CONTENTS
THE BEST BROADWAY SONGS EVER

my Funny Valentine

ALL I ASK OF YOU

(From "THE PHANTOM OF THE OPERA")

Music by ANDREW LLOYD WEBBER
Lyrics by CHARLES HART
Additional Lyrics by RICHARD STILGOE

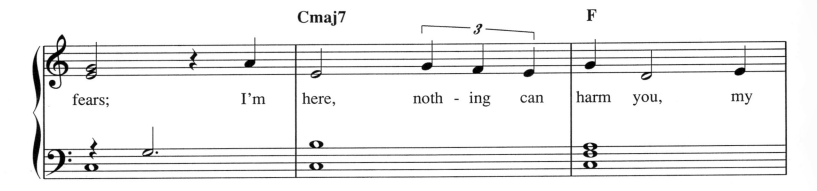

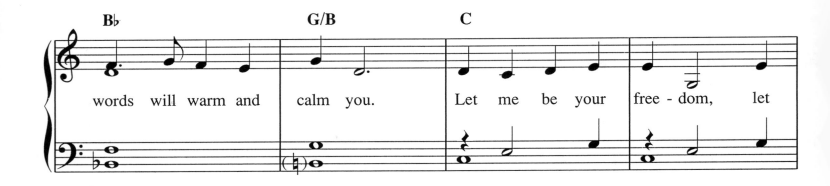

CHRISTINE:

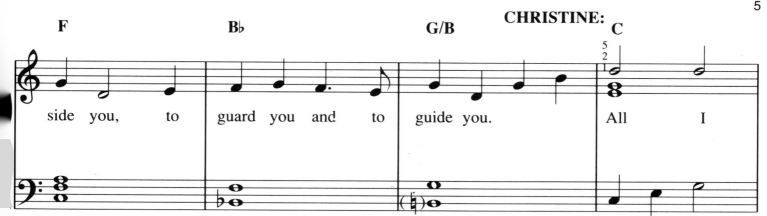

side you, to guard you and to guide you. All I

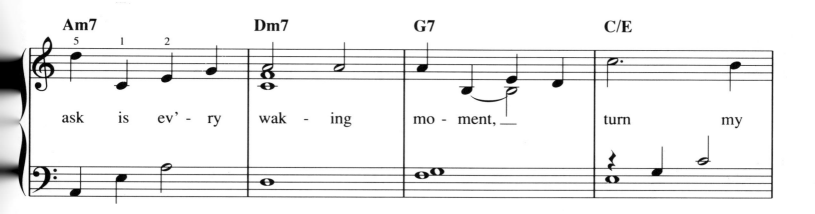

ask is ev' - ry wak - ing mo - ment, ___ turn my

head with talk of sum - mer - time.

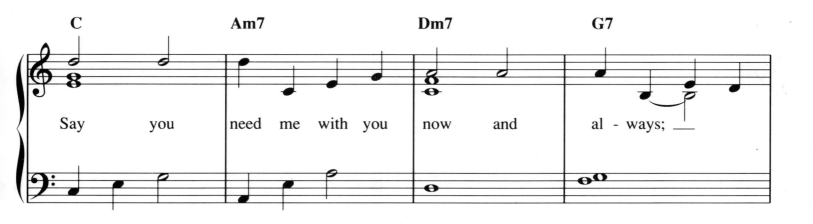

Say you need me with you now and al - ways; ___

C/E   F   C/E   G

pro - mise me that all you say is true, that's all I ask of

rit.

RAOUL:

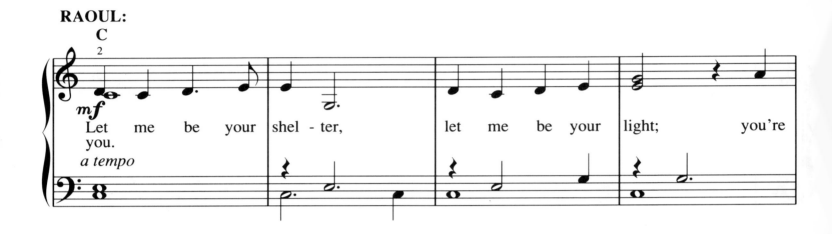

C   Cmaj7   F   B♭

mf

Let me be your shel - ter, let me be your light; you're

you.

a tempo

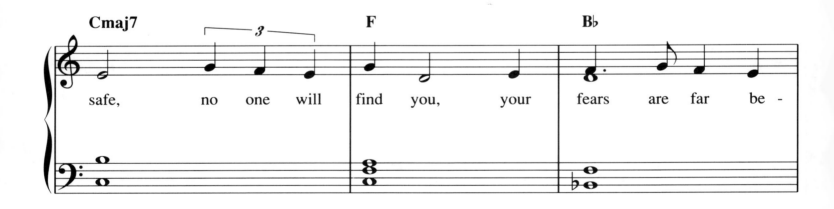

Cmaj7   3   F   B♭

safe, no one will find you, your fears are far be -

CHRISTINE:

G/B   C

hind you. All I want is free - dom, a world with no more

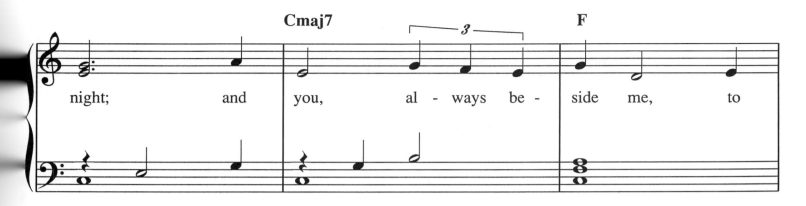

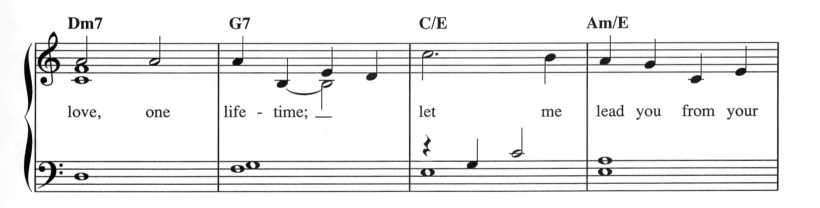

8

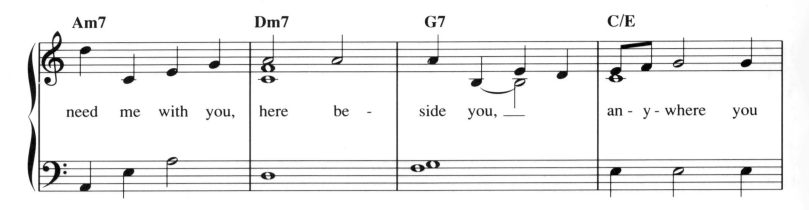

Am7 ... **Dm7** ... **G7** ... **C/E**

need me with you, here be - side you, ___ an - y - where you

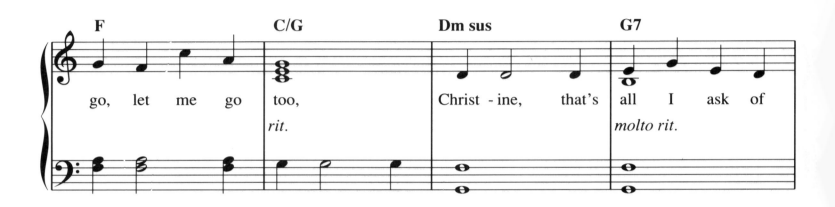

F ... **C/G** ... **Dm sus** ... **G7**

go, let me go too, Christ - ine, that's all I ask of

rit. *molto rit.*

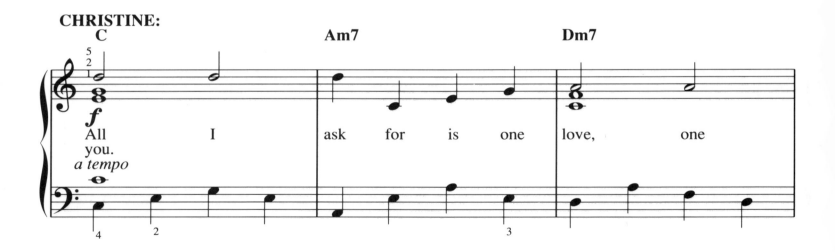

CHRISTINE:

C ... **Am7** ... **Dm7**

f

All I ask for is one love, one

you.

a tempo

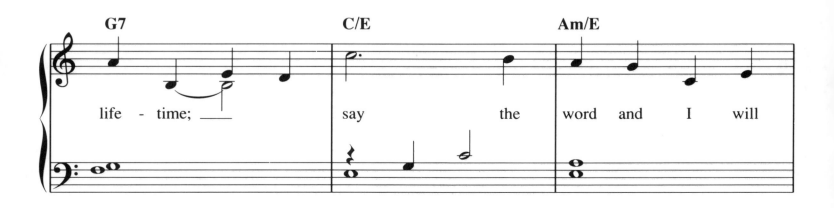

G7 ... **C/E** ... **Am/E**

life - time; ___ say the word and I will

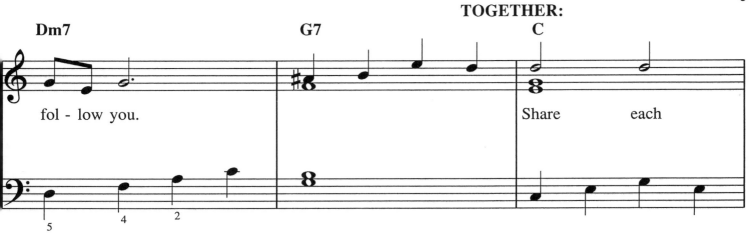

TOGETHER:

fol - low you.

Share each

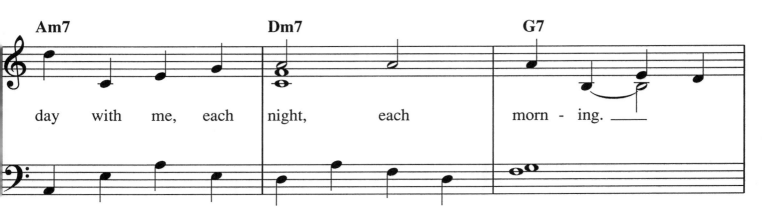

day with me, each night, each morn - ing. ____

Slower

An - y - where you go, let me go too;

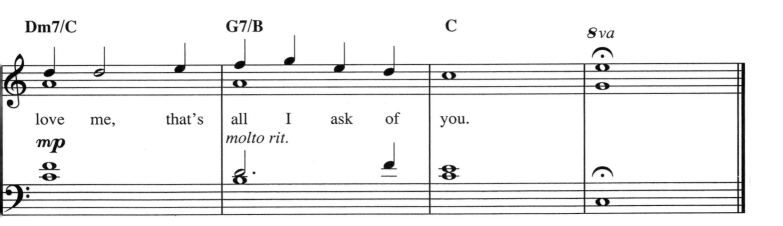

love me, that's all I ask of you.

ANOTHER OP'NIN', ANOTHER SHOW

(From "KISS ME, KATE")

Words and Music by
COLE PORTER

Brightly, in 2 (= 1 beat)

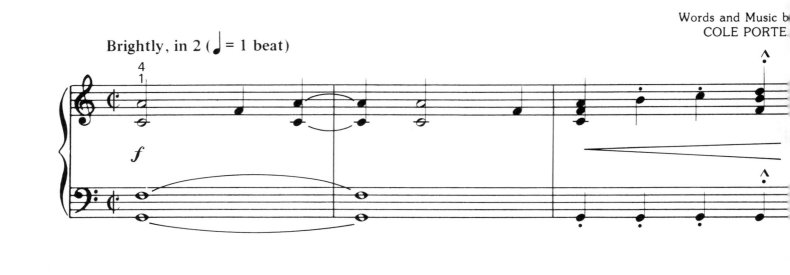

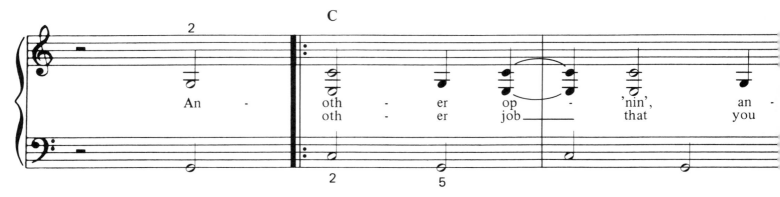

An -
oth -   er   op -   'nin',   an   you
oth -   er   job   that

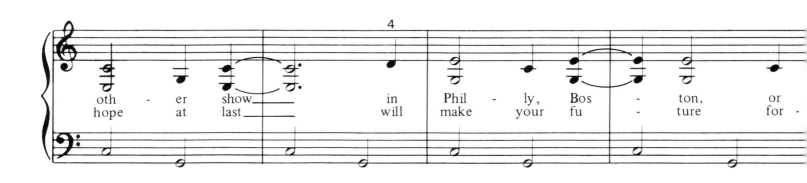

oth -   er   show   in   Phil -   ly,   Bos -   ton,   or
hope   at   last   will   make   your   fu -   ture   for -

Balt -   i -   mo'e,   A   chance   for   stage   folks   to
get   your   past,   An -   oth -   er   pain   where   the

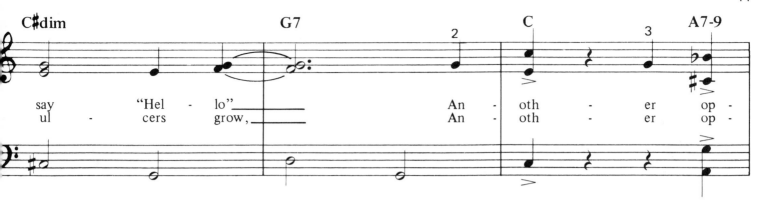

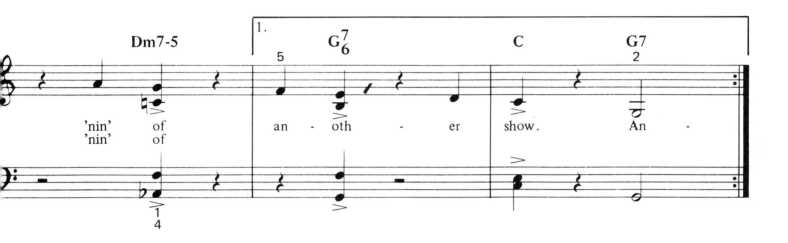

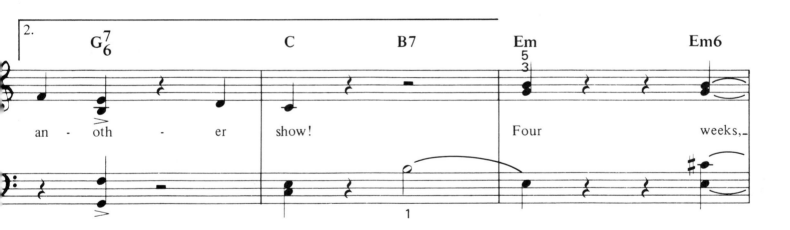

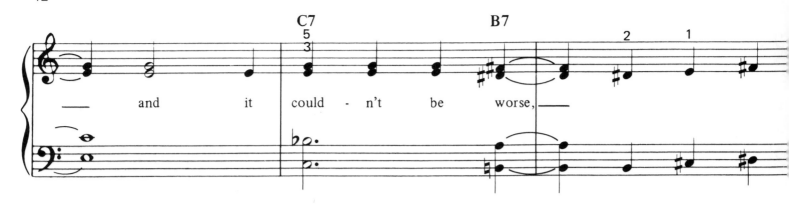

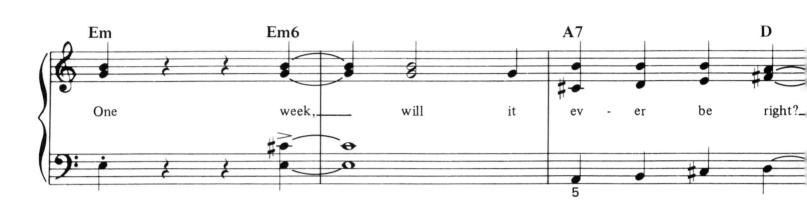

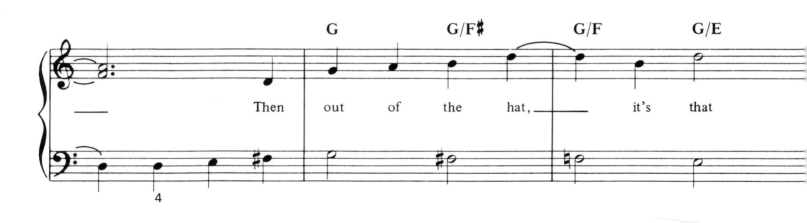

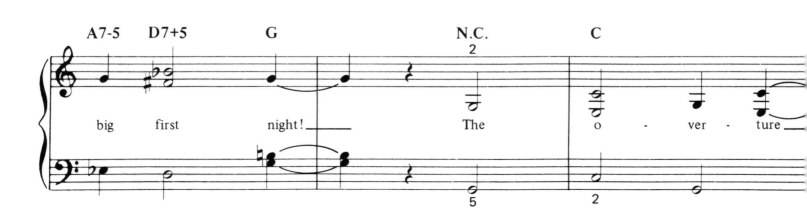

is a - bout to start,____ you cross your fin -

- gers and hold your heart.____ It's cur - tain time.__

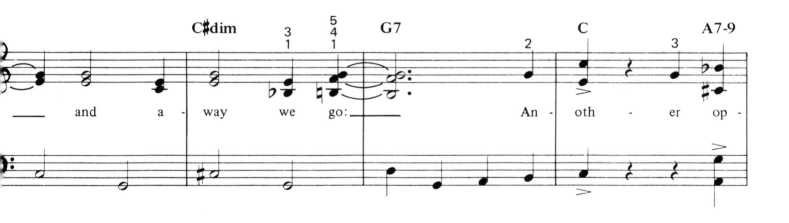

C#dim — G7 — C — A7-9

____ and a - way we go:____ An - oth - er op -

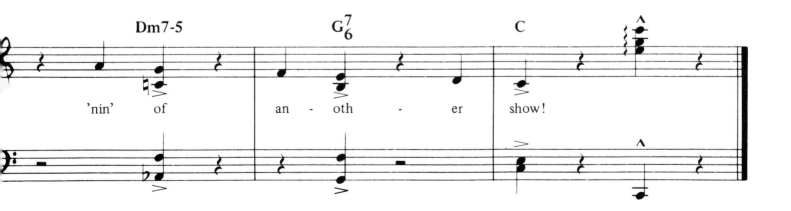

Dm7-5 — G7/6 — C

'nin' of an - oth - er show!

AS LONG AS HE NEEDS ME

(From the Columbia Pictures-Romulus film "OLIVER")

Words and Music by LIONEL BART

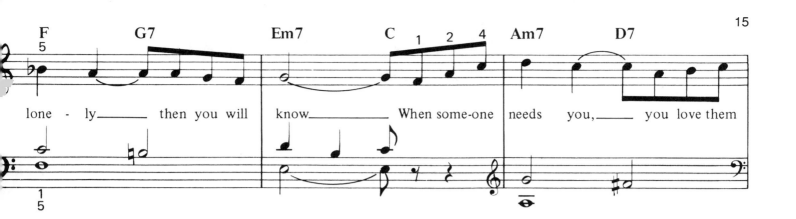

lone - ly_____ then you will know_____ When some-one needs you,_____ you love them

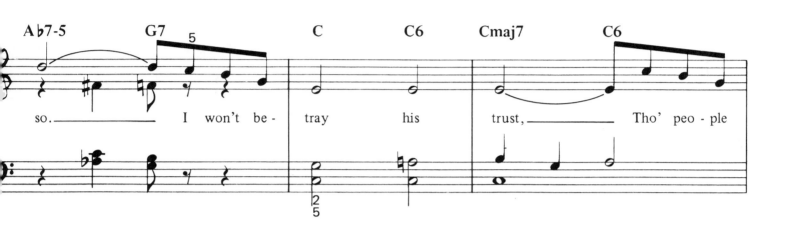

so._____ I won't be - tray his trust,_____ Tho' peo - ple

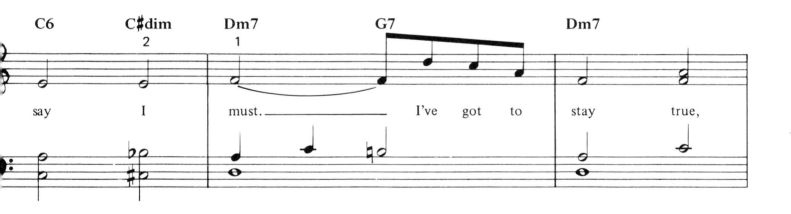

say I must._____ I've got to stay true,

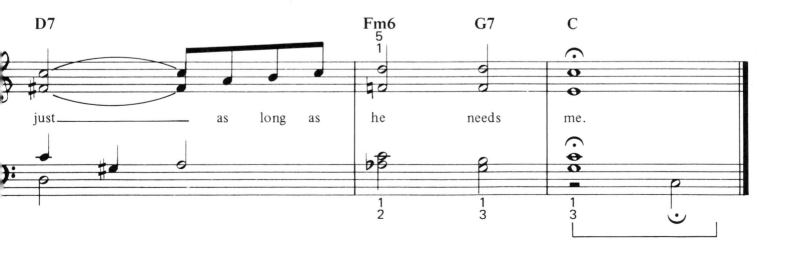

just_____ as long as he needs me.

BESS, YOU IS MY WOMAN

(From "PORGY AND BESS")

Words by DUBOSE HEYWARD & IRA GERSHWIN
Music by GEORGE GERSHWIN

Moderately

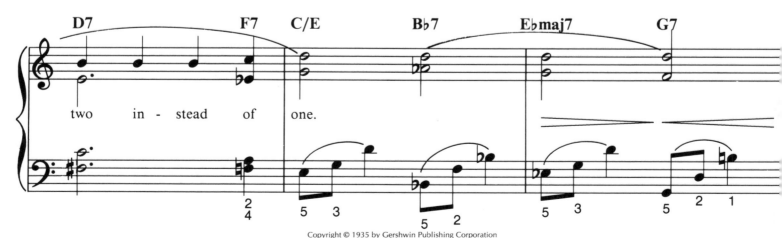

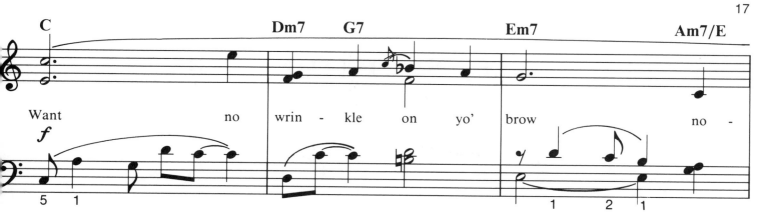

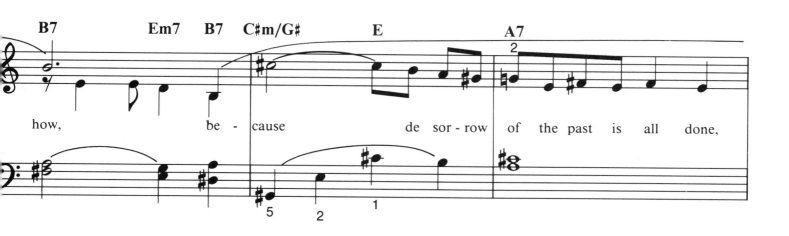

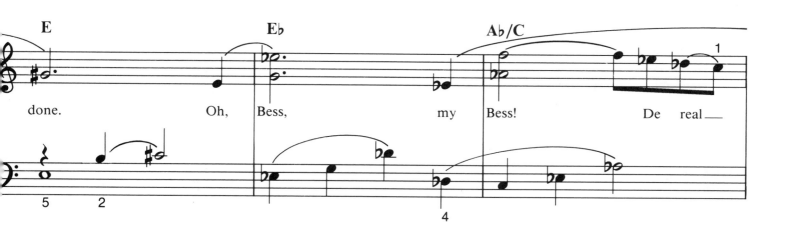

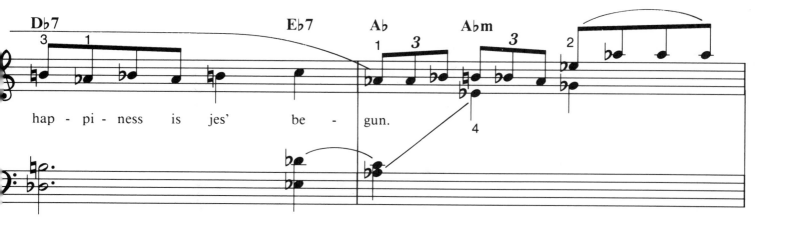

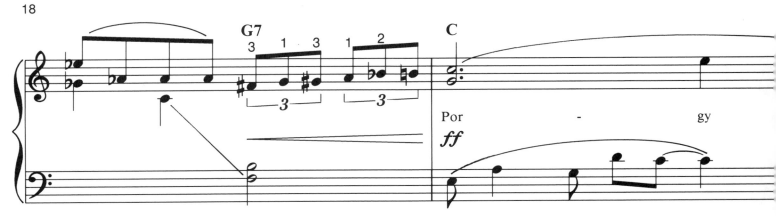

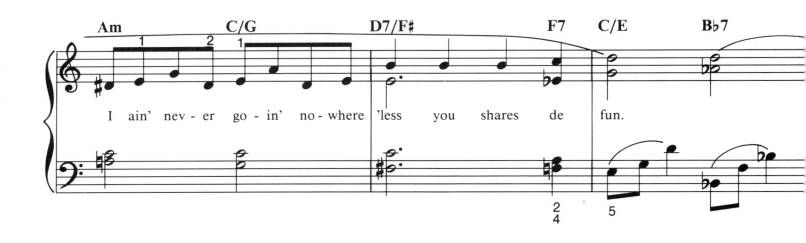

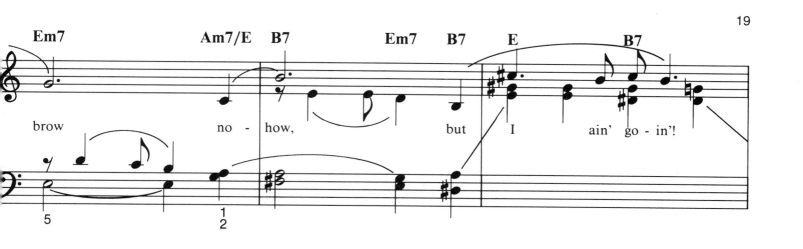

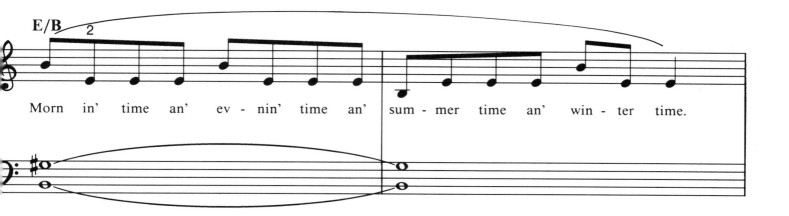

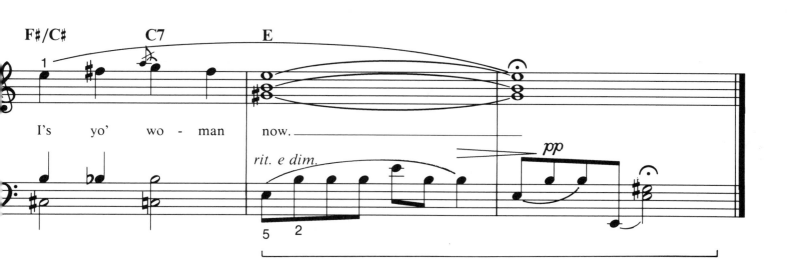

ALL THE THINGS YOU ARE

(From "VERY WARM FOR MAY")

Lyrics by OSCAR HAMMERSTEIN II
Music by JEROME KERN

Moderately Slow (𝅗𝅥 = 1 count)

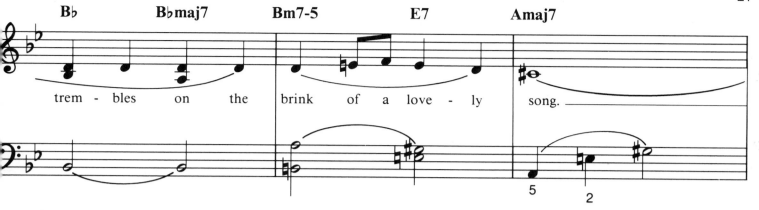

trem - bles   on   the   brink   of a   love - ly   song.

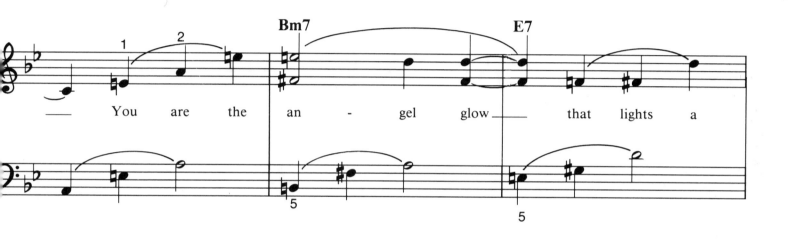

You   are   the   an - gel   glow   that   lights   a

star,   The   dear - est   things   I   know

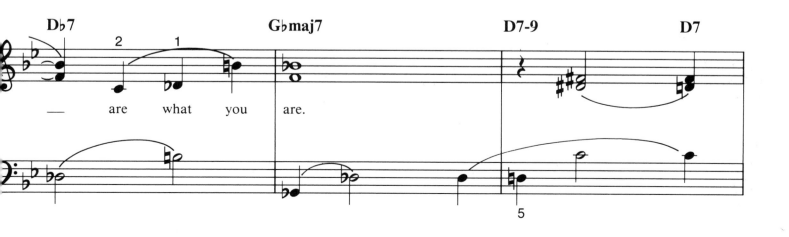

are   what   you   are.

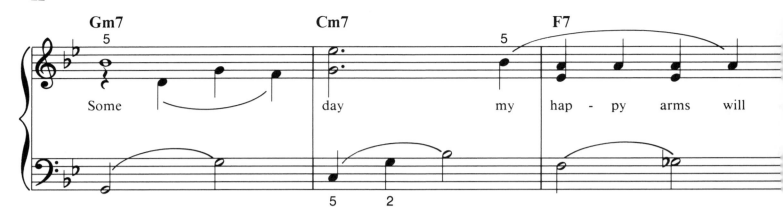

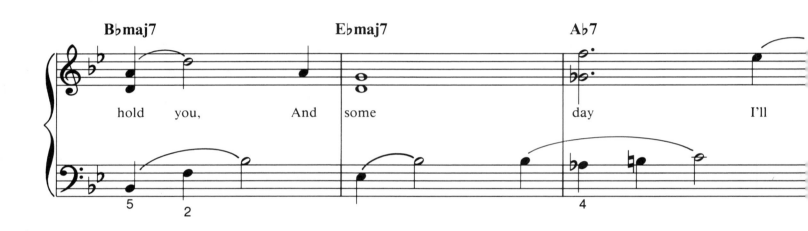

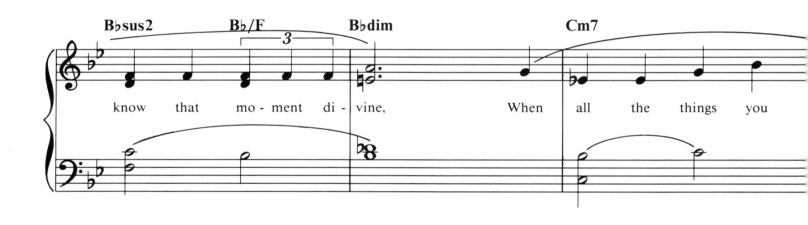

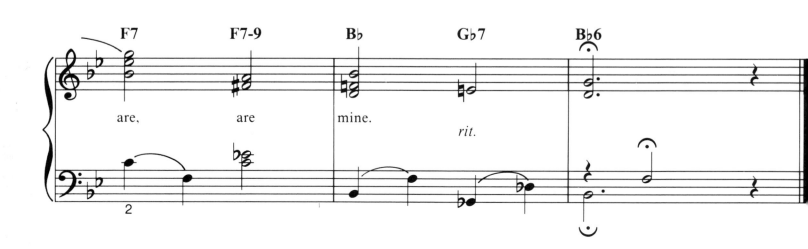

BEWITCHED

(From "PAL JOEY")

Words by LORENZ HART
Music by RICHARD RODGERS

Moderately, in 2 (𝅗𝅥 = 1 beat)

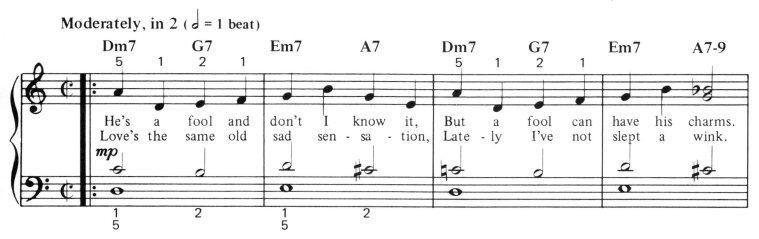

He's a fool and don't I know it, But a fool can have his charms.
Love's the same old sad sen - sa - tion, Late - ly I've not slept a wink.

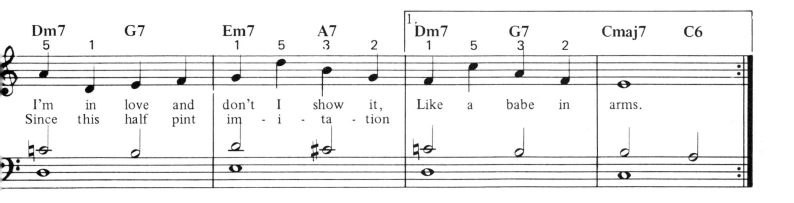

I'm in love and don't I show it, Like a babe in arms.
Since this love half pint im - i - ta - tion

Put me on the blink. I'm wild a - gain! Be - guiled a - gain! A

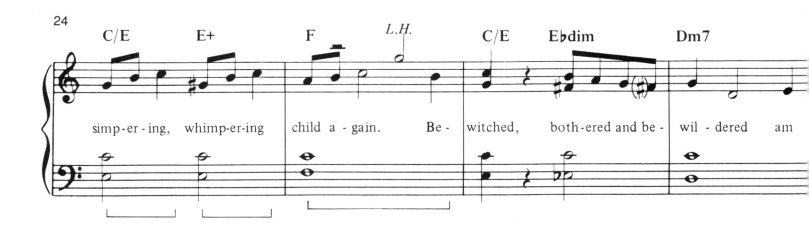

simp-er-ing, whimp-er-ing child a - gain. Be - witched, both-ered and be - wil - dered am

Could-n't sleep And would-n't sleep When

love came and told me I should-n't sleep. Be - witched, both-ered and be- wil - dered am

Lost my heart, but what of it?

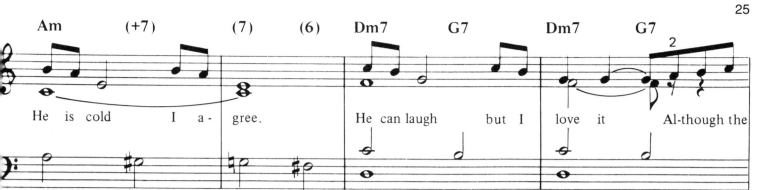

He is cold I a-gree. He can laugh but I love it Al-though the

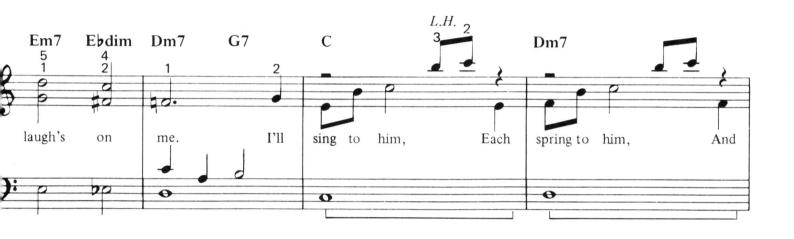

laugh's on me. I'll sing to him, Each spring to him, And

long for the day when I'll cling to him, Be-witched, both-ered and be-wil-dered am

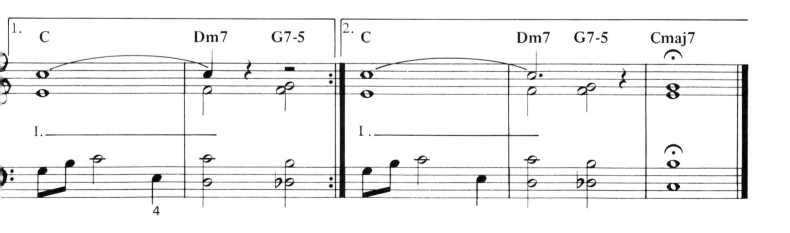

CABARET
(From the Musical "CABARET")

Music by JOHN KANDE[R]
Words by FRED EB[B]

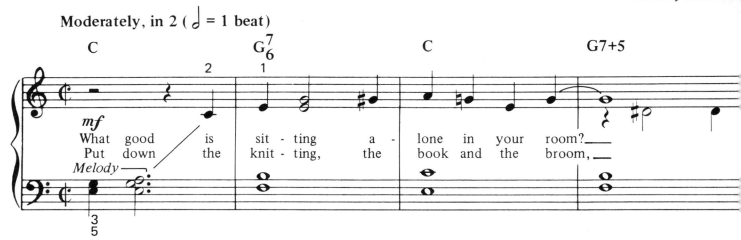

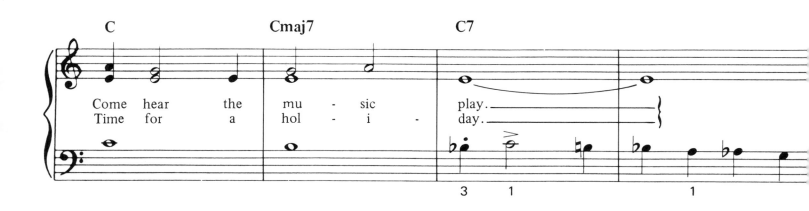

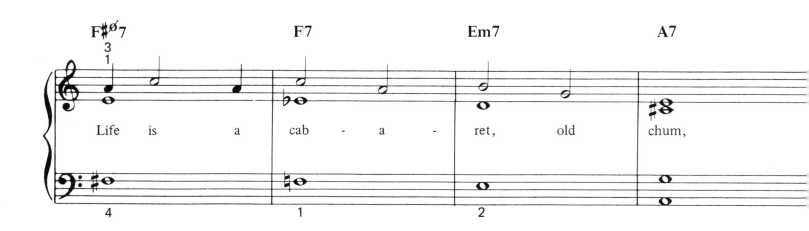

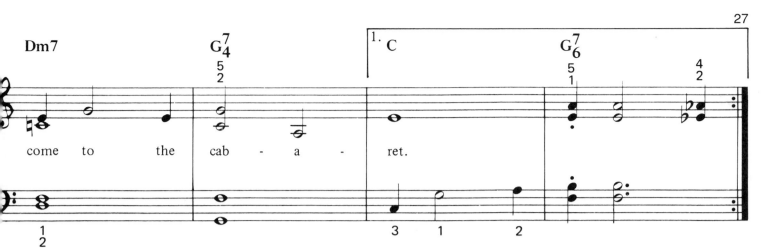

come to the cab - a - ret.

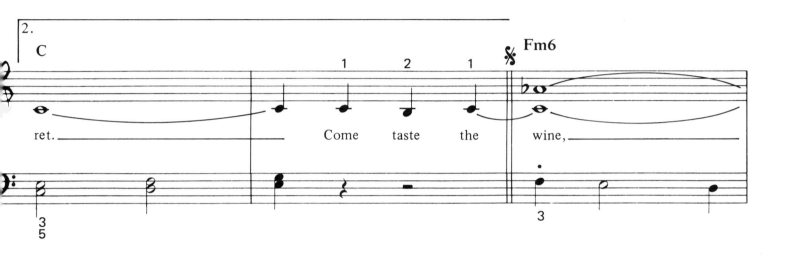

ret. Come taste the wine,

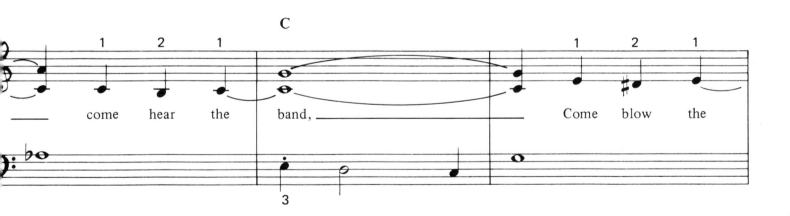

come hear the band, Come blow the

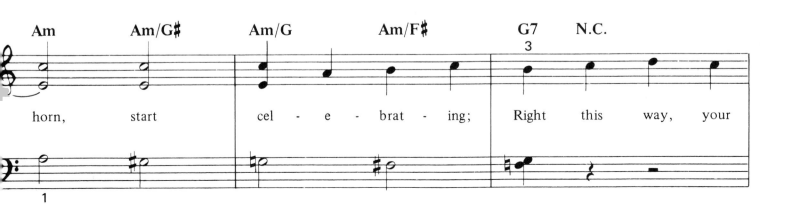

horn, start cel - e - brat - ing; Right this way, your

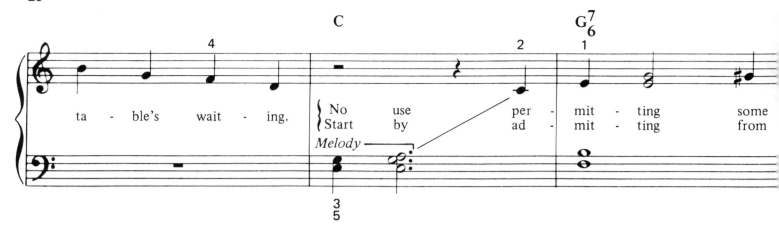

ta - ble's wait - ing. { No use per - mit - ting some
{ Start by ad - mit - ting some from

Melody

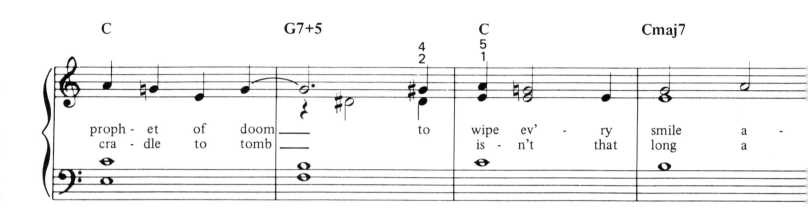

proph - et of doom ___ to wipe ev' - ry smile a -
cra - dle to tomb ___ is - n't that long a

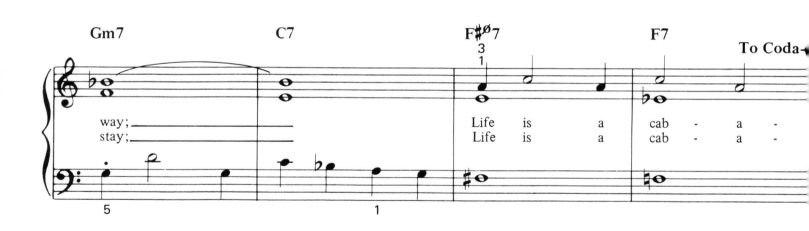

way; ___ Life is a cab - a -
stay; ___ Life is a cab - a -

To Coda

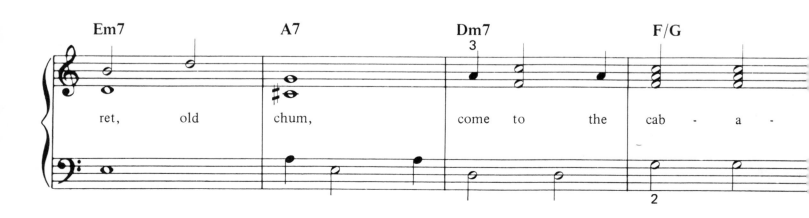

ret, old chum, come to the cab - a -

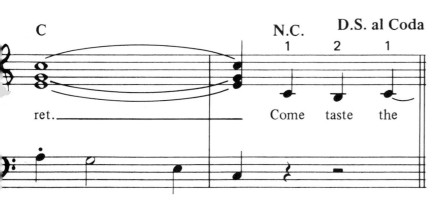

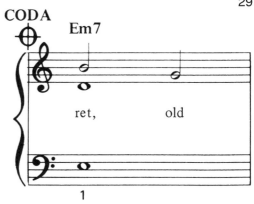

ret._____ Come taste the

ret, old

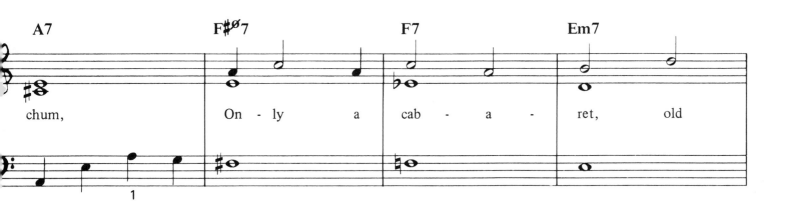

chum, On - ly a cab - a - ret, old

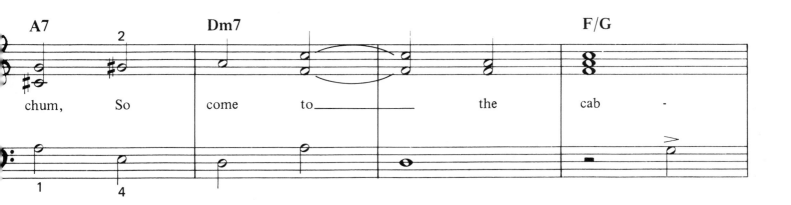

chum, So come to_____ the cab -

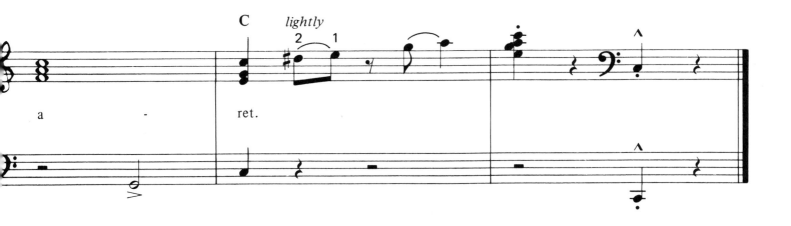

a - ret.

CAMELOT
(From "CAMELOT")

Words by ALAN JAY LERNE[R]
Music by FREDERICK LOEW[E]

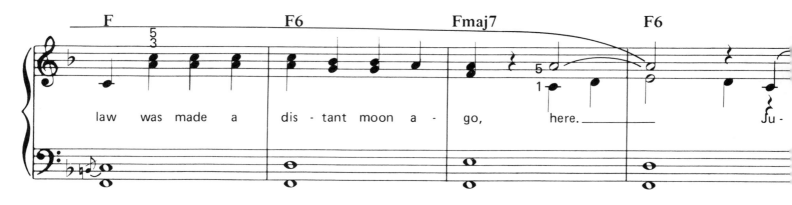

law was made a dis-tant moon a-go, here. _____ Ju-

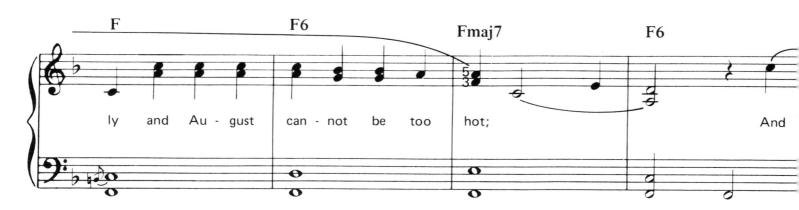

ly and Au-gust can-not be too hot; And

there's a le - gal lim - it to the snow here _____ In

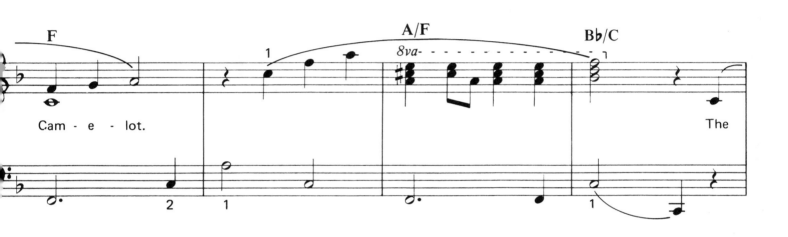

Cam - e - lot. The

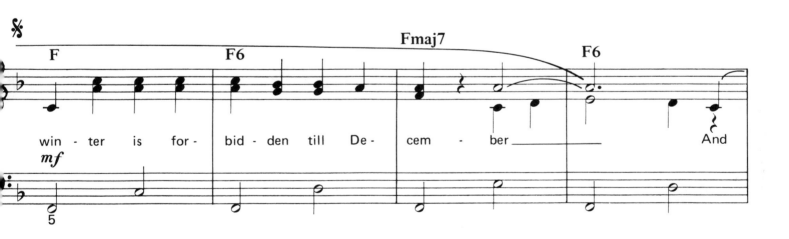

win - ter is for - bid - den till De - cem - ber _____ And

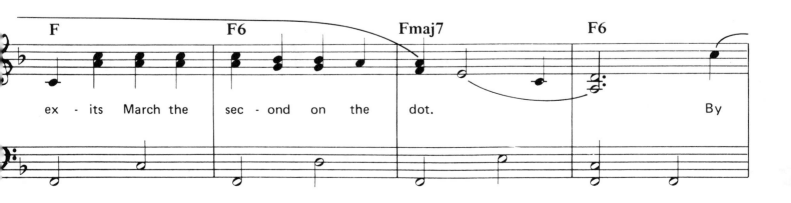

ex - its March the sec - ond on the dot. By

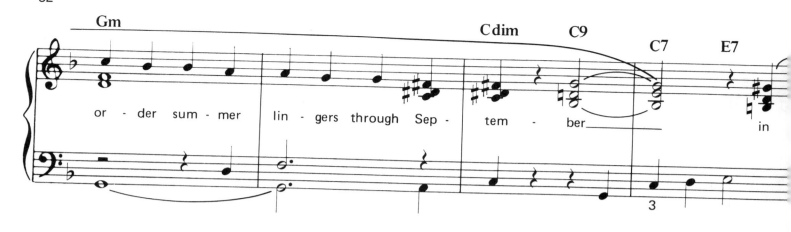

or - der sum - mer lin - gers through Sep - tem - ber___ in

Cam - e - lot.

cresc.

Cam - e - lot! Cam - e - lot! I know it

f

I know it

sounds a bit bi - zarre,

gives a per - son pause,

But in

But in

Cam - e - lot,
Cam - e - lot,

Cam - e - lot,
Cam - e - lot,

that's
those

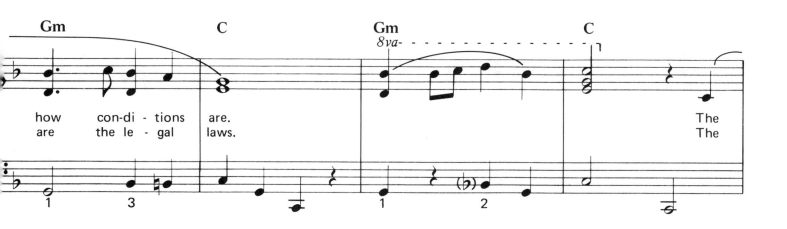

how con-di - tions are.
are the le - gal laws.

The
The

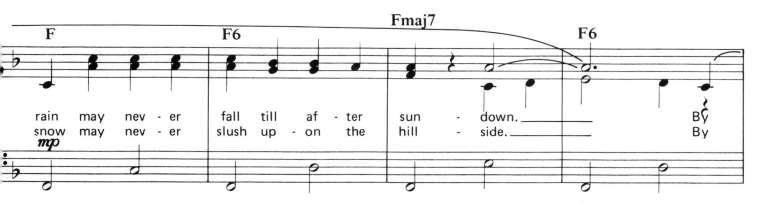

rain may nev - er fall till af - ter sun - down.
snow may nev - er slush up - on the hill - side.

By
By

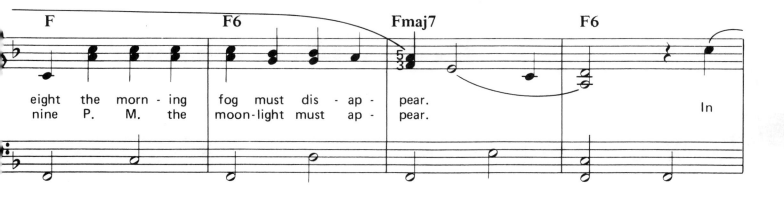

eight the morn - ing fog must dis - ap - pear.
nine P. M. the moon-light must ap - pear.

In

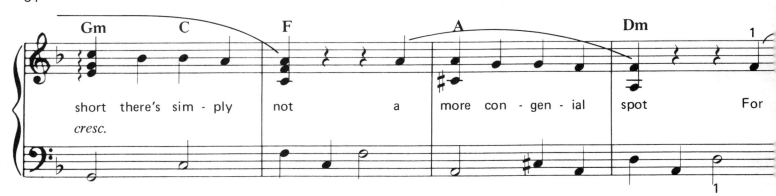

short there's sim - ply not a more con - gen - ial spot

cresc.

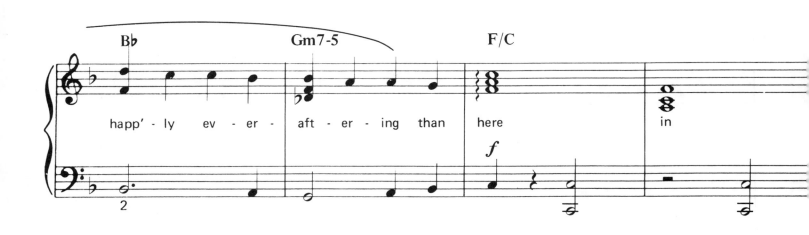

happ' - ly ev - er - aft - er - ing than here in

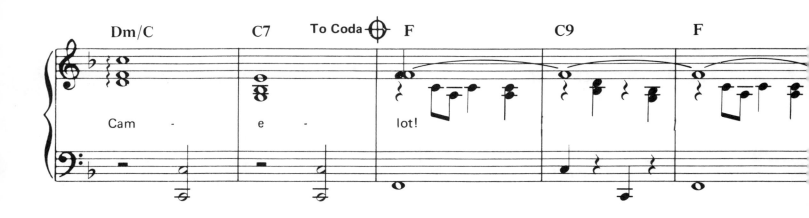

Cam - e - lot!

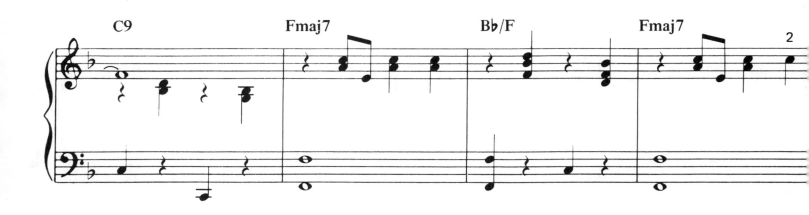

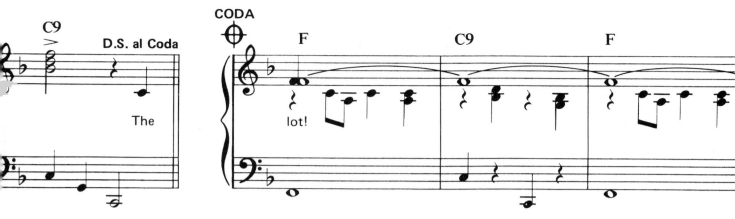

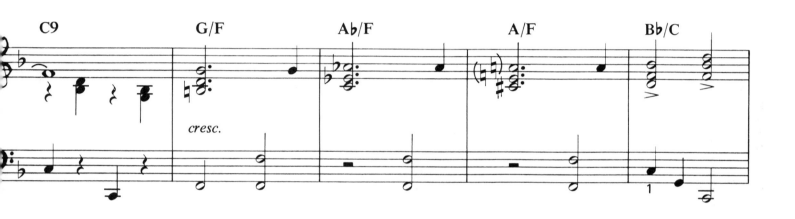

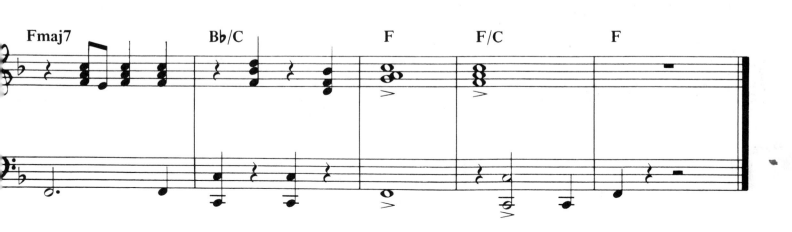

CLIMB EV'RY MOUNTAIN
(From "THE SOUND OF MUSIC")

Lyrics by OSCAR HAMMERSTEIN II
Music by RICHARD RODGERS

Majestically

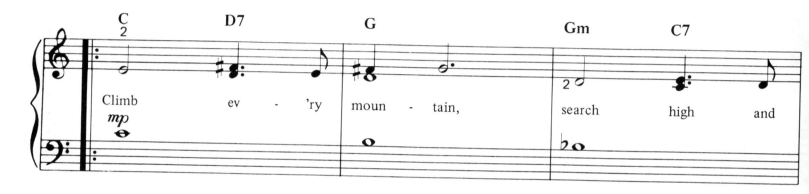

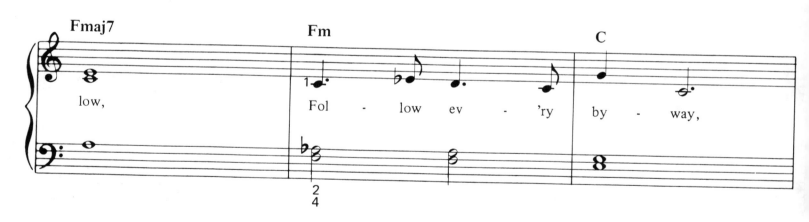

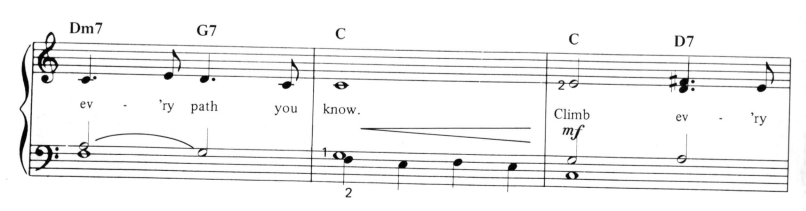

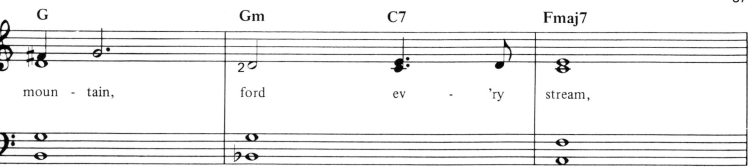

G   **Gm**   **C7**   **Fmaj7**

moun - tain,   ford   ev - 'ry   stream,

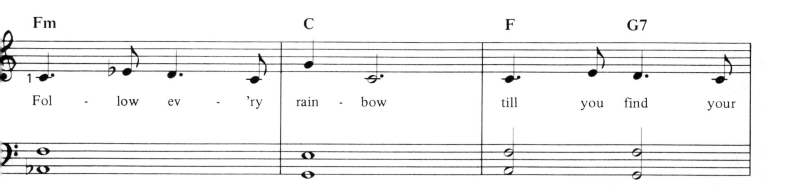

Fm   **C**   **F**   **G7**

Fol - low ev - 'ry   rain - bow   till   you find   your

C   **F**   **Dm7**   **G7**

dream!   A   dream that will need   all the love you can

C   **D7**   **G**

give.   Ev - 'ry   day   of your life

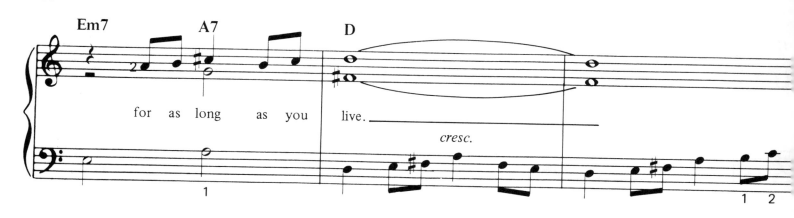

for as long as you live.

cresc.

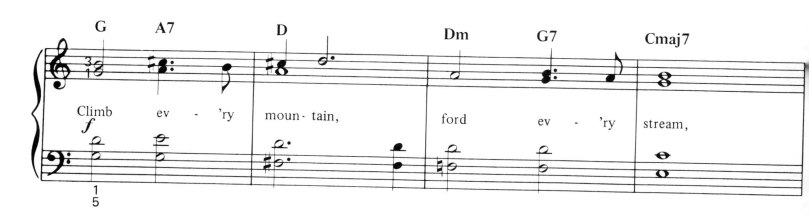

Climb ev - 'ry moun - tain, ford ev - 'ry stream,

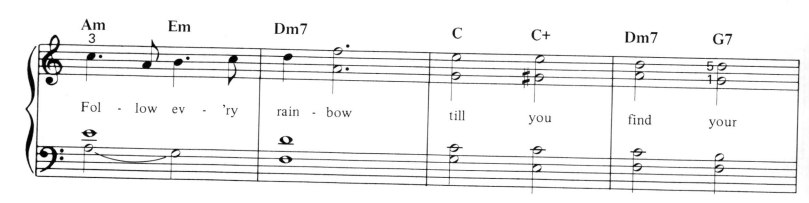

Fol - low ev - 'ry rain - bow till you find your

dream! _____   dream! _____

COMEDY TONIGHT
(From "A FUNNY THING HAPPENED ON THE WAY TO THE FORUM")

Words and Music by
STEPHEN SONDHEIM

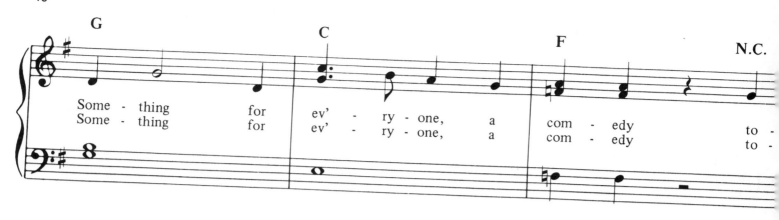

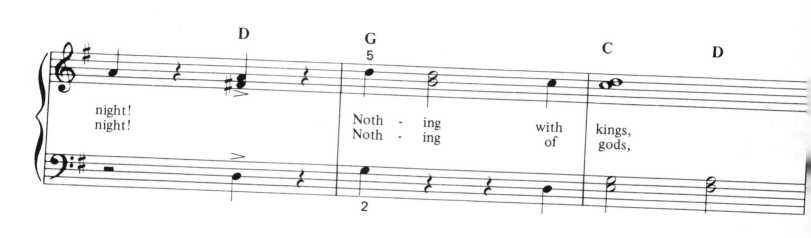

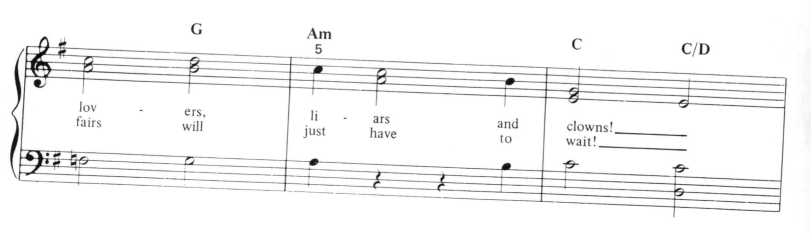

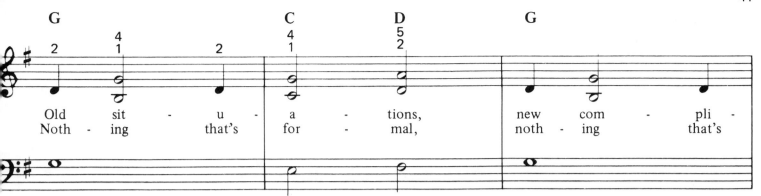

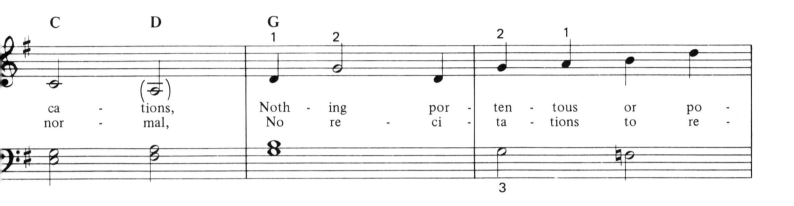

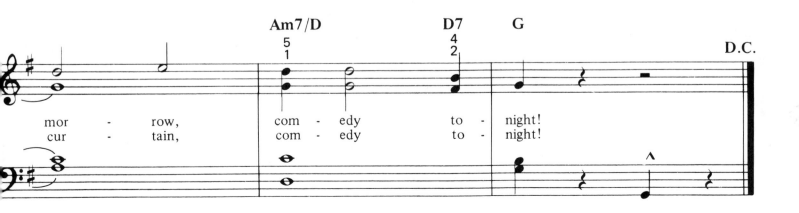

DON'T CRY FOR ME ARGENTINA

(From The Opera "EVITA")

Lyric by TIM RICE
Music by ANDREW LLOYD WEBBER

MCA MUSIC PUBLISHING

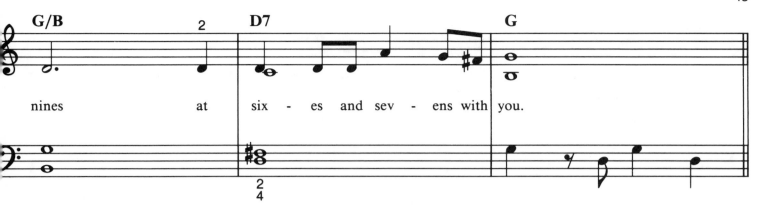

nines   at   six - es   and   sev - ens   with   you.

I had to let it hap - pen, I had to change;   Could - n't
And as for for - tune and as for fame,   I

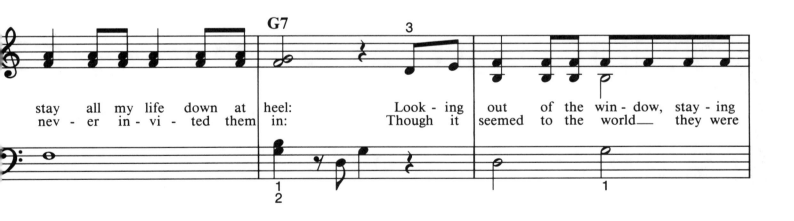

stay all my life down at heel: Look - ing out of the win - dow, stay - ing
nev - er in - vi - ted them in: Though it seemed to the world___ they were

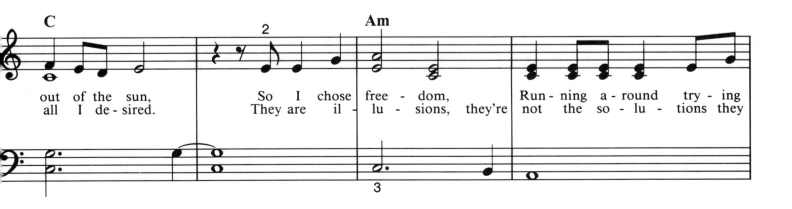

out of the sun,   So I chose free - dom,   Run - ning a - round try - ing
all I de - sired.   They are il - lu - sions, they're not the so - lu - tions they

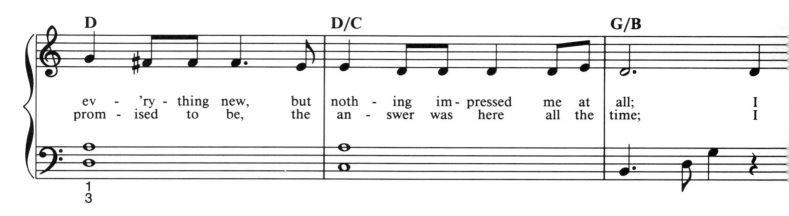

D   **D/C**   **G/B**

ev - 'ry - thing new,   but   noth - ing im - pressed   me   at   all;   I
prom - ised   to   be,   the   an - swer was   here   all   the   time;   I

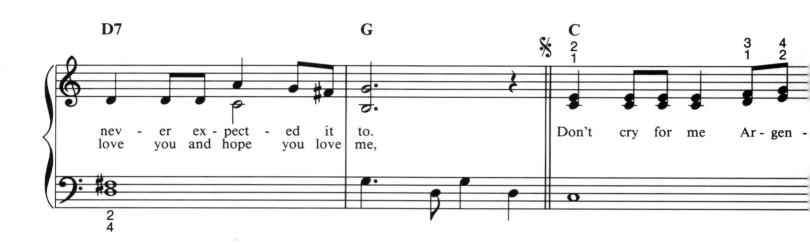

D7   **G**   **C**

nev - er ex - pect - ed   it   to.   Don't   cry   for   me   Ar - gen -
love   you and hope   you love   me,

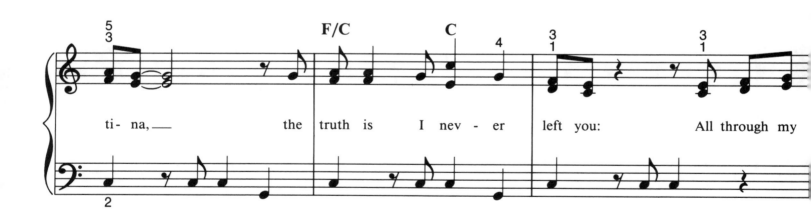

                 F/C   **C**

ti - na,   the   truth   is   I   nev - er   left   you: All through my

G   **Am**   **C**   **To Coda**

wild days,   my mad ex - ist - ence,   I   kept   my   prom - ise,   don't keep your

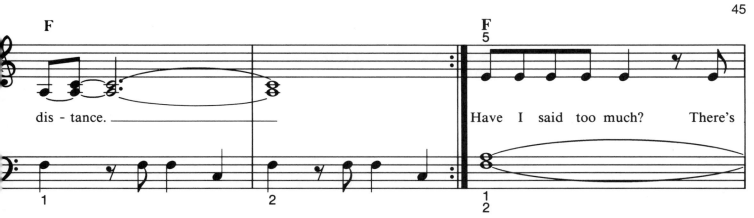

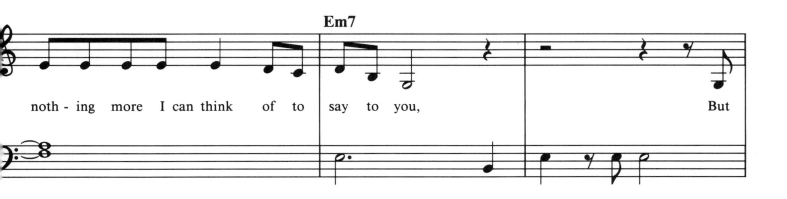

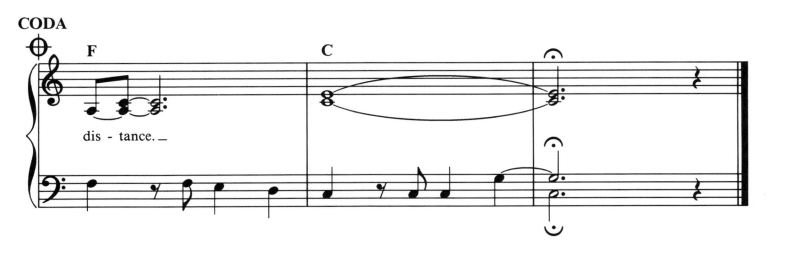

DON'T RAIN ON MY PARADE

(From "FUNNY GIRL")

Words by BOB MERRILL
Music by JULE STYNE

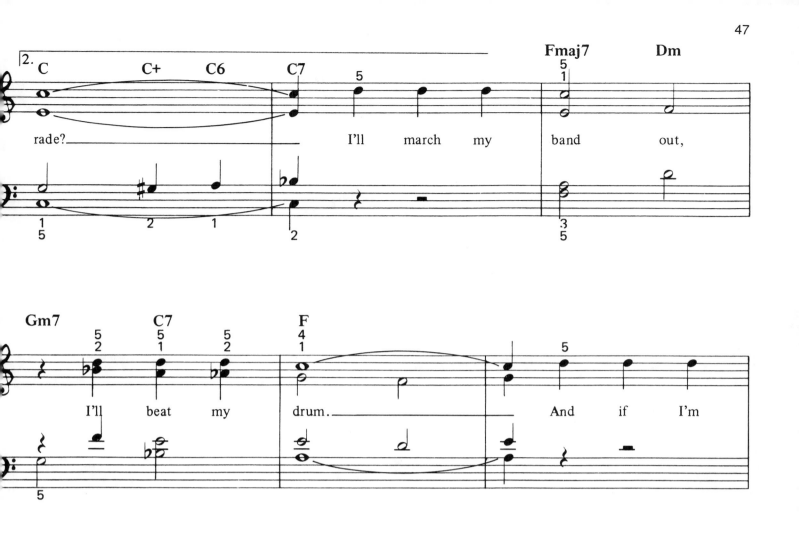

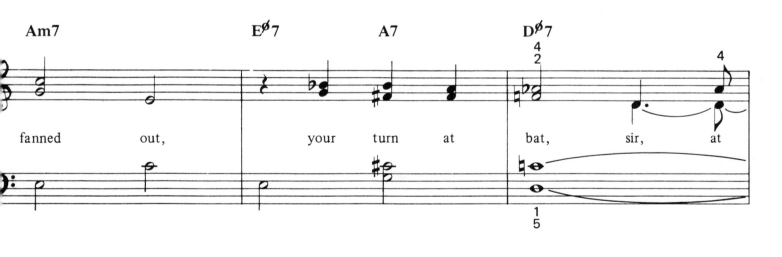

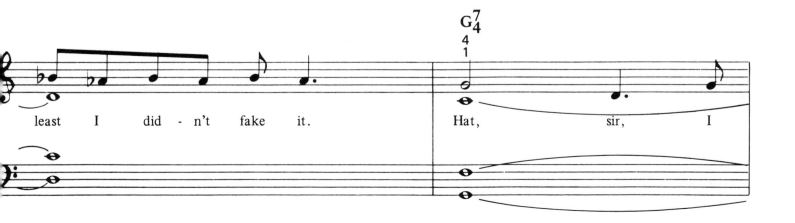

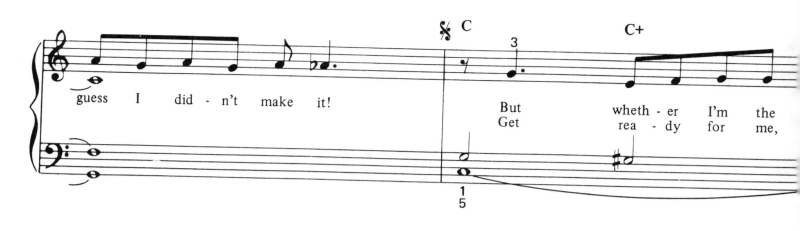

guess I did - n't make it! But / Get

wheth - er I'm the / rea - dy for me,

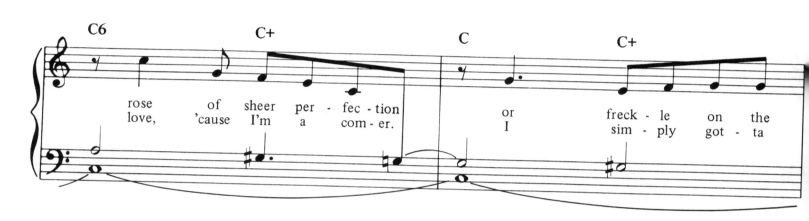

C6 **C+** **C** **C+**

rose of sheer per - fec - tion / love, 'cause I'm a com - er.

or / I

freck - le on the / sim - ply got - ta

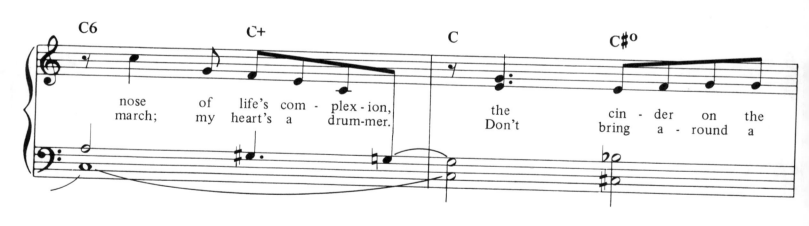

C6 **C+** **C** **C#o**

nose of life's com - plex - ion, / march; my heart's a drum-mer.

the / Don't

cin - der on the / bring a - round a

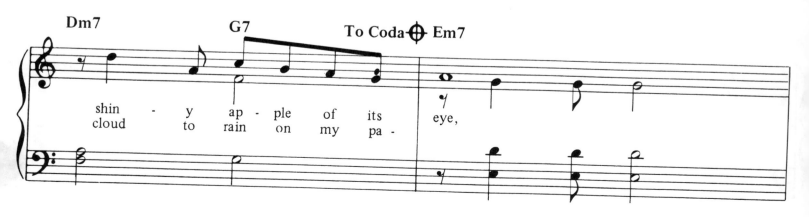

Dm7 **G7** **To Coda** **Em7**

shin - y ap - ple of its / cloud to rain on my pa -

eye,

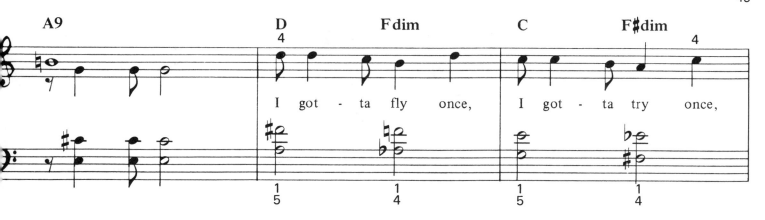

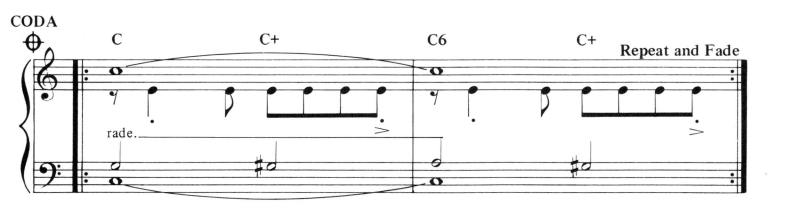

EVERYTHING'S COMING UP ROSES

(From "GYPSY")

Words by STEPHEN SONDHEIM
Music by JULE STYNE

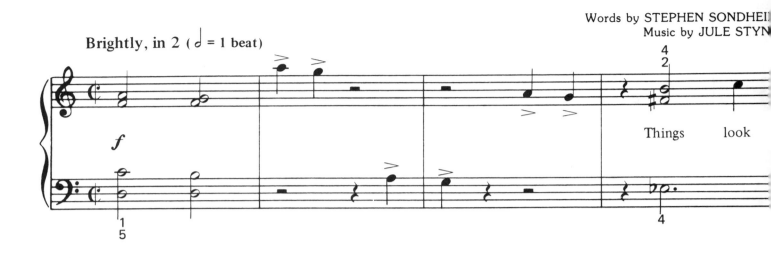

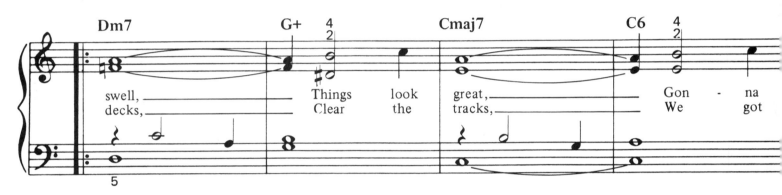

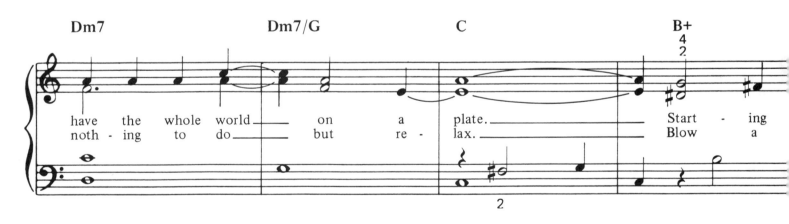

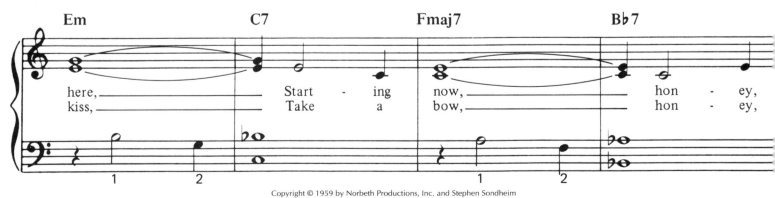

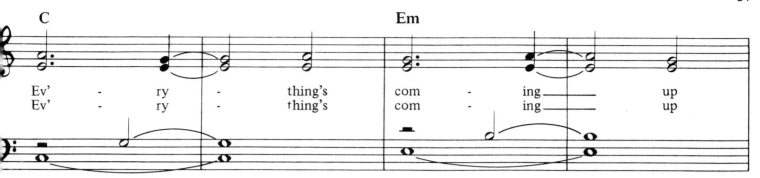

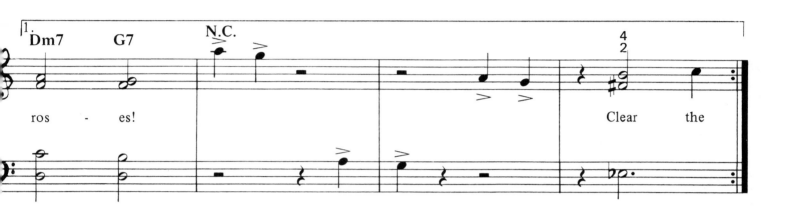

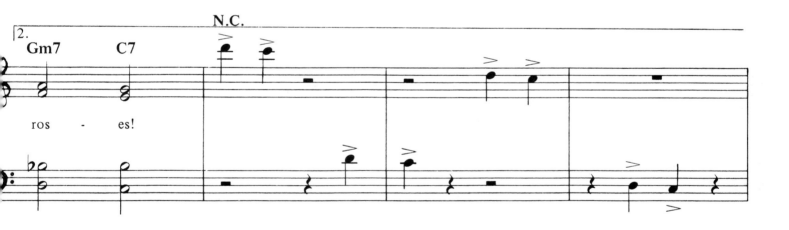

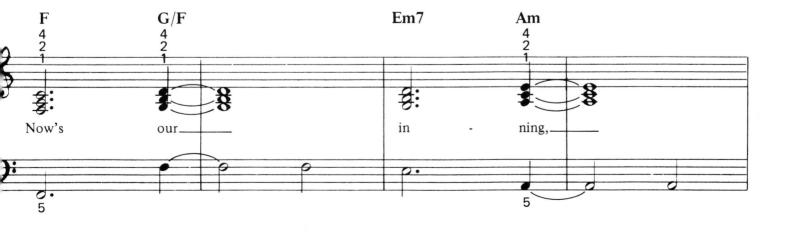

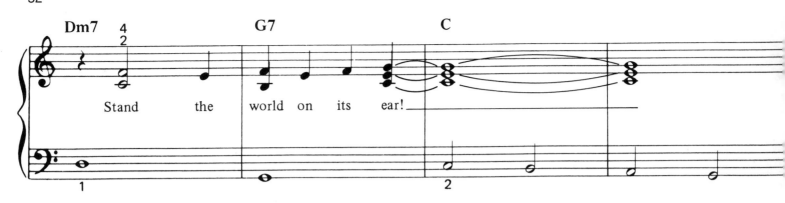

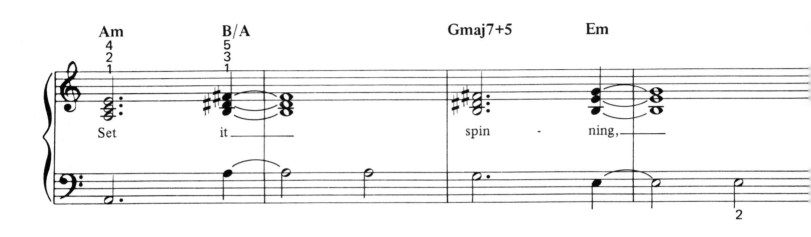

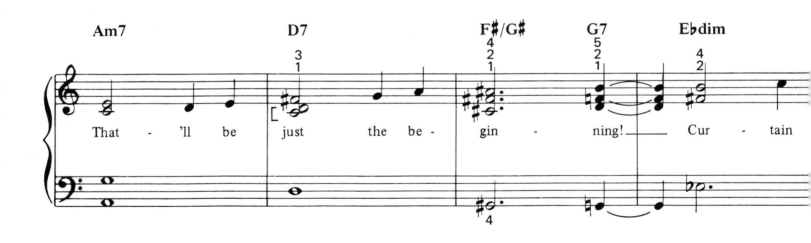

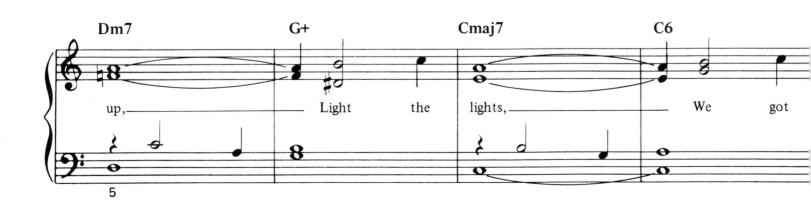

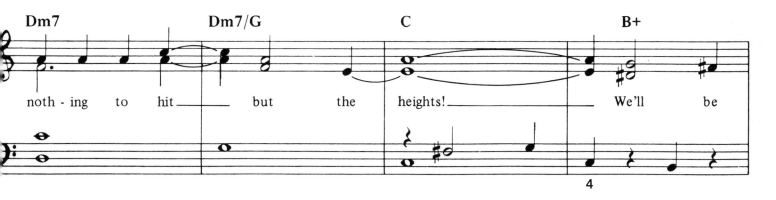

noth - ing to hit ____ but the heights! _____ We'll be

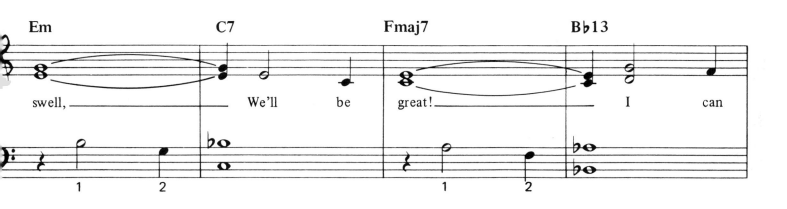

swell, _____ We'll be great! _____ I can

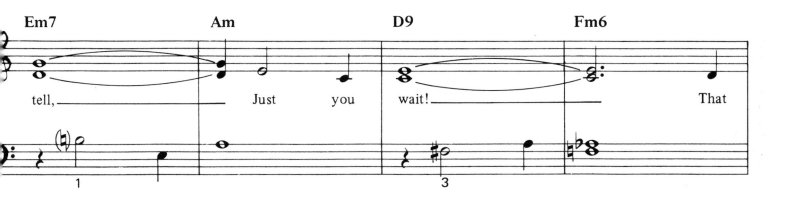

tell, _____ Just you wait! _____ That

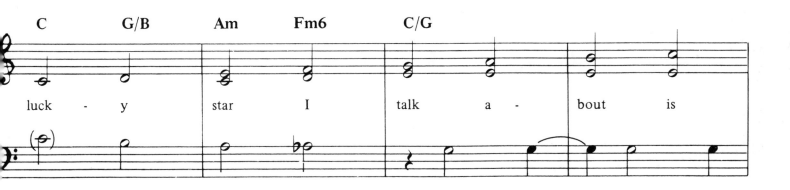

luck - y star I talk a - bout is

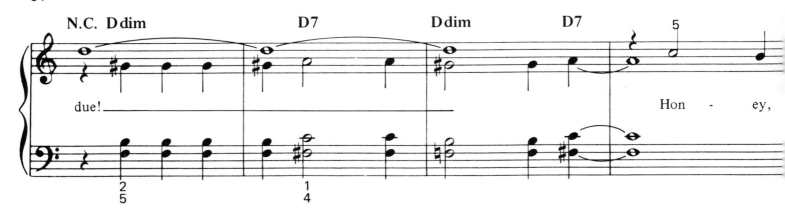

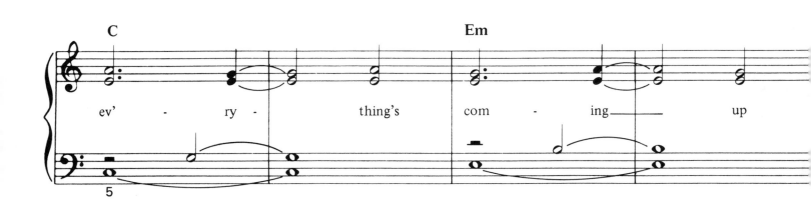

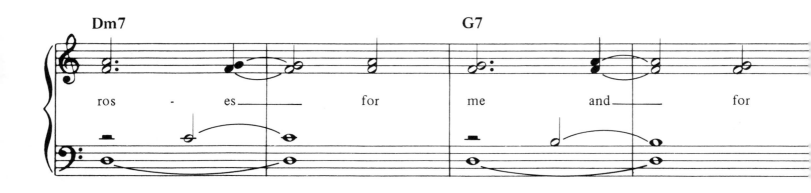

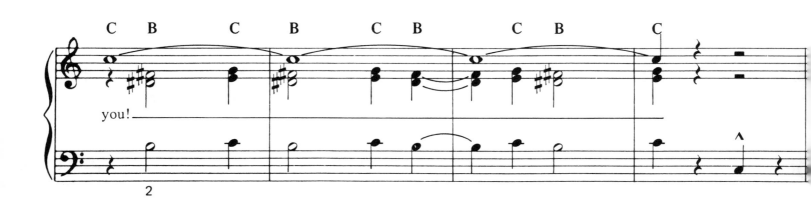

FALLING IN LOVE WITH LOVE

(From "THE BOYS FROM SYRACUSE")

Moderate Waltz Tempo

Words by LORENZ HART
Music by RICHARD RODGERS

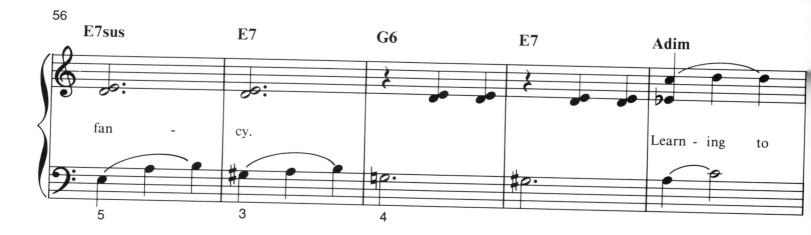

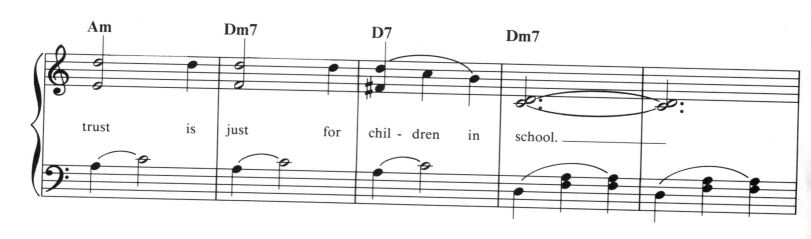

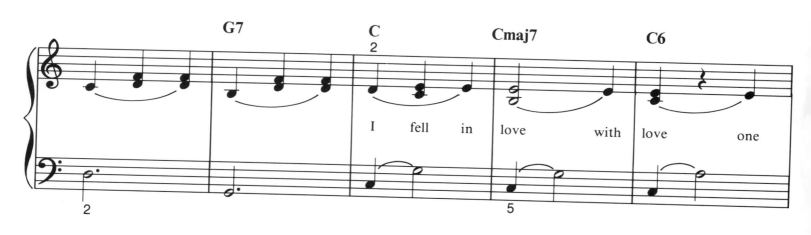

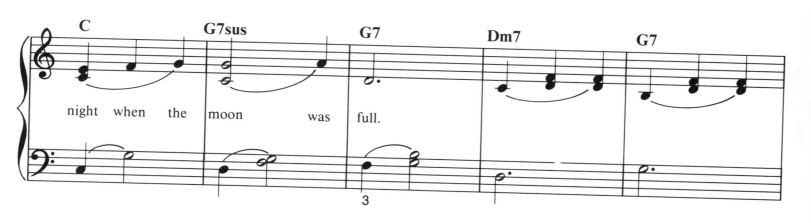

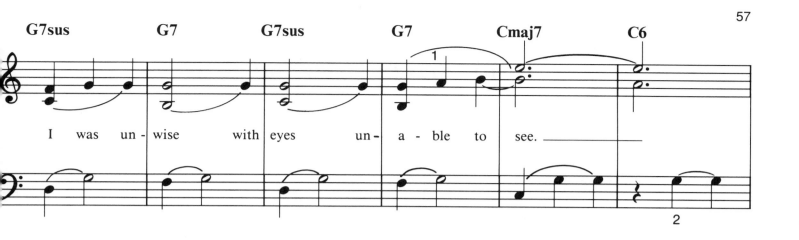

I was un- wise with eyes un- a - ble to see. _____

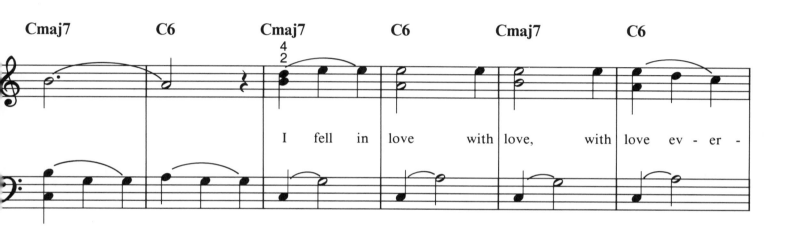

I fell in love with love, with love ev - er -

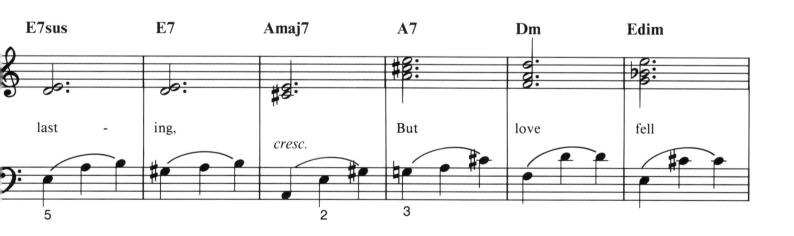

last - ing, *cresc.* But love fell

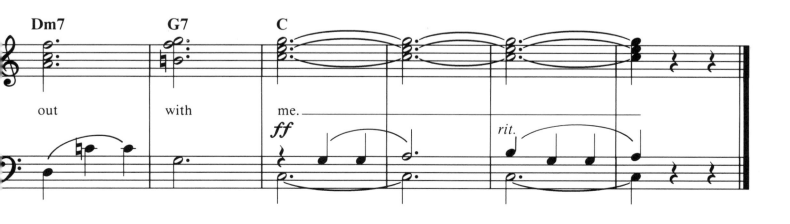

out with me. _____ *ff* *rit.*

FROM THIS MOMENT ON

(From "OUT OF THIS WORLD")

Words and Music b
COLE PORTE

Rhythmically

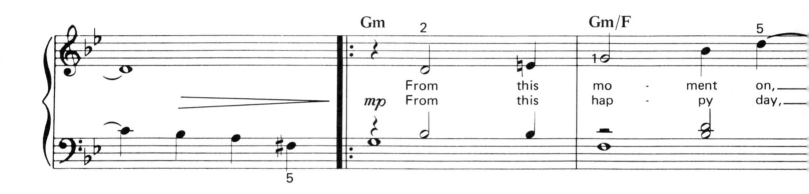

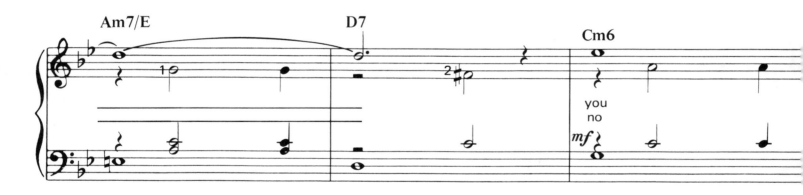

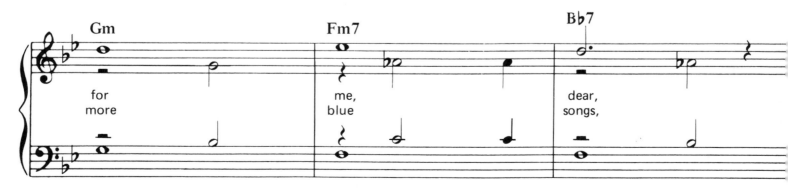

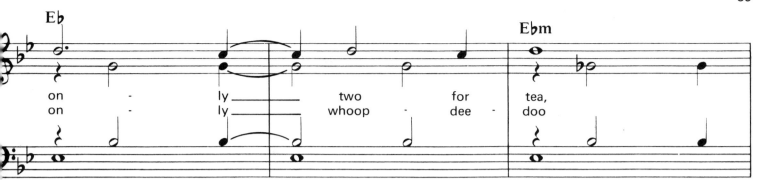

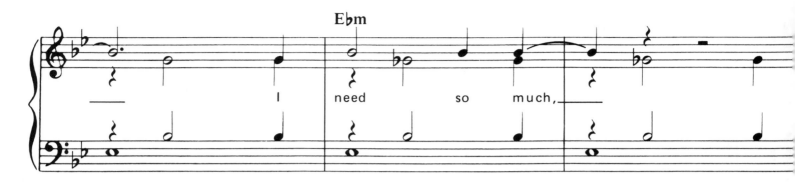

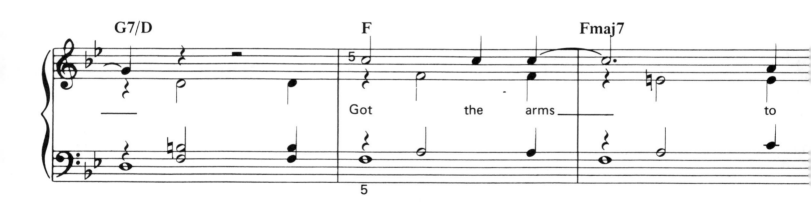

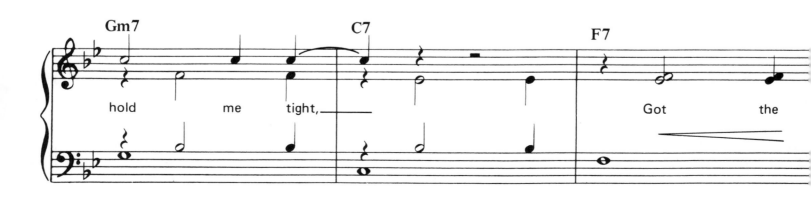

sweet lips___ to kiss me good - night,___

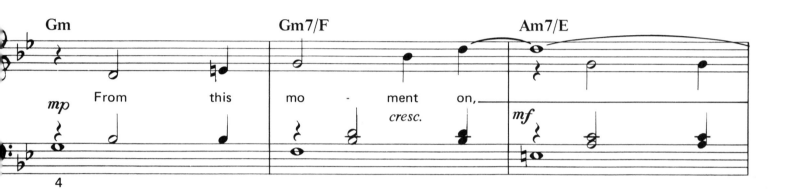

From this mo - ment on,___ you

and

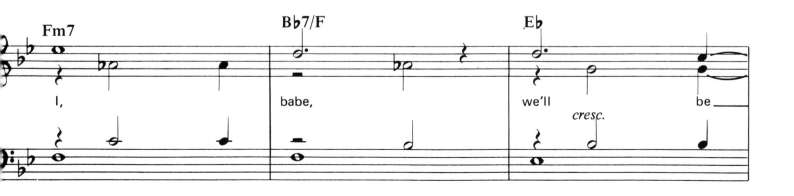

I, babe, we'll be___

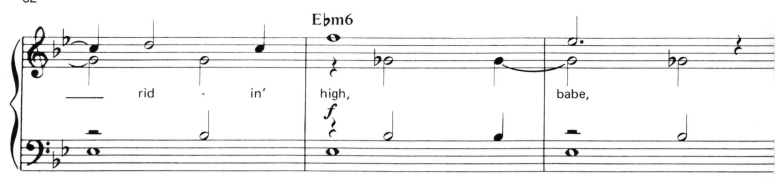

rid - in' high, babe,

Ev' - ry care is gone ___

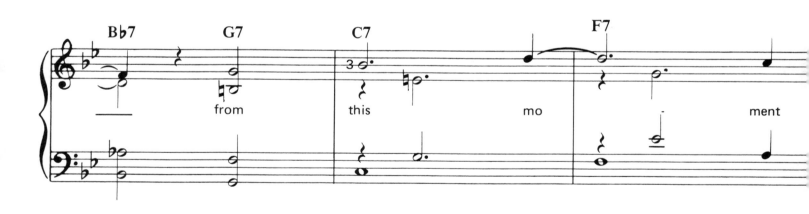

from this mo - ment

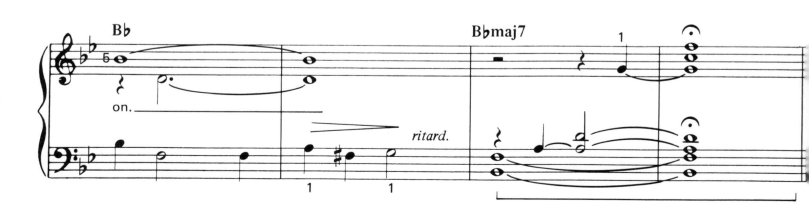

on. ___

ritard.

GETTING TO KNOW YOU
(From "THE KING AND I")

Lyrics by OSCAR HAMMERSTEIN II
Music by RICHARD RODGERS

Without Hurry

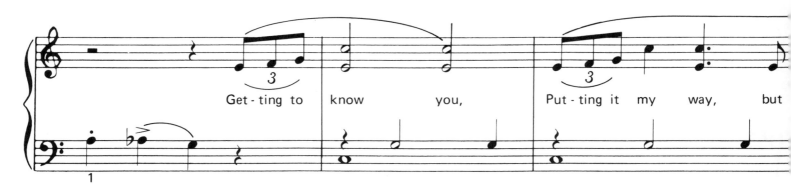

Get-ting to know you, Put-ting it my way, but

nice - ly, You are pre - cise - ly

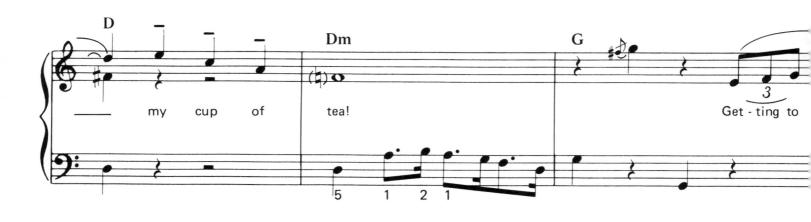

my cup of tea! Get - ting to

know you, get-ting to feel free and eas - y,

When I am with you, get-ting to know what to

say. Have-n't you no - ticed?

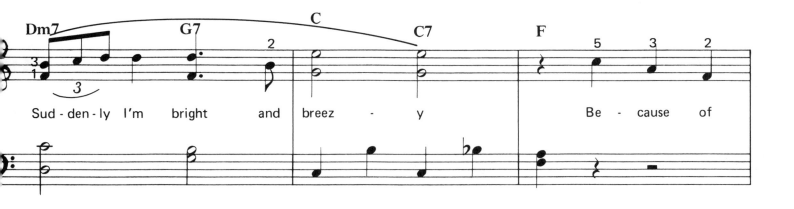

Sud - den - ly I'm bright and breez - y Be - cause of

all the beau-ti - ful and new things I'm

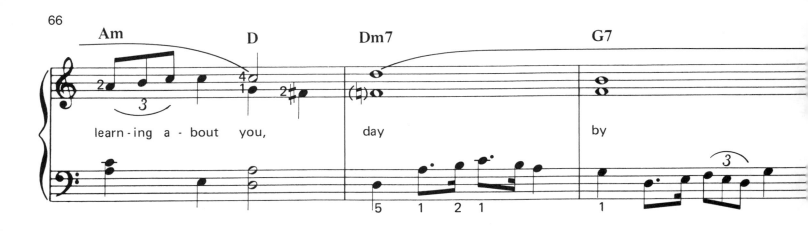

learn - ing a - bout you,   day   by

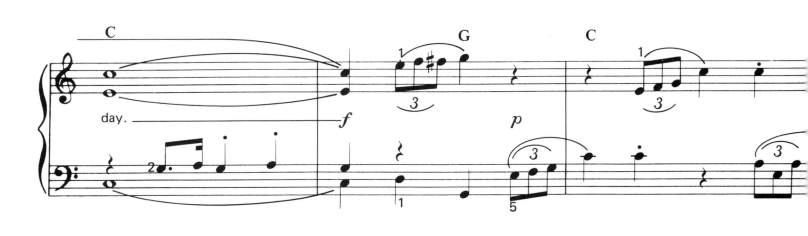

day.

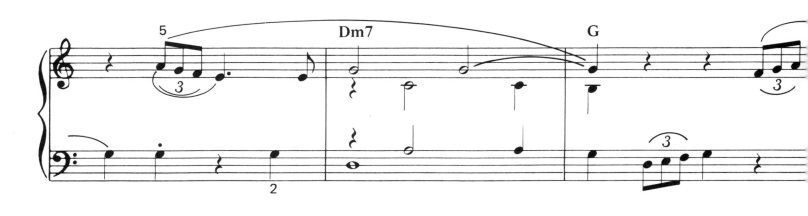

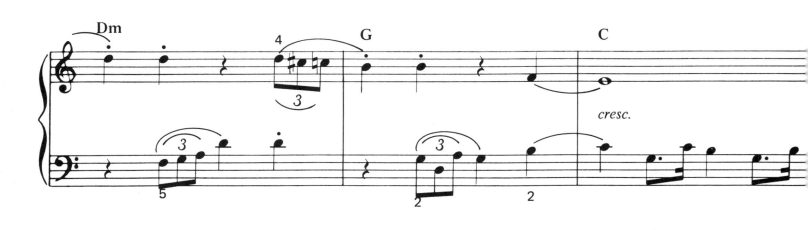

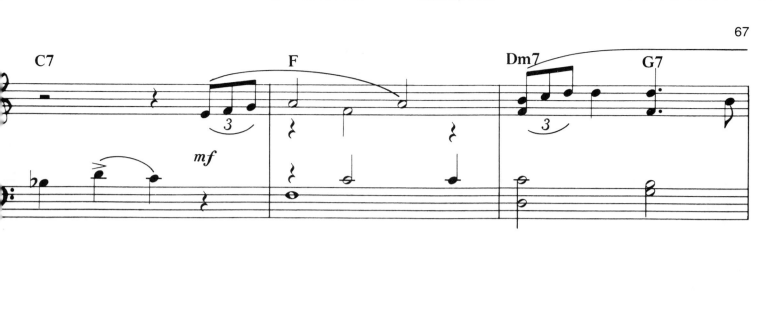

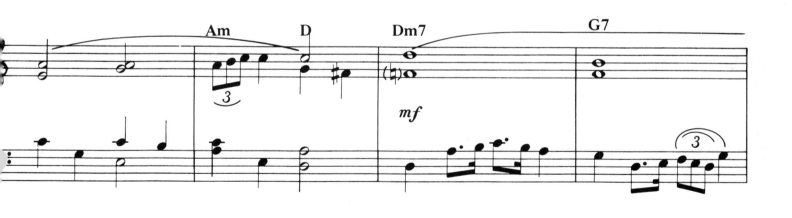

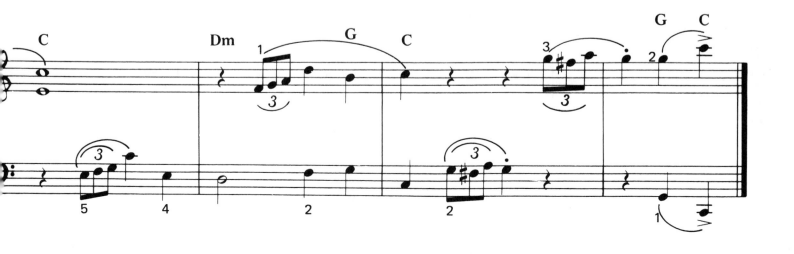

HELLO, YOUNG LOVERS
(From "THE KING AND I")

Lyrics by OSCAR HAMMERSTEIN
Music by RICHARD RODGER

Very moderately

Hel - lo, young lov - ers, who - ev - er you
brave young young lov - ers, and fol - low your

are, I hope your trou - bles are few.
star, Be brave your faith - ful and true.

All my good wish - es go with you to -
Cling ver - y close to each oth - er to -

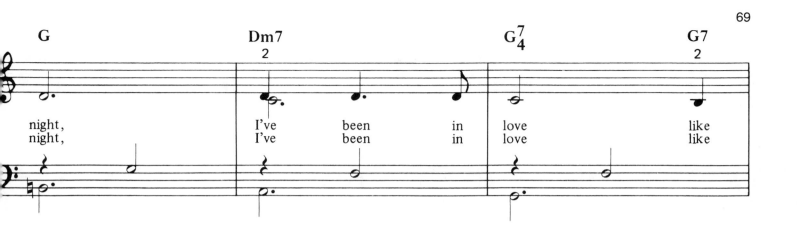

G | Dm7 | G⁷₄ | G7

night,
night,

I've been in love
I've been in love like

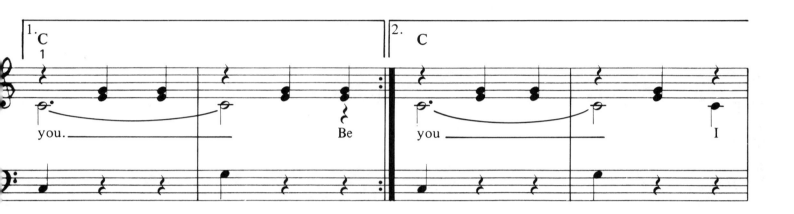

1. C | 2. C

you. _____ Be | you _____ I

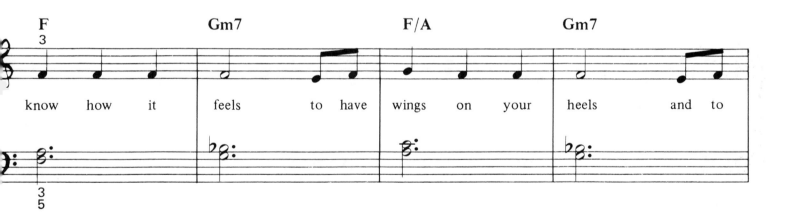

F | Gm7 | F/A | Gm7

know how it feels to have wings on your heels and to

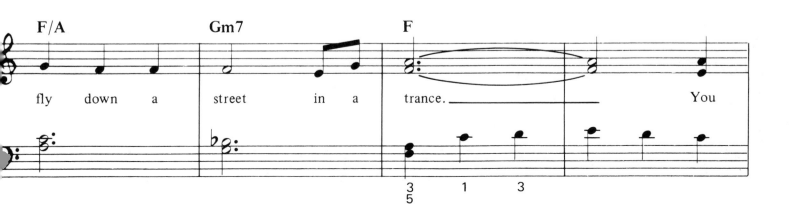

F/A | Gm7 | F

fly down a street in a trance. _____ You

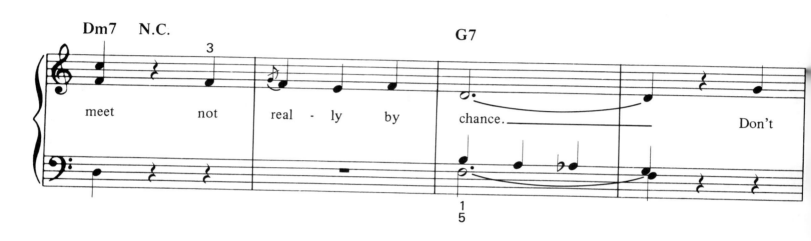

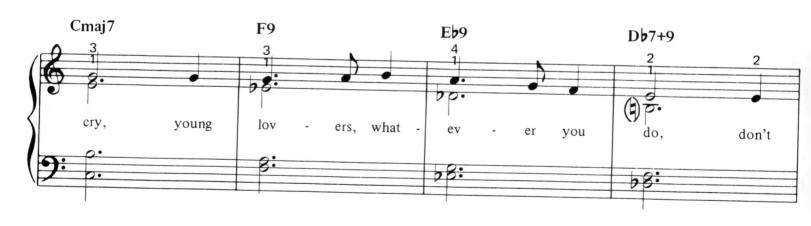

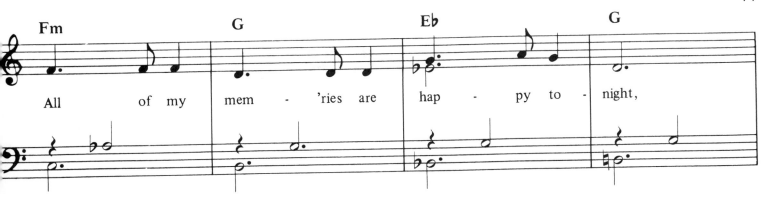

All of my mem - 'ries are hap - py to - night,

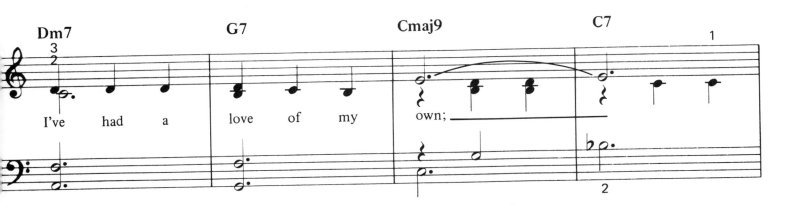

I've had a love of my own;

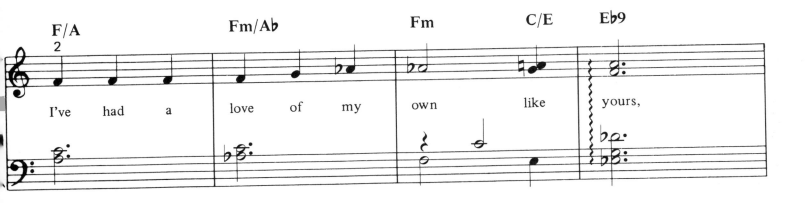

I've had a love of my own like yours,

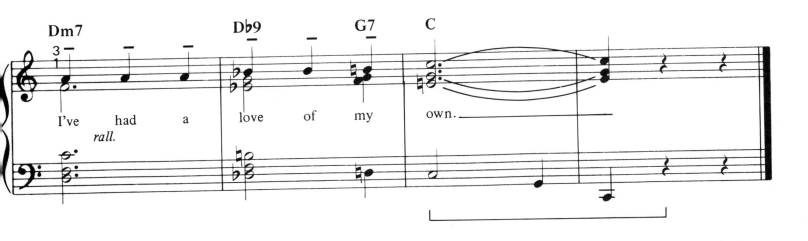

I've had a love of my own.

rall.

HOW ARE THINGS IN GLOCCA MORRA

(From "FINIAN'S RAINBOW")

Words by E.Y. HARBURG
Music by BURTON LANE

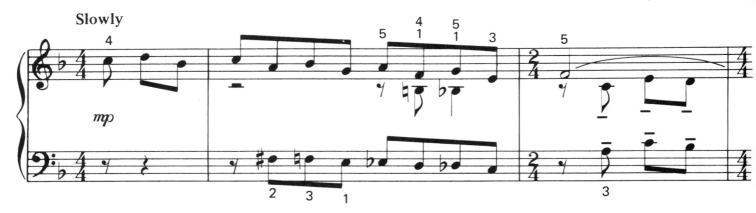

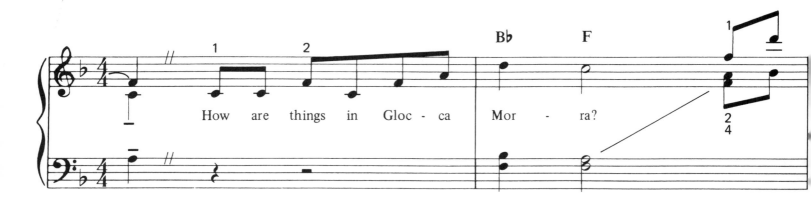

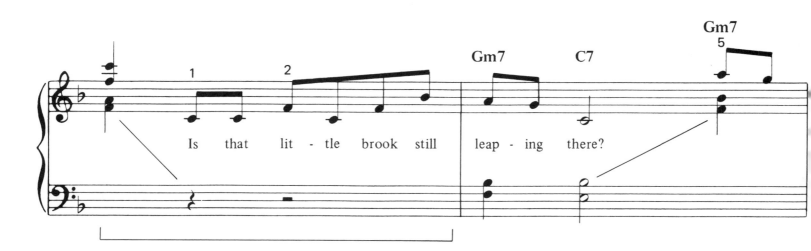

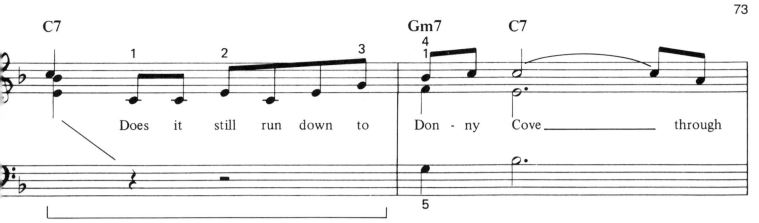

Does it still run down to Don - ny Cove _____ through

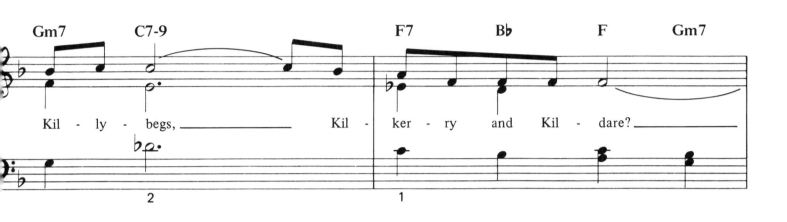

Kil - ly - begs, _____ Kil - ker - ry and Kil - dare? _____

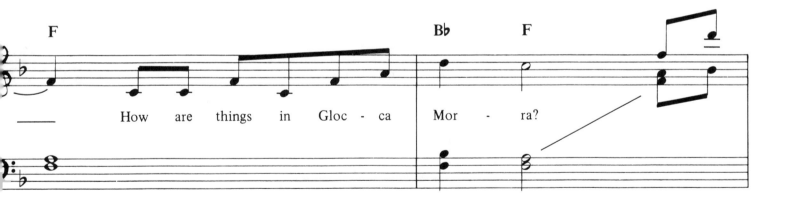

_____ How are things in Gloc - ca Mor - ra?

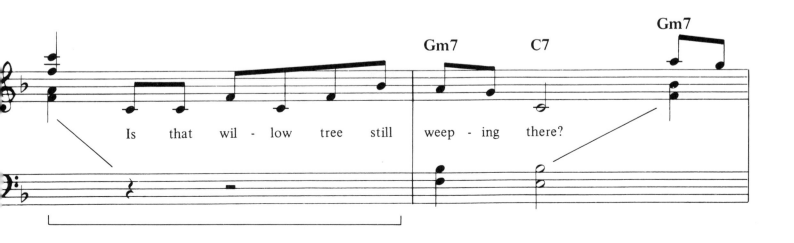

Is that wil - low tree still weep - ing there?

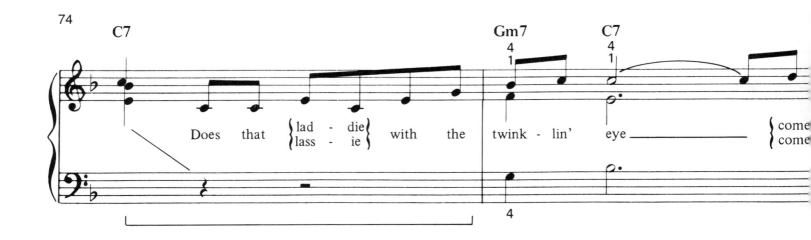

Does that {lad - die / lass - ie} with the twink - lin' eye _____ {come / come

whist - lin' by _____ and does he walk a - way} sad and
smil - in' by _____ and does she walk a - way} sad and

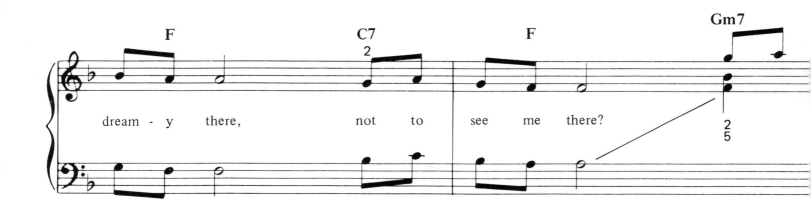

dream - y there, not to see me there?

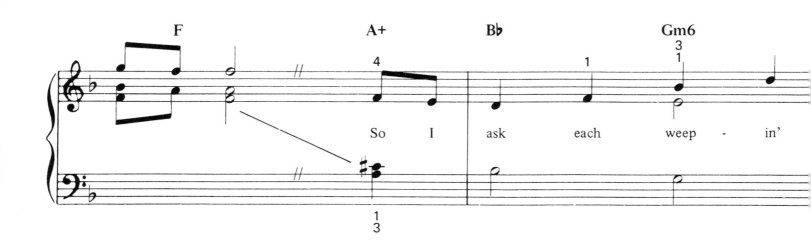

So I ask each weep - in'

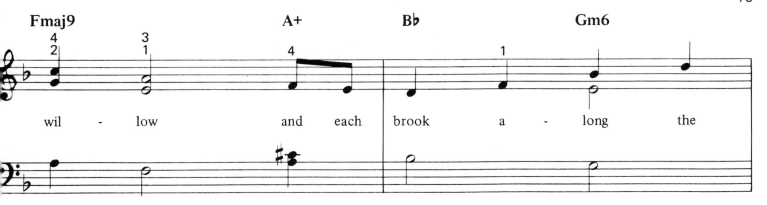

wil - low   and   each   brook   a - long   the

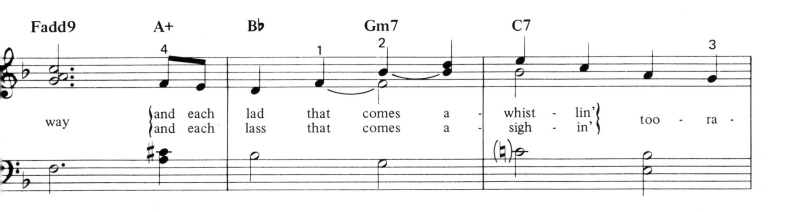

way   {and each   lad   that   comes   a -   whist - lin'}   too - ra -
        {and each   lass   that   comes   a -   sigh - in'}

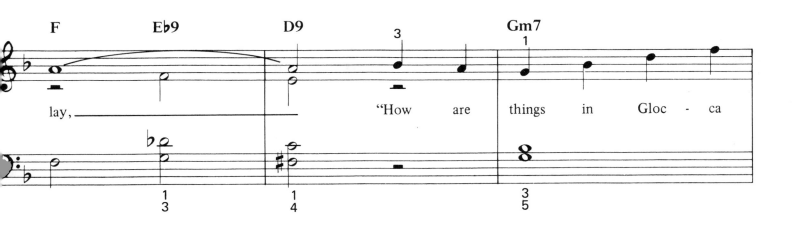

lay,_____   "How   are   things   in   Gloc - ca

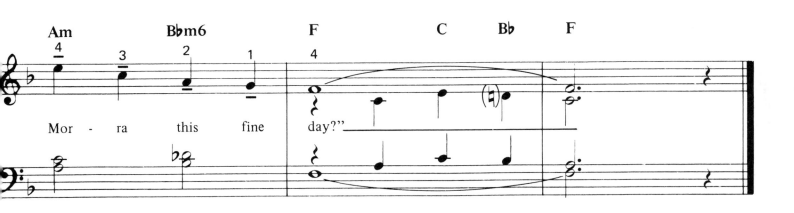

Mor - ra   this   fine   day?"_____

I BELIEVE IN YOU

(From "HOW TO SUCCEED IN BUSINESS WITHOUT REALLY TRYING")

Words and Music by FRANK LOESSER

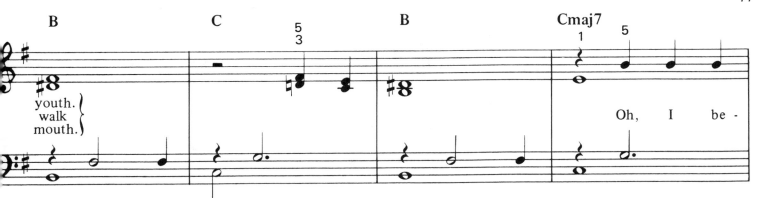

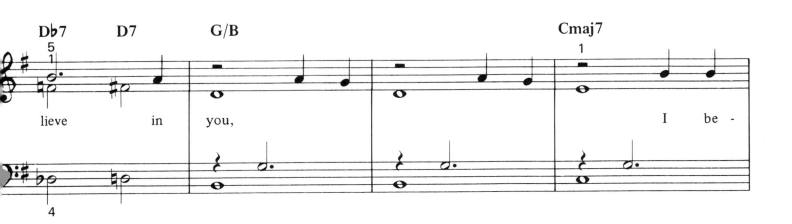

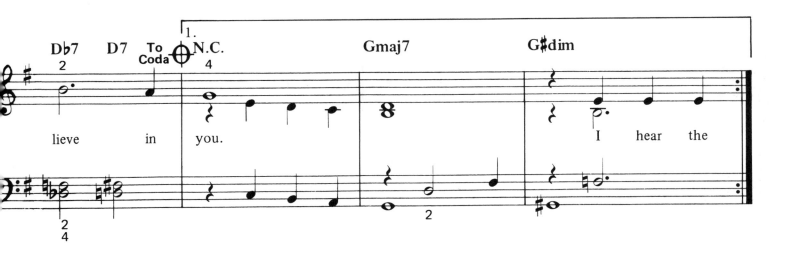

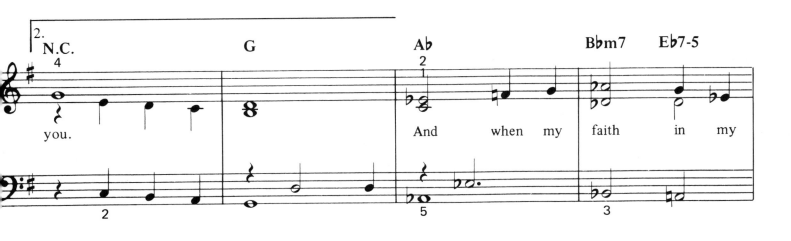

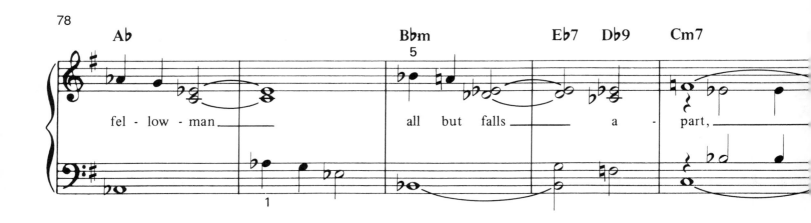

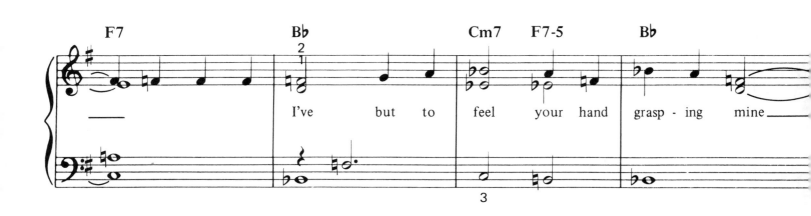

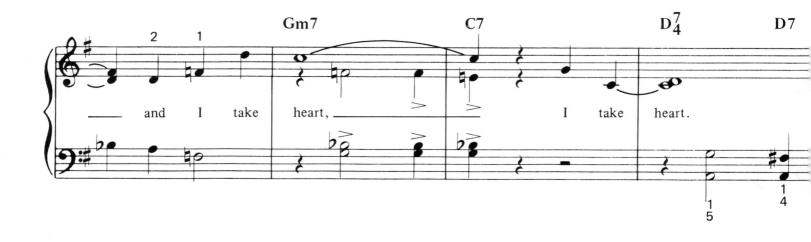

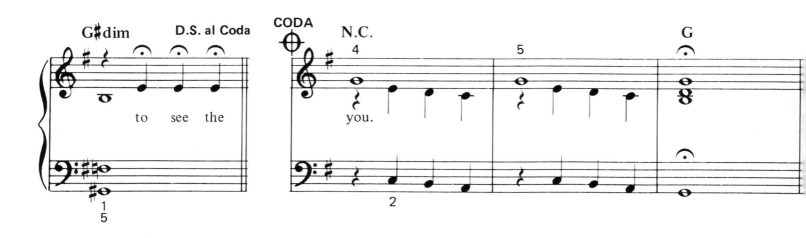

I COULD HAVE DANCED ALL NIGHT

(From "MY FAIR LADY")

Words by ALAN JAY LERNER
Music by FREDERICK LOEWE

Brightly, in 2 (♩ = 1 beat)

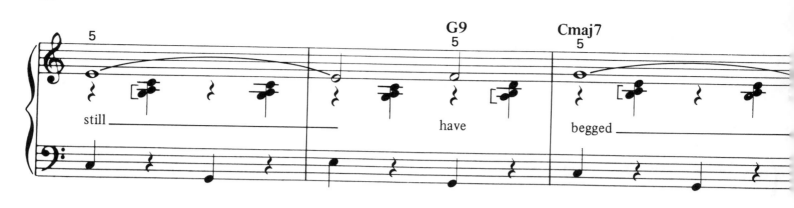

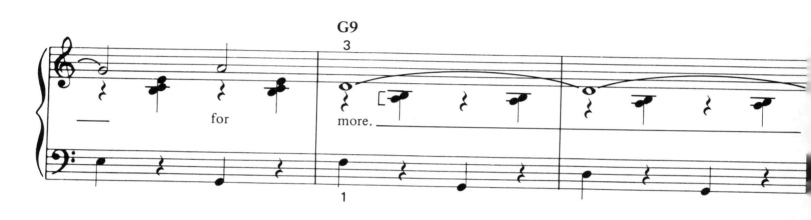

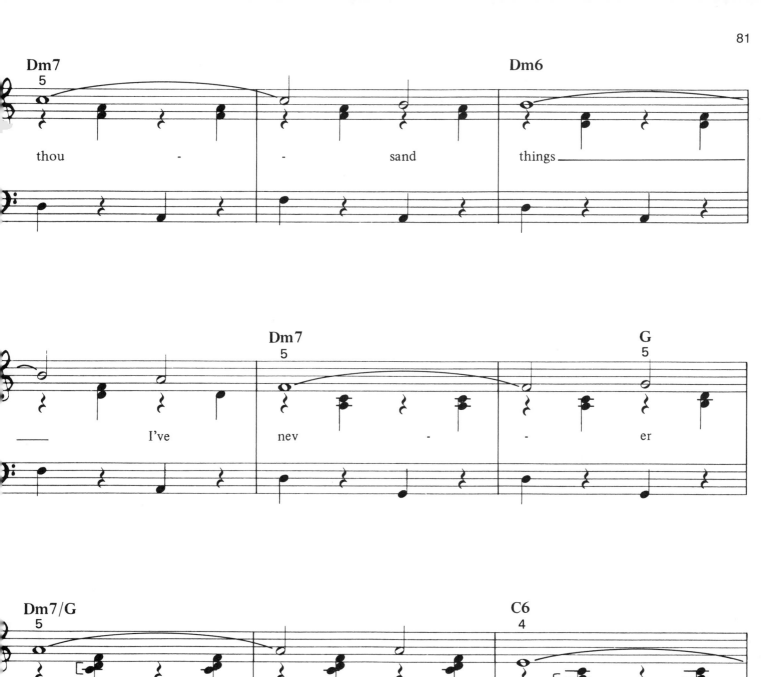

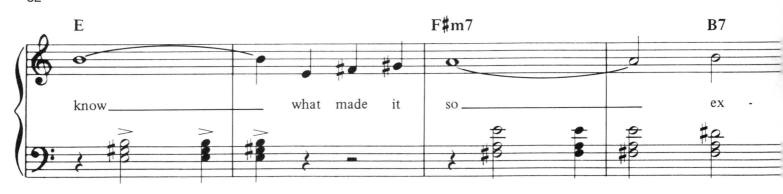

know _____ what made it so _____ ex -

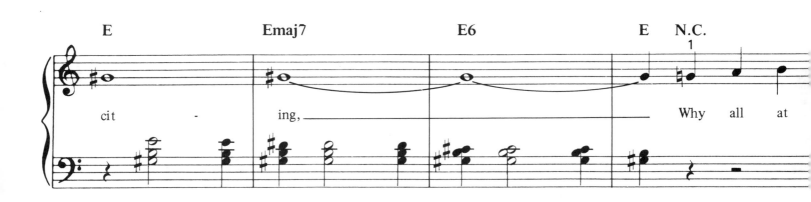

cit - ing, _____ Why all at

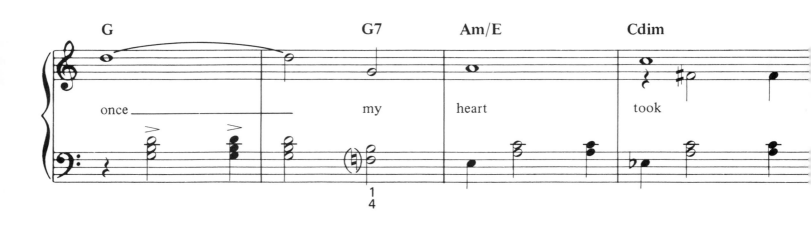

once _____ my heart took

flight. _____ I on - ly

know_____ when he_____ be - gan to

dance_____ with me,_____ I could have

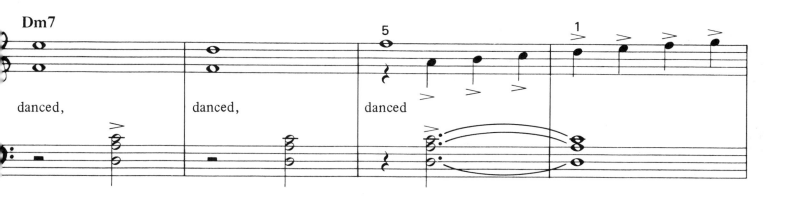

danced, danced, danced

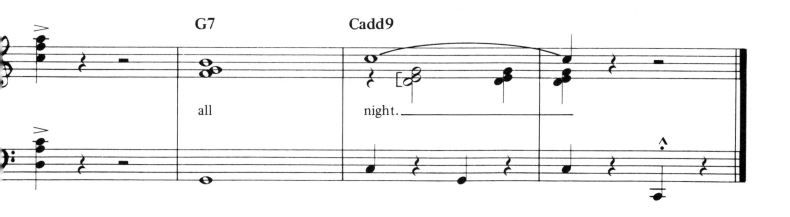

all night._____

I DREAMED A DREAM
(From "LES MISERABLES")

Lyrics by HERBERT KRETZME
Original Text by ALAIN BOUBLIL & JEAN-MARC NATE
Music by CLAUDE-MICHEL SCHÖNBER

FANTINE:
I dreamed a dream in days gone by

when hope was high and life worth liv- ing.

I dreamed that love would nev- er die.

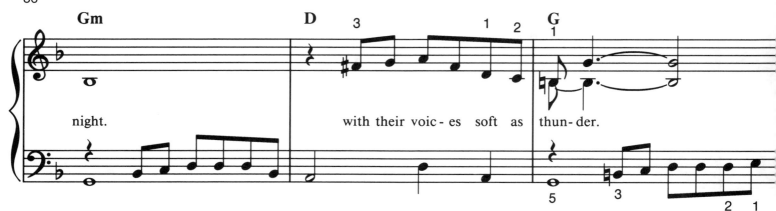

Gm night. **D** with their voic - es soft as **G** thun - der.

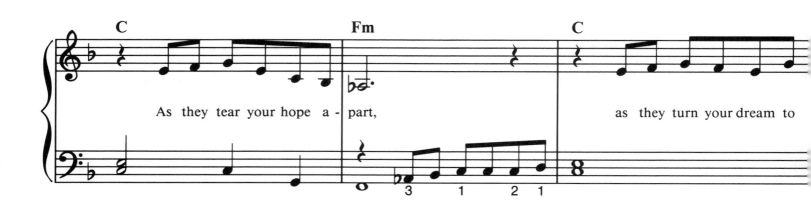

C As they tear your hope a - part, **Fm** **C** as they turn your dream to

F **Gm/F** **F** **Bb/F** **C** *rall.*
shame.

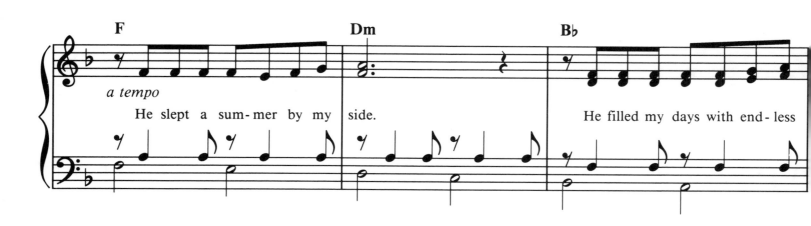

F *a tempo* He slept a sum - mer by my **Dm** side. **Bb** He filled my days with end - less

I REMEMBER IT WELL

(From "GIGI")

Words by ALAN JAY LERNER
Music by FREDERICK LOEWE

90

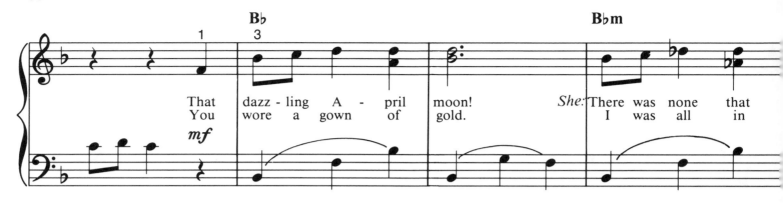

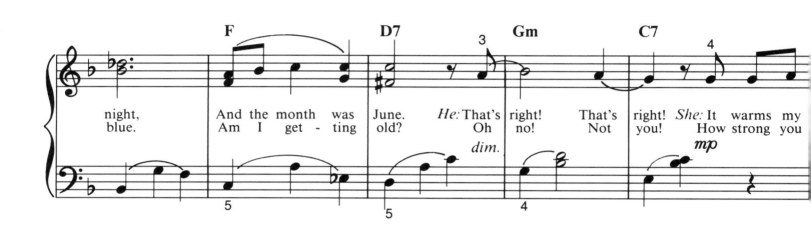

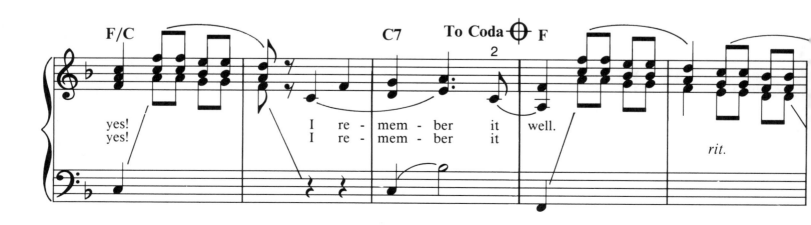

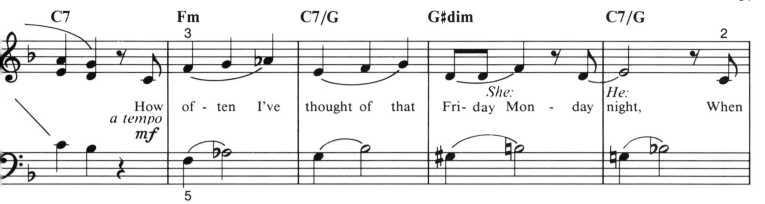

C7   Fm   C7/G   G♯dim   C7/G

a tempo *mf*

How of-ten I've thought of that Fri-day Mon-day night, When

She: *He:*

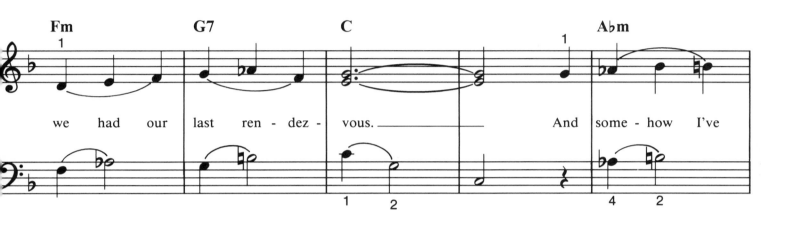

Fm   G7   C   A♭m

we had our last ren-dez- vous._____ And some-how I've

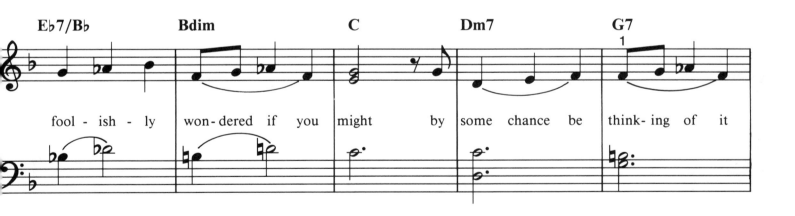

E♭7/B♭   Bdim   C   Dm7   G7

fool-ish - ly won-dered if you might by some chance be think-ing of it

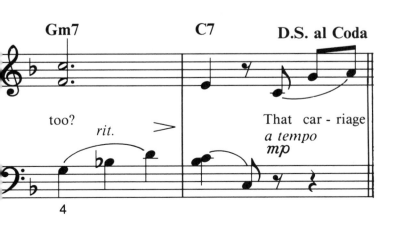

Gm7   C7   D.S. al Coda

too? *rit.* That car - riage

a tempo *mp*

CODA

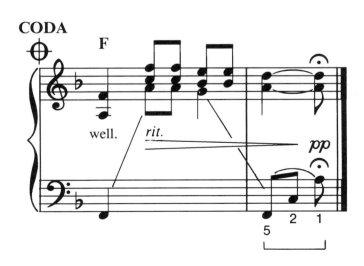

F

well. *rit.* *pp*

I GOT PLENTY O' NUTTIN'
(From "PORGY AND BESS")

Words by IRA GERSHWIN
and DuBOSE HEYWARD
Music by GEORGE GERSHWIN

Moderately

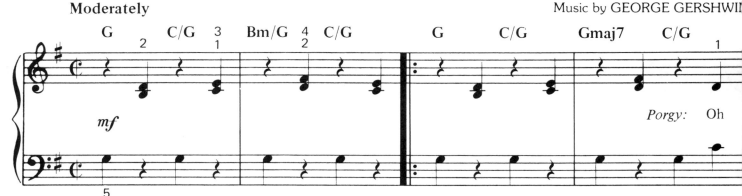

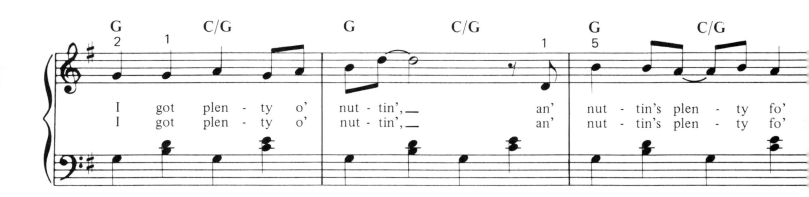

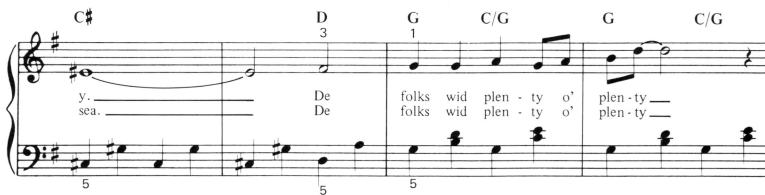

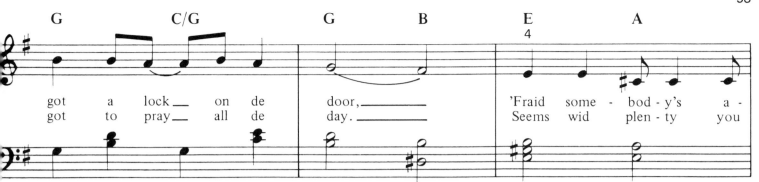

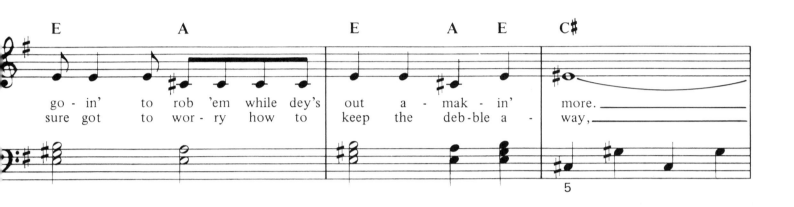

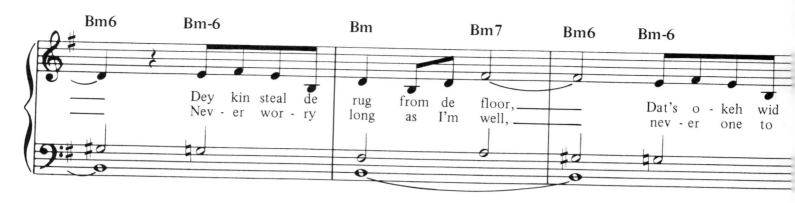

Dey kin steal de rug from de floor,____ Dat's o - keh wid
Nev - er wor - ry long as I'm well,____ nev - er one to

me 'cause de things dat I prize, like de stars in de skies, all are free.____
strive to be good, to be bad, What the hell? I is glad I's a - live.____

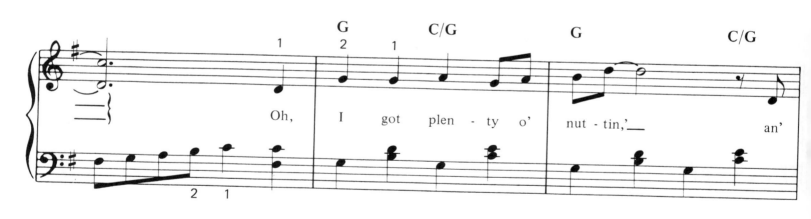

Oh, I got plen - ty o' nut - tin,'____ an'

nut - tin's plen - ty fo' me. I got my gal, got my song, got

heb-ben the whole day long. No use com-plain - in'! Got my

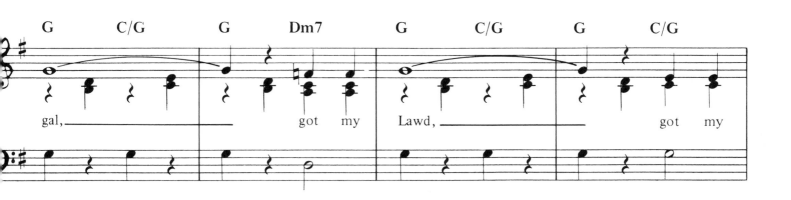

gal,_____ got my Lawd,_____ got my

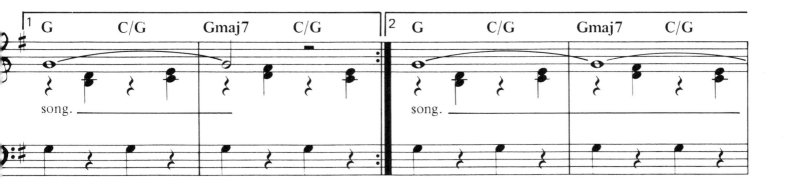

song._____ song._____

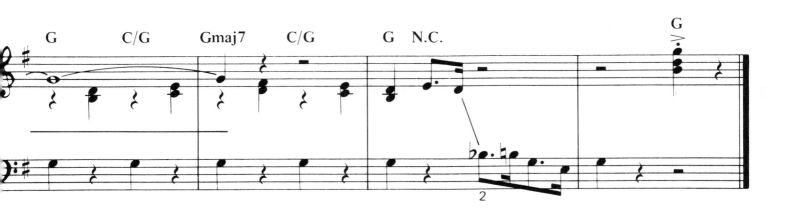

I'LL BE SEEING YOU

(From "RIGHT THIS WAY")

Lyrics by IRVING KAHAL
Music by SAMMY FAIN

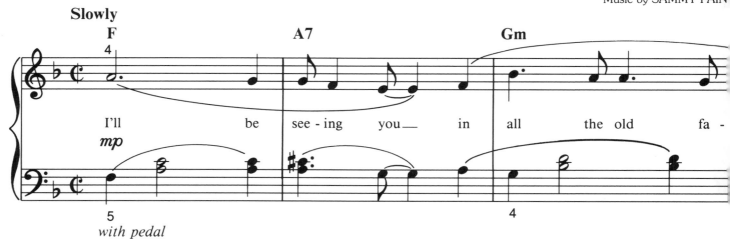

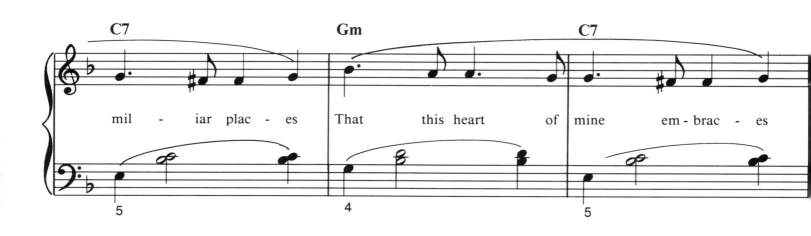

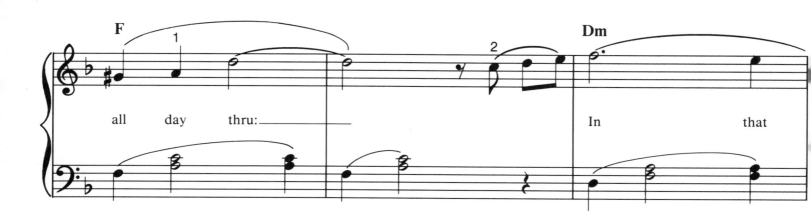

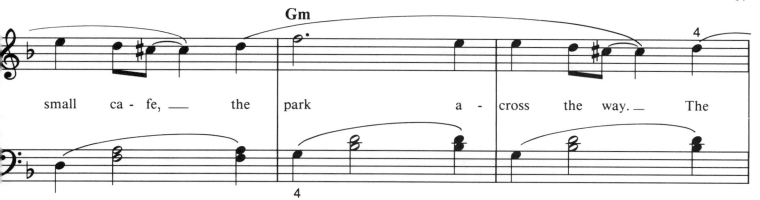

small ca - fe, ___ the park a - cross the way. ___ The

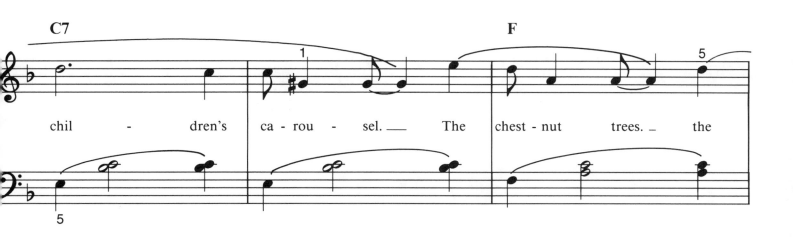

chil - dren's ca - rou - sel. ___ The chest - nut trees. ___ the

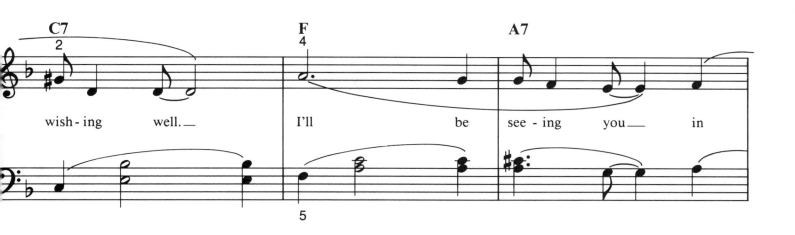

wish - ing well. ___ I'll be see - ing you ___ in

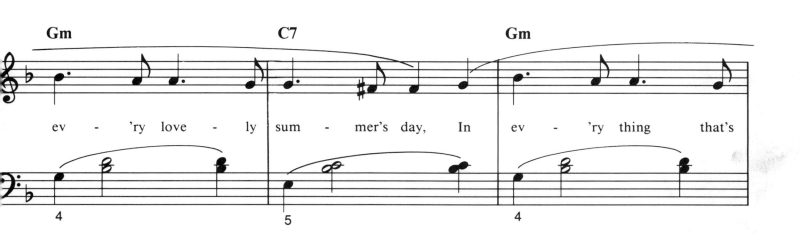

ev - 'ry love - ly sum - mer's day, In ev - 'ry thing that's

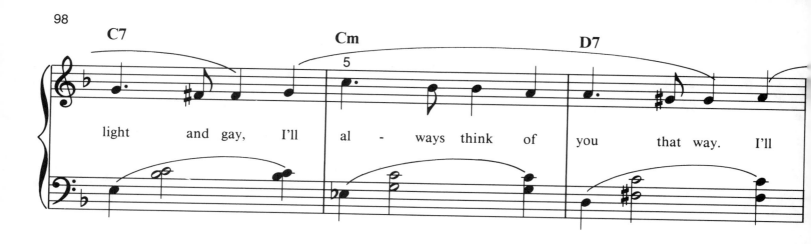

light and gay, I'll al - ways think of you that way. I'll

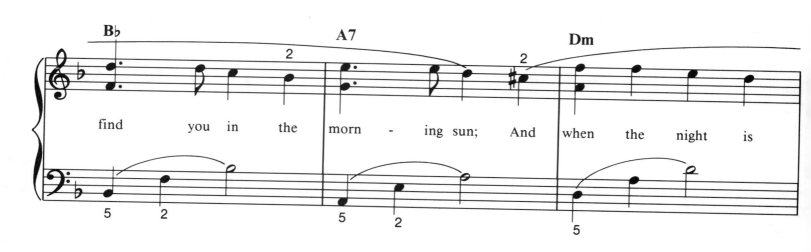

find you in the morn - ing sun; And when the night is

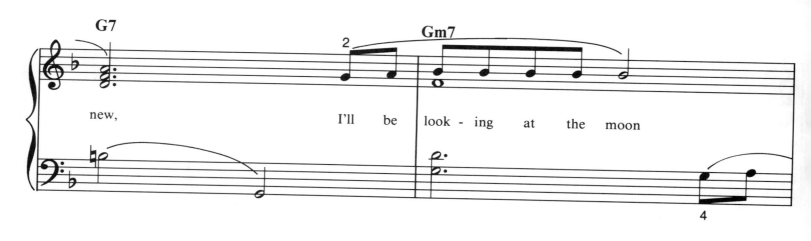

new, I'll be look - ing at the moon

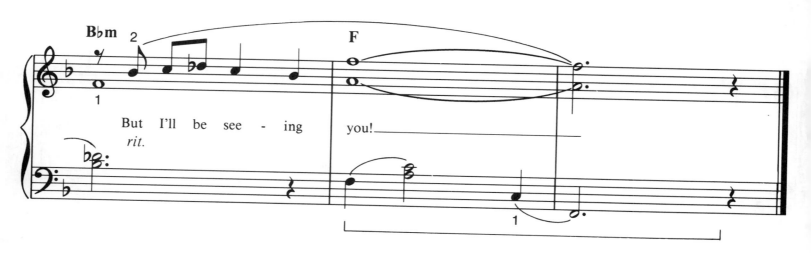

But I'll be see - ing you!
rit.

I'VE GROWN ACCUSTOMED TO HER FACE

(From "MY FAIR LADY")

Words by ALAN JAY LERNER
Music by FREDERICK LOEWE

smiles,   her frowns,   her   ups,   her downs are se - cond
joys,   her woes,   her   highs,   her lows are se - cond

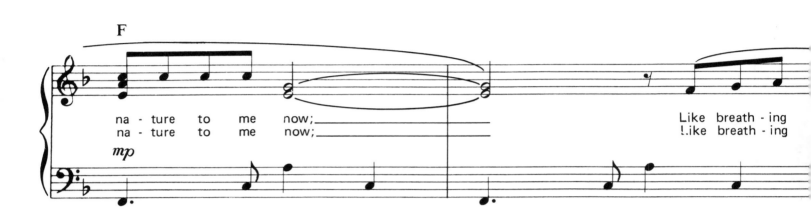

na - ture to me now;_____   Like breath - ing
na - ture to me now;_____   Like breath - ing

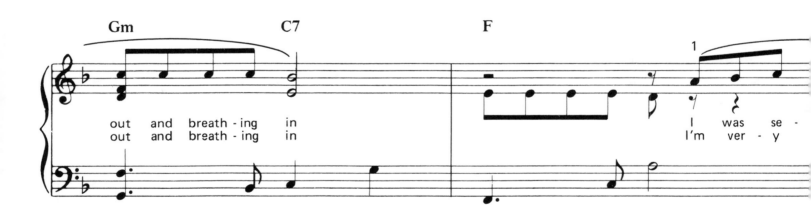

out and breath - ing in   I was se -
out and breath - ing in   I'm ver - y

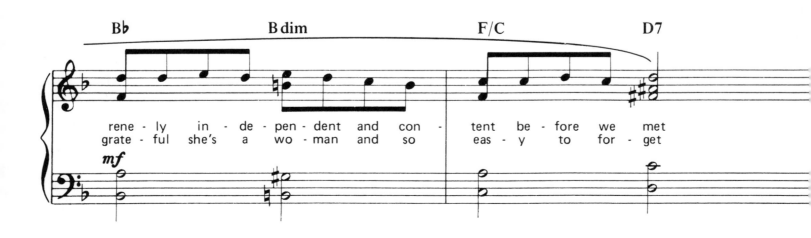

rene - ly in - de - pen - dent and con -   tent be - fore we met
grate - ful she's a wo - man and so   eas - y to for - get

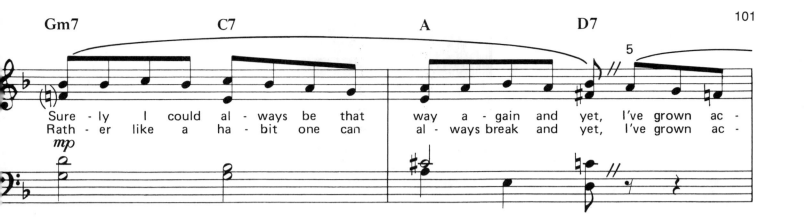

Gm7 ... C7 ... A ... D7

Sure -ly I could al - ways be that way a - gain and yet, I've grown ac -
Rath -er like a ha - bit one can al - ways break and yet, I've grown ac -

mp

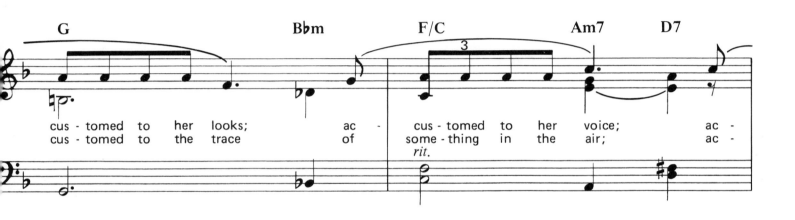

G ... Bbm ... F/C ... Am7 ... D7

cus - tomed to her looks; ac - cus - tomed to her voice; ac -
cus - tomed to the trace of some - thing in the air; ac -

rit.

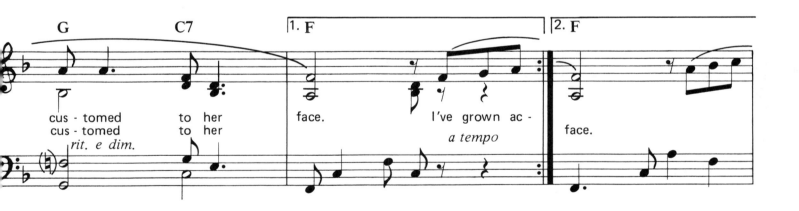

G ... C7 ... 1. F ... 2. F

cus - tomed to her face. I've grown ac -
cus - tomed to her face.

rit. e dim. ... *a tempo*

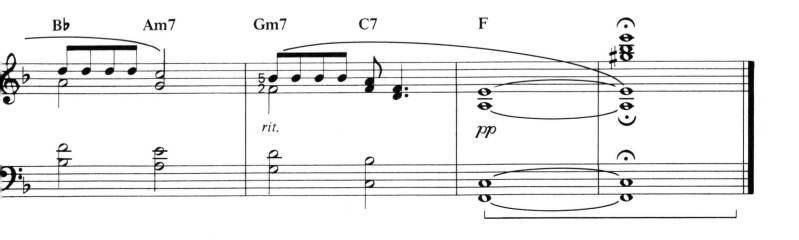

Bb ... Am7 ... Gm7 ... C7 ... F

rit. ... *pp*

IF EVER I WOULD LEAVE YOU

(From "CAMELOT")

Words by ALAN JAY LERNER
Music by FREDERICK LOEWE

Moderately fast

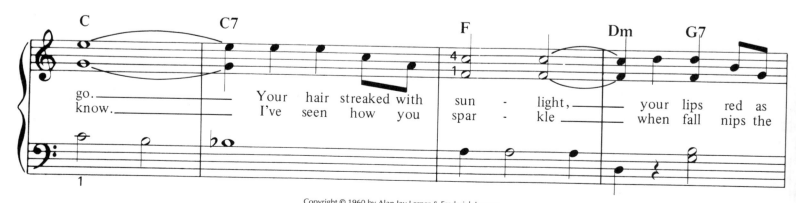

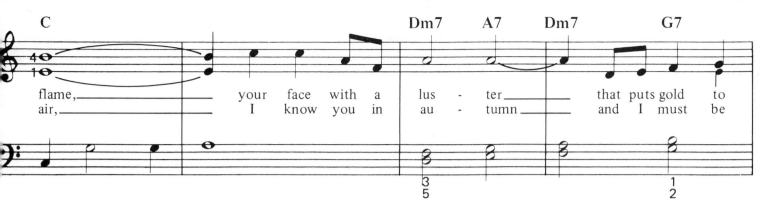

C

flame,_____ your face with a lus-ter_____ that puts gold to
air,_____ I know you in au-tumn_____ and I must be

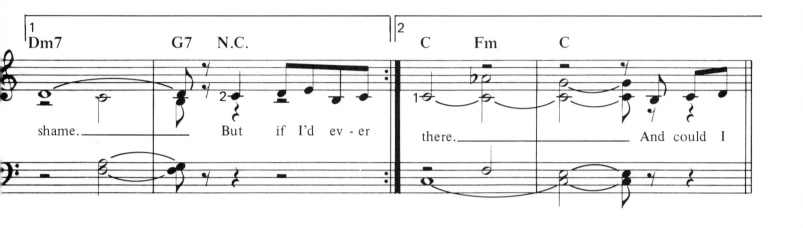

Dm7 G7 N.C.
shame._____ But if I'd ev-er

C Fm C
there._____ And could I

Rather freely

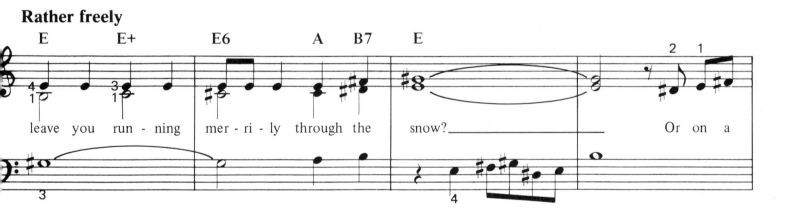

E   E+   E6   A   B7   E

leave you run-ning mer-ri-ly through the snow?_____ Or on a

Again in strict tempo

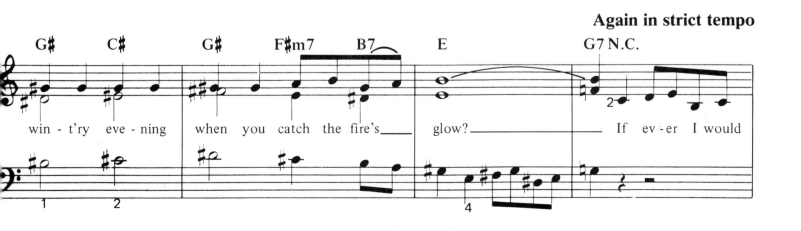

G♯   C♯   G♯   F♯m7   B7   E   G7 N.C.

win-t'ry eve-ning when you catch the fire's___ glow?_____ If ev-er I would

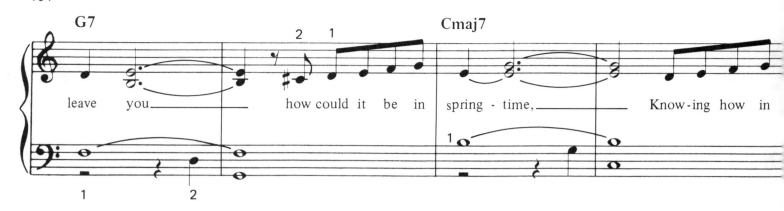

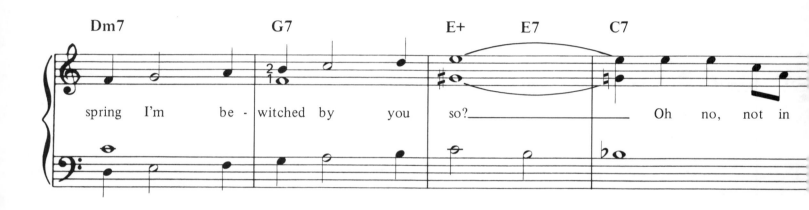

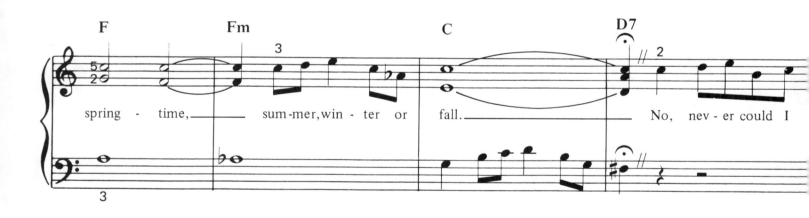

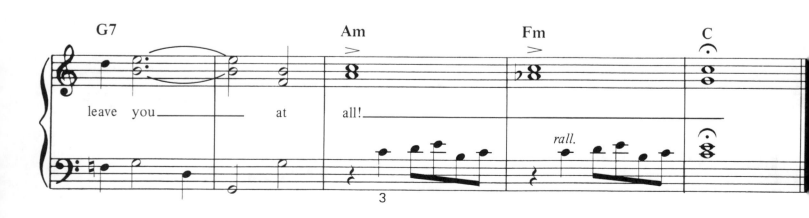

IT MIGHT AS WELL BE SPRING

(From "STATE FAIR")

Lyrics by OSCAR HAMMERSTEIN II
Music by RICHARD RODGERS

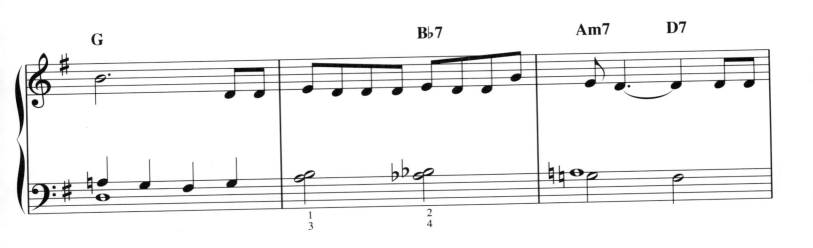

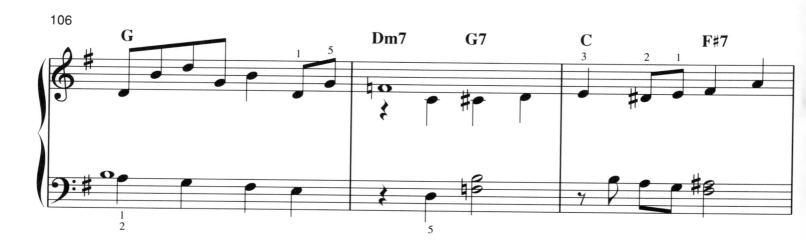

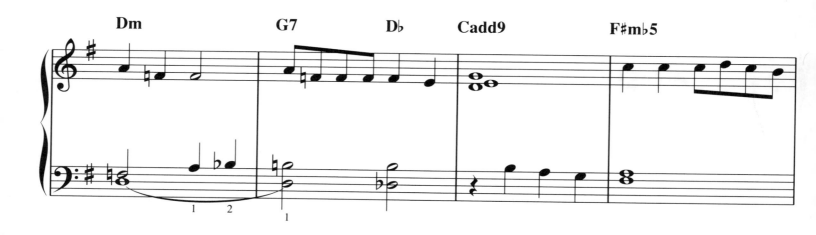

IF I LOVED YOU

(From "CAROUSEL")

Lyrics by OSCAR HAMMERSTEIN II
Music by RICHARD RODGERS

Slowly, but not dragging

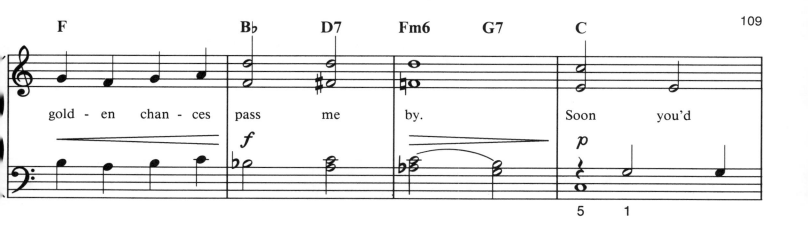

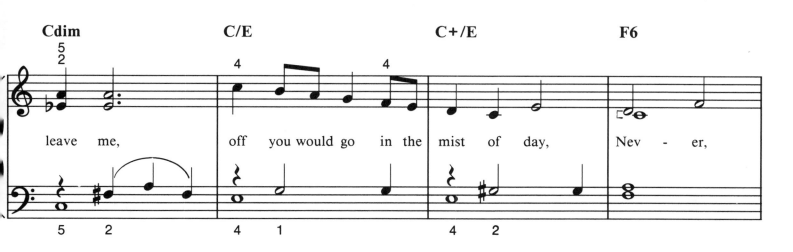

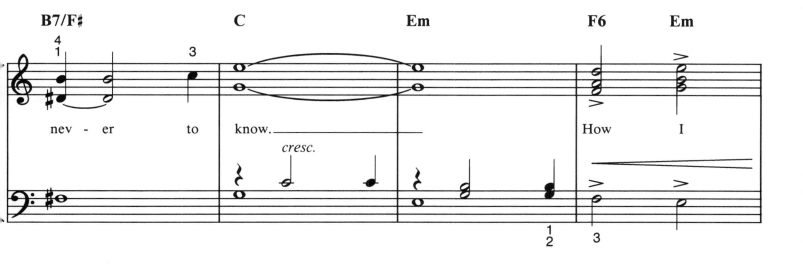

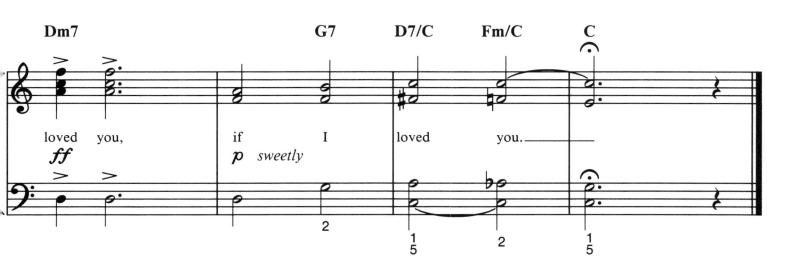

IF I RULED THE WORLD

(From "PICKWICK")

Words by LESLIE BRICUSSE
Music by CYRIL ORNADEL

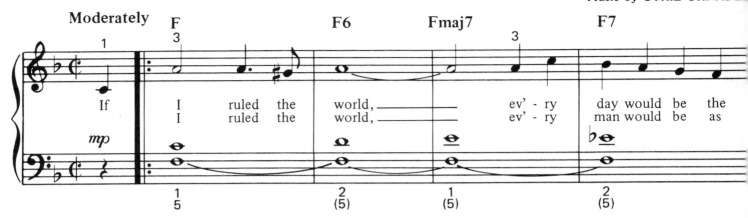

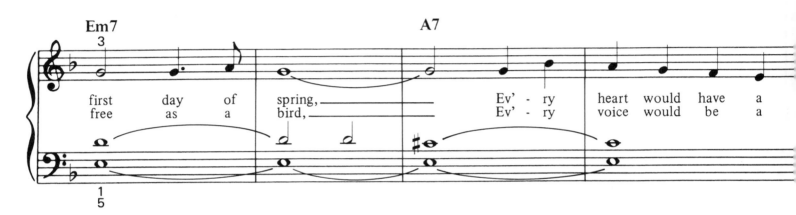

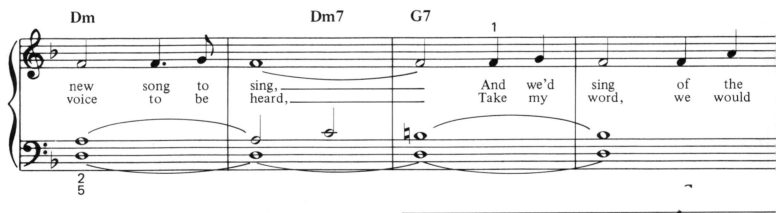

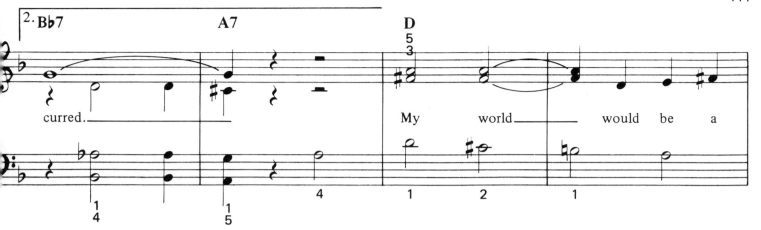

curred._____ My world_____ would be a

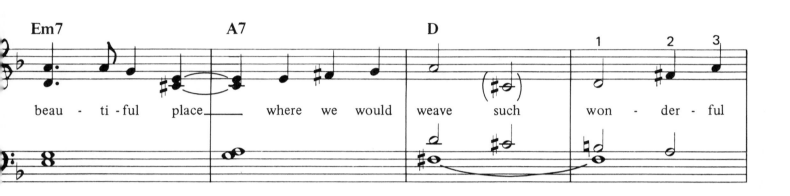

beau - ti -ful place_____ where we would weave such won - der - ful

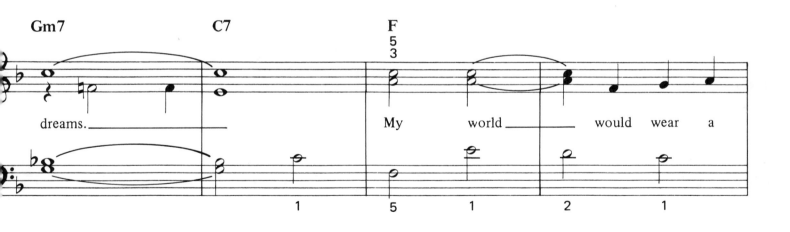

dreams._____ My world_____ would wear a

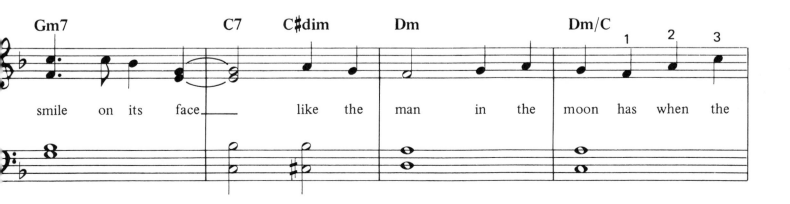

smile on its face_____ like the man in the moon has when the

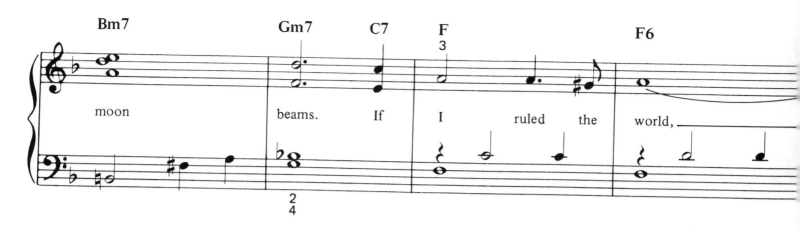

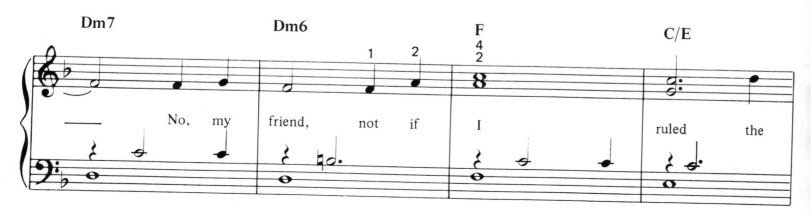

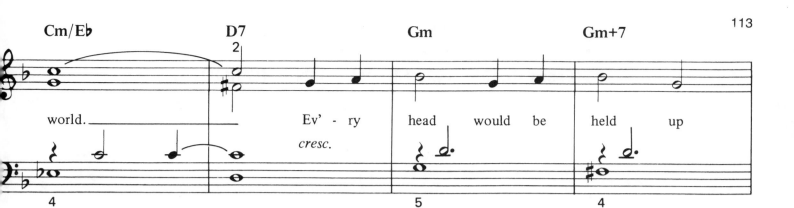

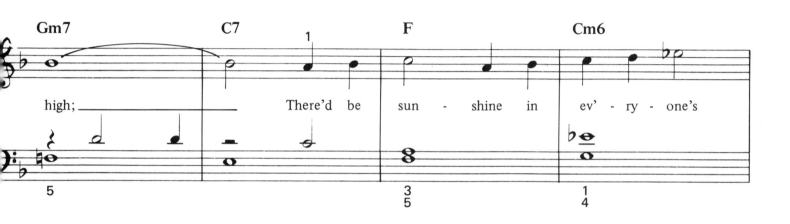

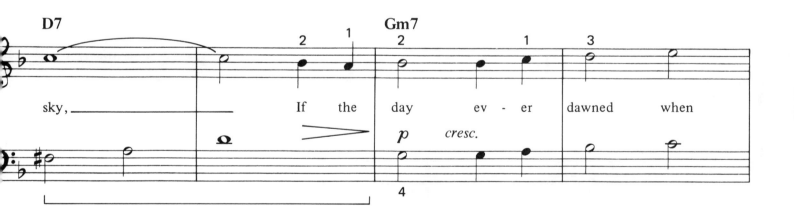

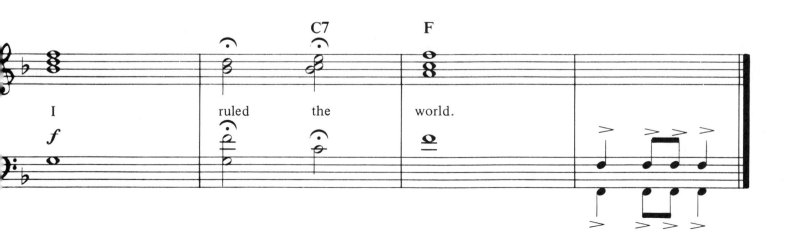

IF I WERE A RICH MAN

(From the Musical "FIDDLER ON THE ROOF")

Words by SHELDON HARNICK
Music by JERRY BOCK

Cm / **1. F♯dim** / **G7**

bid - dy, bid - dy bum,　if I were a wealth - y　man.

2. F♯dim / **G7** / **C** / **C7**

dig - guh, dig - guh, dee - dle dai - dle　man.

I'd　build　a

I　see　my

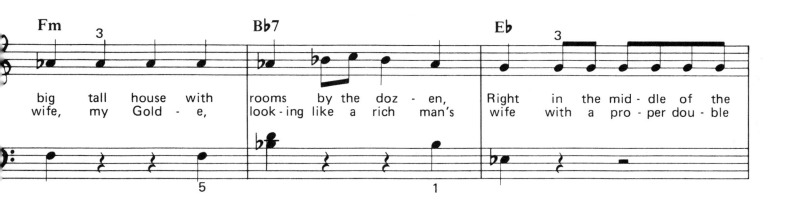

Fm / **B♭7** / **E♭**

big　tall　house with　rooms　by the doz - en,　Right　in the mid - dle of the

wife, my　Gold - e,　look - ing like a rich　man's　wife　with a pro - per dou - ble

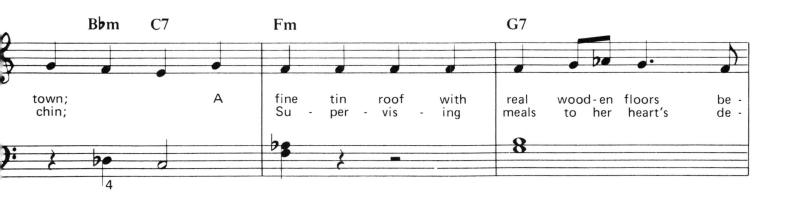

B♭m　**C7** / **Fm** / **G7**

town;　　　A　fine　tin　roof　with　real　wood - en floors　be -

chin;　　Su - per - vis - ing　meals　to her　heart's　de -

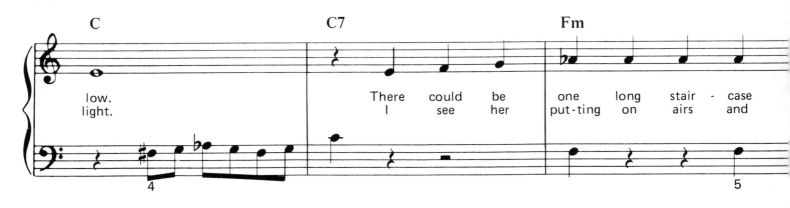

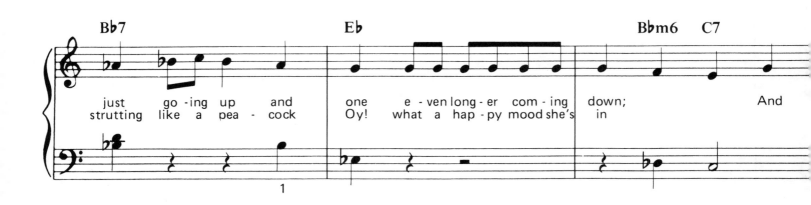

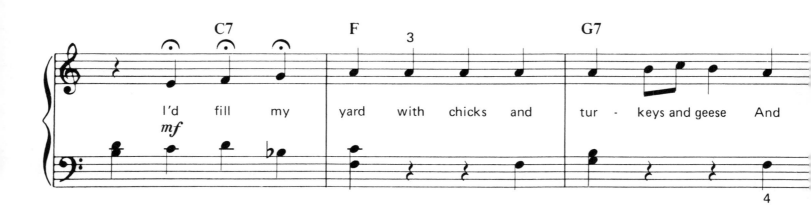

ducks   for the town to see and   hear;   Squawk - ing   just   as

nois - i - ly   as   they   can.   And   each   loud

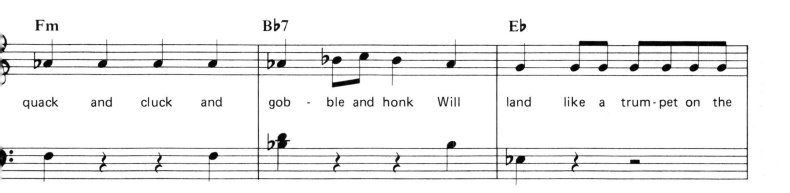

quack   and   cluck   and   gob - ble and honk Will   land   like a trum-pet on the

ear;   As   if   to   say   here   lives   a   weal - thy

D.S. al Coda
(with repeat)

CODA

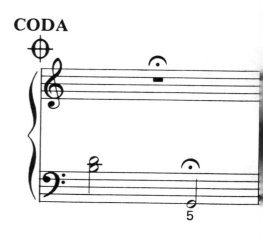

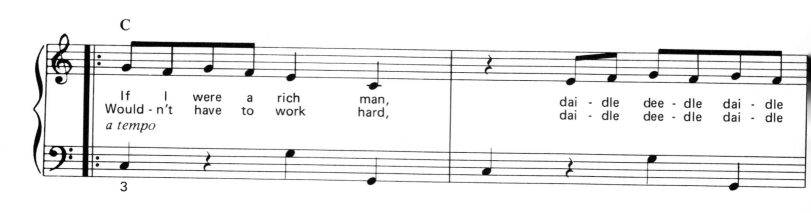

If   I   were   a   rich   man,   dai - dle   dee - dle   dai - dle
Would - n't   have   to   work   hard,   dai - dle   dee - dle   dai - dle
a tempo

dig - guh   dig - guh   dee - dle   dai - dle   dum.
dig - guh   dig - guh   dee - dle   dai - dle   dum.

All   day   long   I'd   bid - dy   bid - dy   bum,   if   I   were   a   wealth - y

man.

Lord, who made the li - on and the lamb,

you de - creed I should be what I am. Would it spoil some

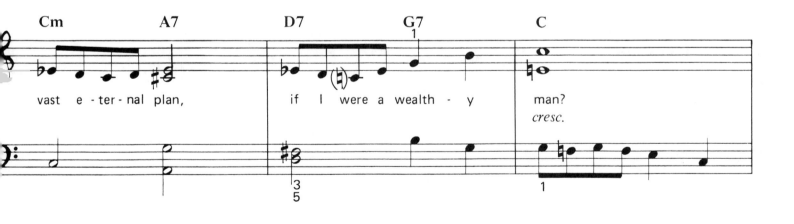

vast e - ter - nal plan, if I were a wealth - y man?
cresc.

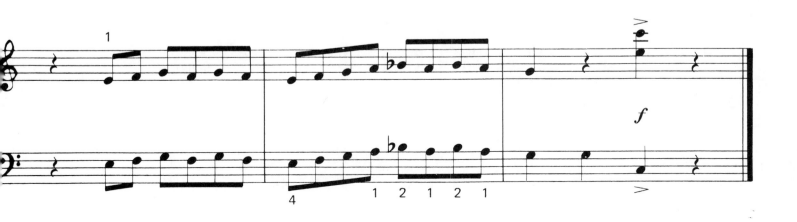

IT'S ALL RIGHT WITH ME

(From "CAN-CAN")

Words and Music by
COLE PORTER

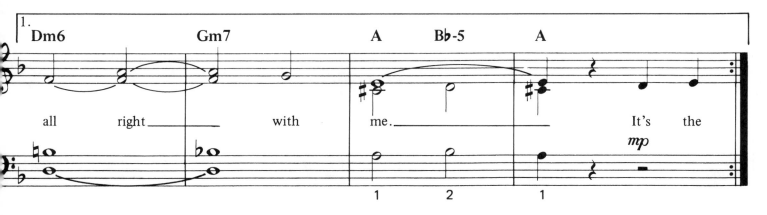

1.

Dm6 Gm7 A Bb-5 A

all right _____ with me. ____ It's the

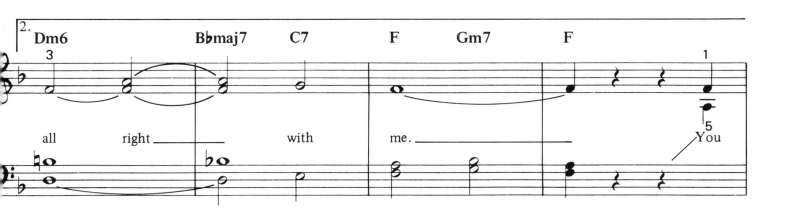

2.

Dm6 Bbmaj7 C7 F Gm7 F

all right _____ with me. ____ You

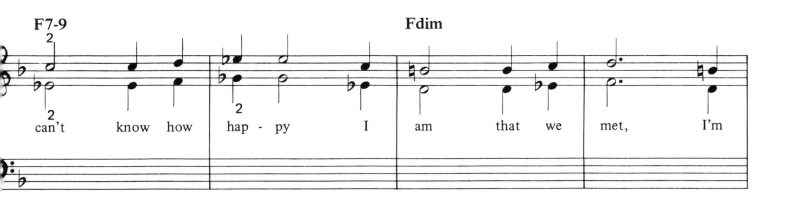

F7-9 Fdim

can't know how hap-py I am that we met, I'm

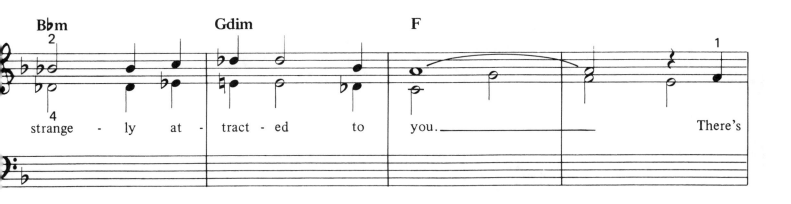

Bbm Gdim F

strange-ly at-tract-ed to you. ____ There's

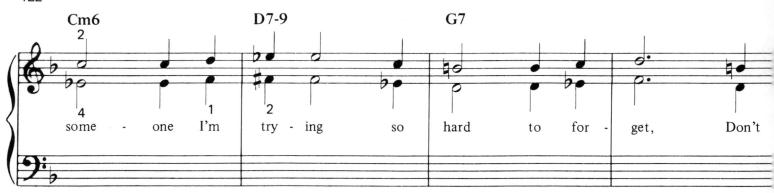

some - one I'm try - ing so hard to for - get, Don't

you want to for - get some - one, too?_____ It's the

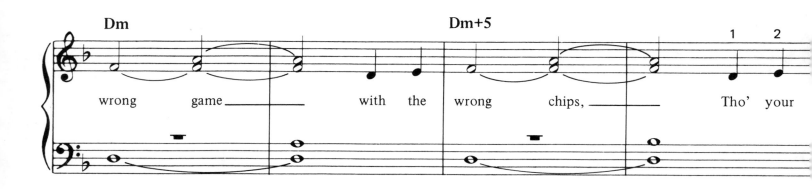

wrong game_____ with the wrong chips, _____ Tho' your

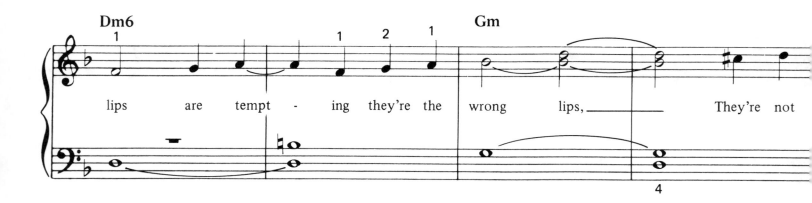

lips are tempt - ing they're the wrong lips, _____ They're not

123

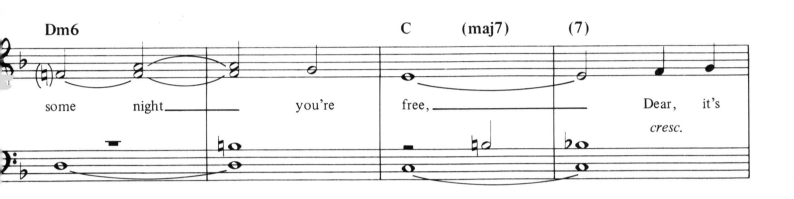

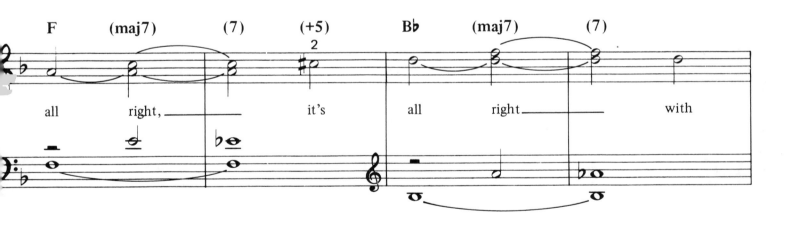

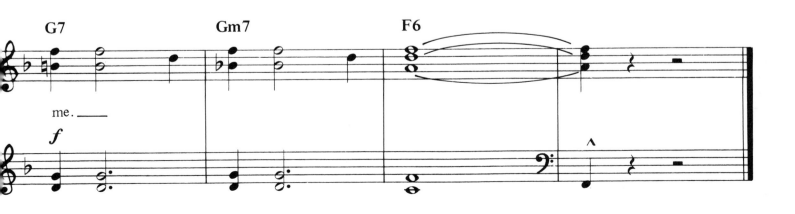

JUST IN TIME
(From "BELLS ARE RINGING")

Words by BETTY COMDEN and ADOLPH GREE[N]
Music by JULE STYN[E]

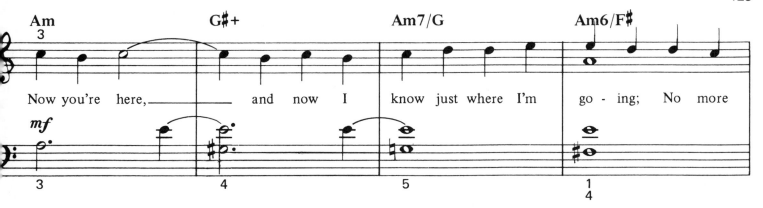

Now you're here,——— and now I know just where I'm go - ing; No more

mf

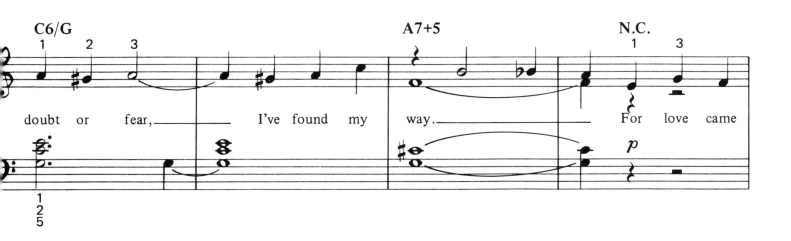

doubt or fear,——— I've found my way.——— For love came

p

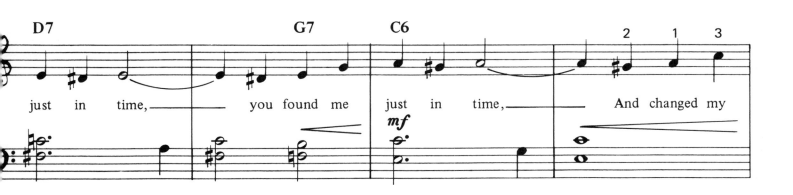

just in time,——— you found me just in time,——— And changed my

mf

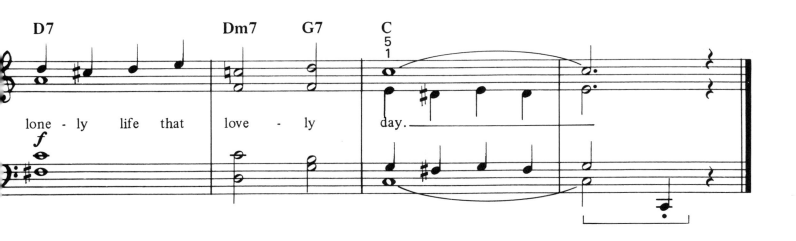

lone - ly life that love - ly day.———

f

THE LADY IS A TRAMP
(From "BABES IN ARMS")

Words by LORENZ HAR
Music by RICHARD RODGER

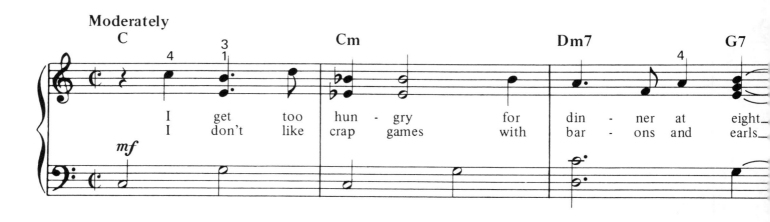

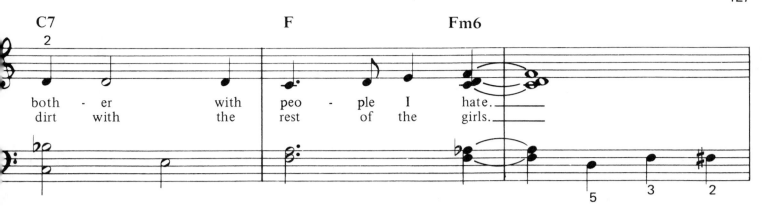

both - er   with   with   the   peo - ple   I   hate.
dirt   with   the   rest   of   the   girls.

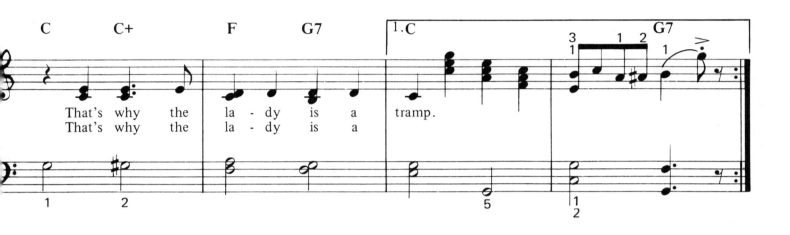

That's   why   the   la - dy   is   a   tramp.
That's   why   the   la - dy   is   a

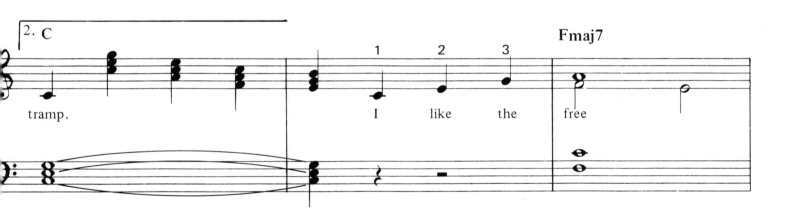

tramp.   I   like   the   free

fresh   wind   in   my   hair,

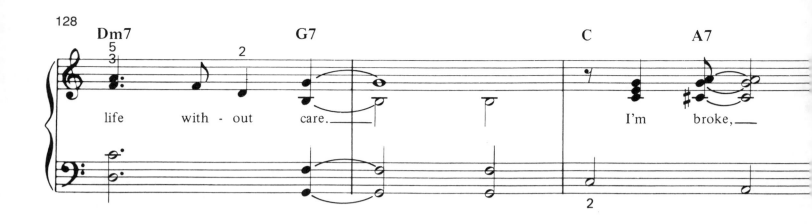

life with - out care.___ I'm broke,___

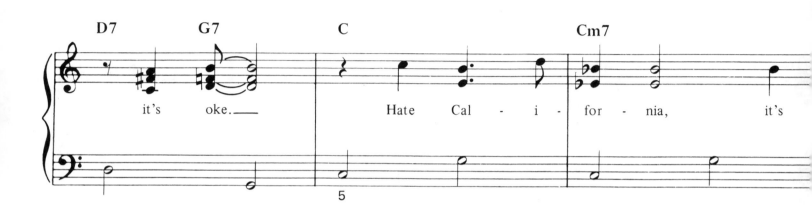

it's oke.___ Hate Cal - i - for - nia, it's

cold and it's damp.___ That's why the

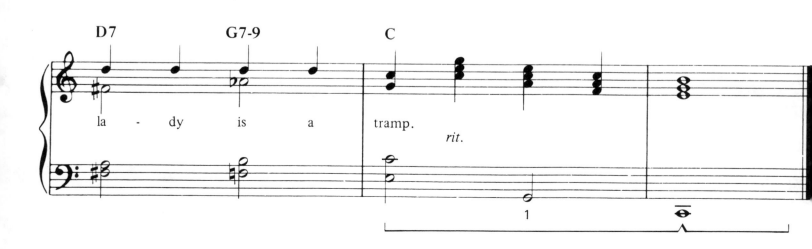

la - dy is a tramp.

rit.

THE LAST NIGHT OF THE WORLD
(From "MISS SAIGON")

Music by CLAUDE-MICHEL SCHÖNBERG
Lyrics by RICHARD MALTBY Jr. & ALAIN BOUBLIL
Adapted From Original French Lyrics by ALAIN BOUBLIL

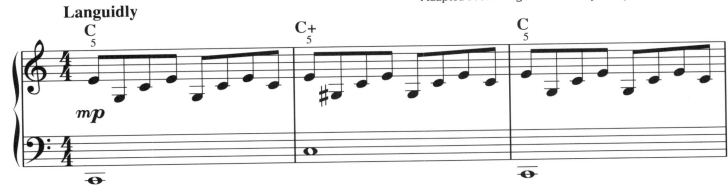

In a place that won't let us feel.

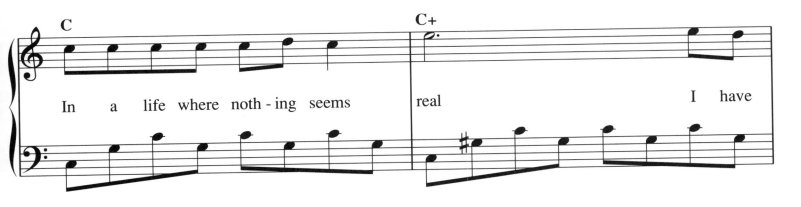

In a life where noth-ing seems real   I have

found   you, _   I have found   you. ___

In a world that's mov-ing too fast.

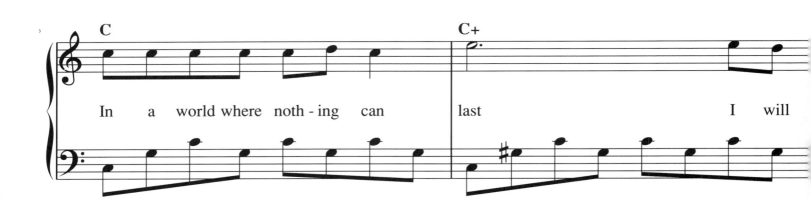

In a world where noth-ing can last I will

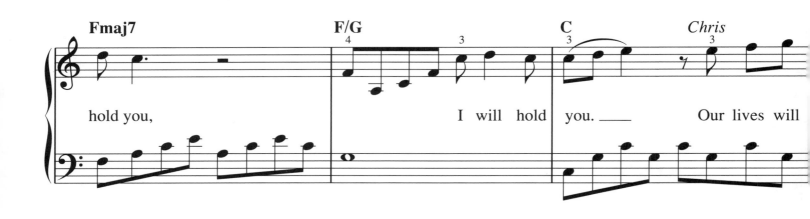

hold you, I will hold you. Our lives will

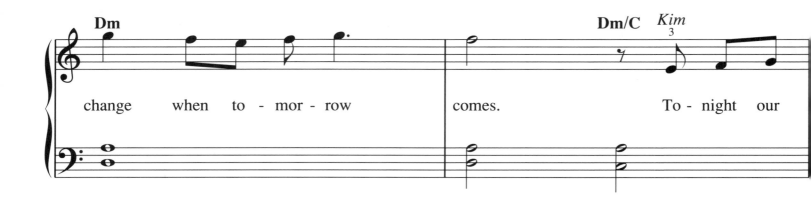

change when to-mor-row comes. To-night our

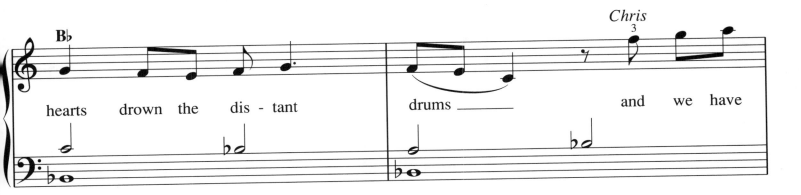

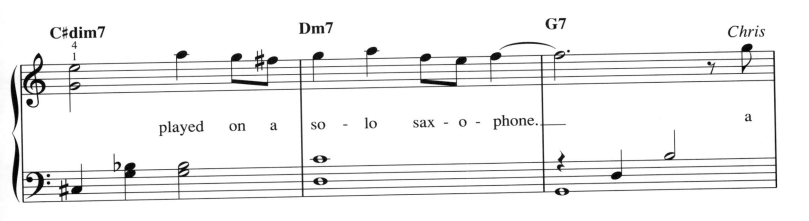

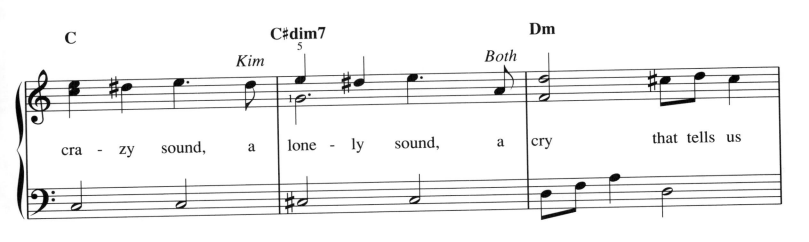

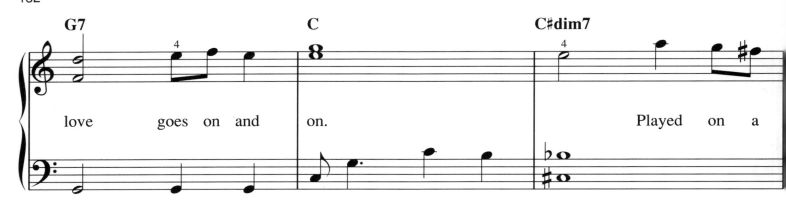

love   goes   on   and   on.   Played   on   a

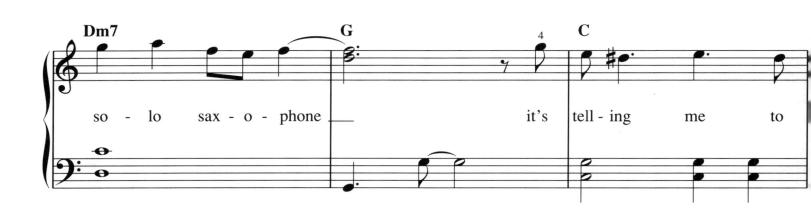

so - lo   sax - o - phone ___   it's tell - ing   me   to

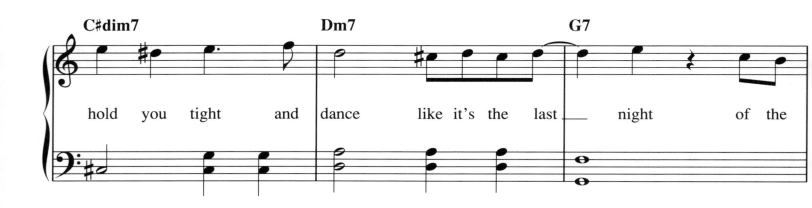

hold   you   tight   and   dance   like it's the last ___ night   of the

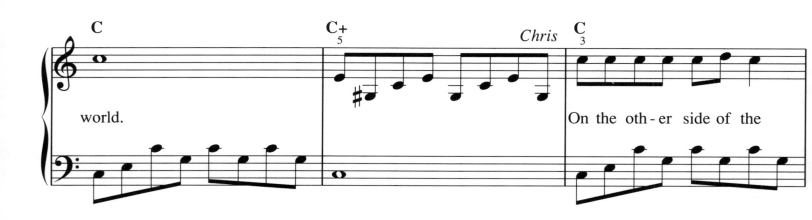

world.   *Chris*

On the oth - er side of the

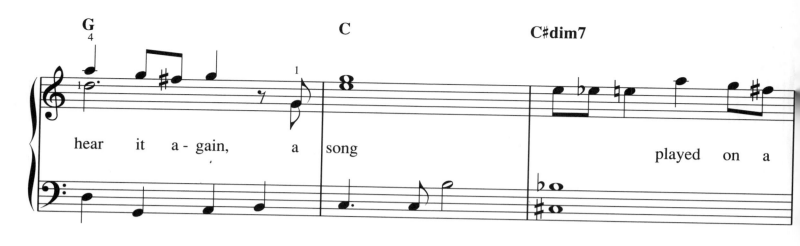

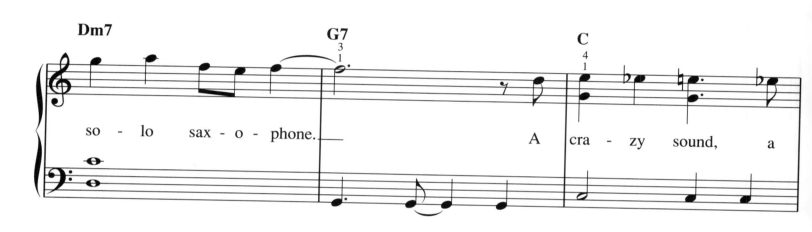

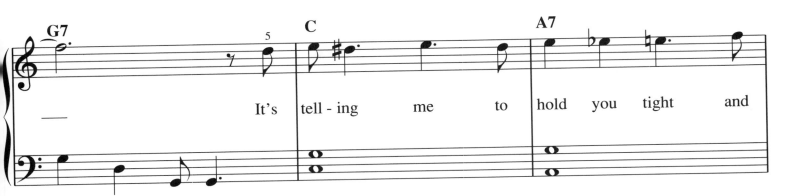

It's tell-ing me to hold you tight and

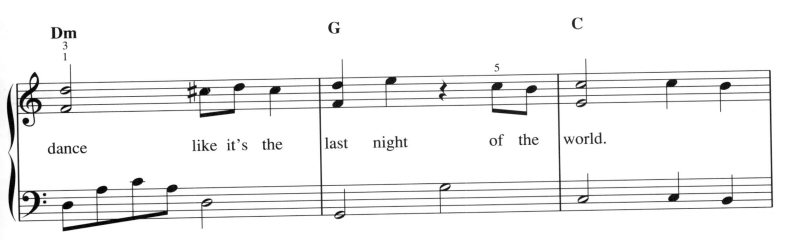

dance like it's the last night of the world.

Kim Dreams _____ were all I ev - er knew. *Chris* Dreams _____ you won't need

when I'm through. *Both* An - y-where we may be,

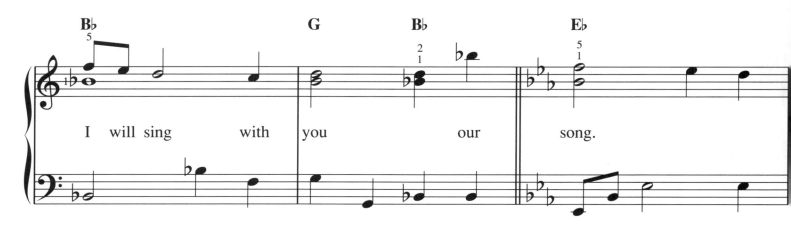

I will sing with you our song.

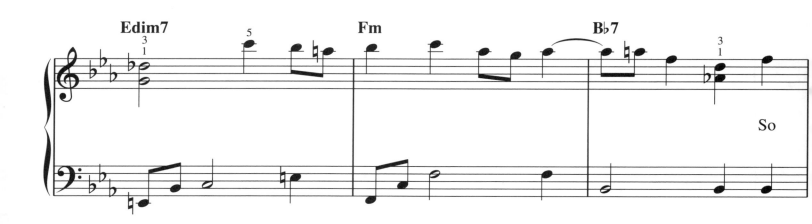

So

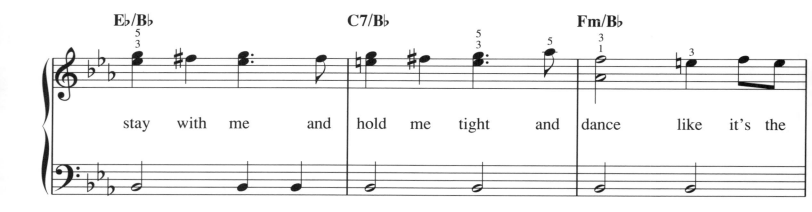

stay with me and hold me tight and dance like it's the

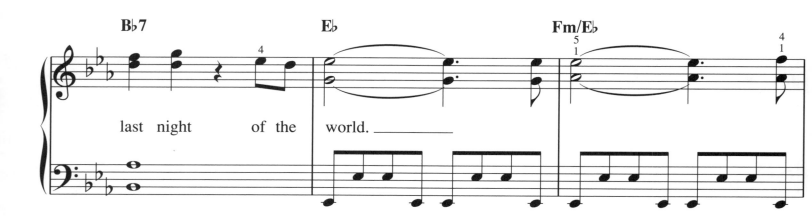

last night of the world. _____

137

LOVE CHANGES EVERYTHING

(From "ASPECTS OF LOVE")

Music by ANDREW LLOYD WEBBER
Lyrics by DON BLACK and CHARLES HART

sum-mer fly   or a   night   seem like   a   life-time.   Yes

love,   love chan-ges   ev-ery-thing: now I   trem-ble   at your

name.   Noth-ing in the world will ev-er   be   the

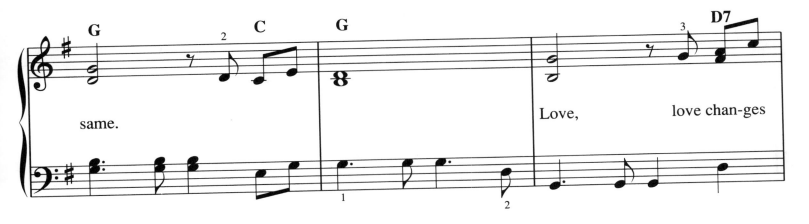

same.   Love,   love chan-ges

ev - ery-thing: days are   long - er,   words mean   more.

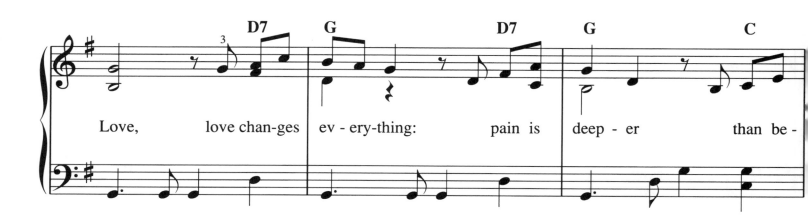

Love,   love chan-ges   ev - ery-thing: pain is   deep - er   than be -

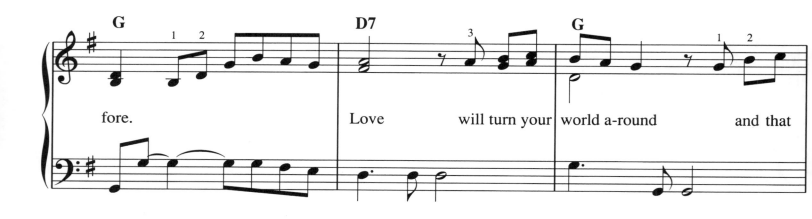

fore.   Love   will turn your   world a-round   and that

world   will last   for   ev - er.   Yes   love,   love chan-ges

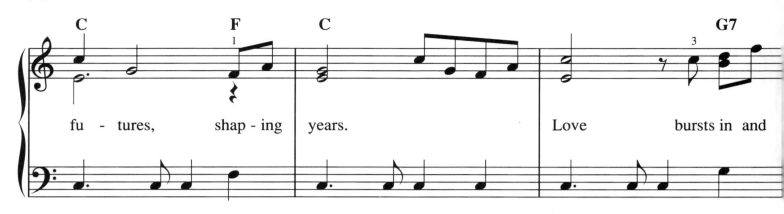

fu - tures, shap - ing years. Love bursts in and

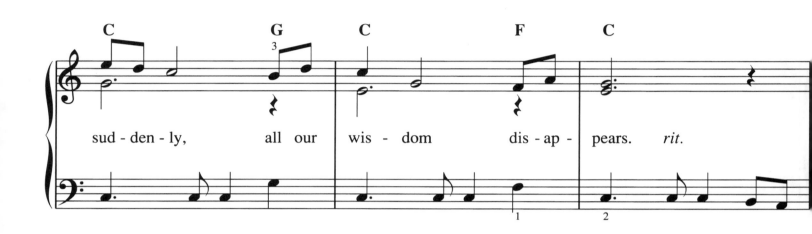

sud - den - ly, all our wis - dom dis - ap - pears. *rit.*

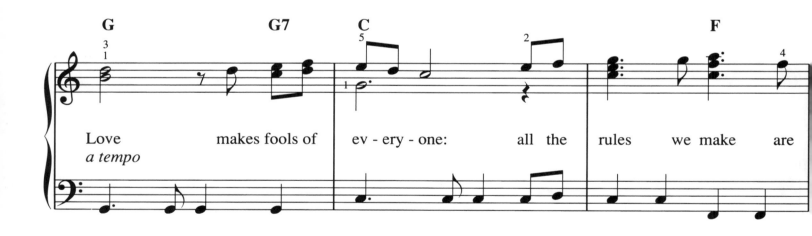

Love makes fools of ev - ery - one: all the rules we make are

a tempo

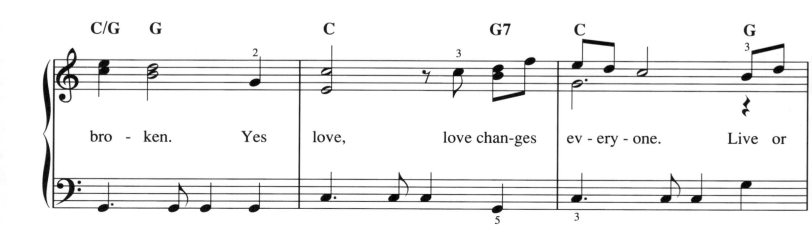

bro - ken. Yes love, love chan - ges ev - ery - one. Live or

MAKE BELIEVE

(From "SHOW BOAT")

Lyrics by OSCAR HAMMERSTEIN II
Music by JEROME KERN

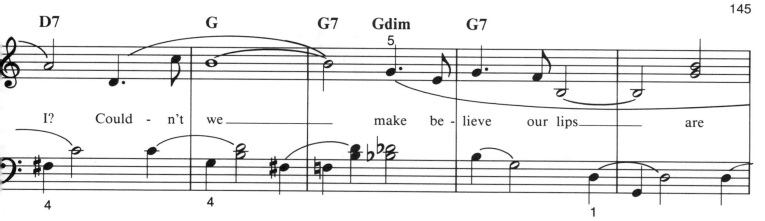

I? Could - n't we _____ make be - lieve our lips _____ are

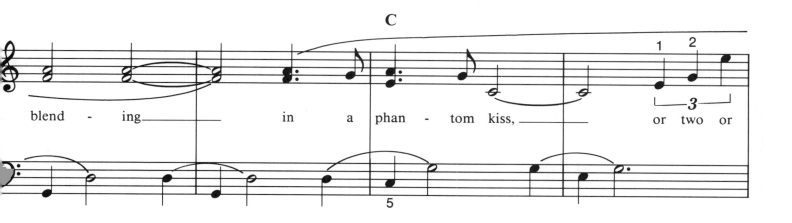

blend - ing _____ in a phan - tom kiss, _____ or two or

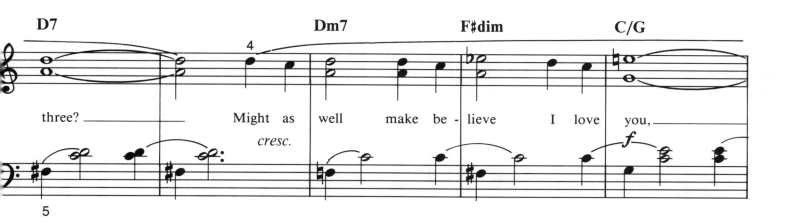

three? _____ Might as well make be - lieve I love you, _____

cresc.

For to tell the truth, _____ I do. _____

MEMORY
(From "CATS")

Music by ANDREW LLOYD WEBBER
Text by TREVOR NUNN after T.S. ELIOT

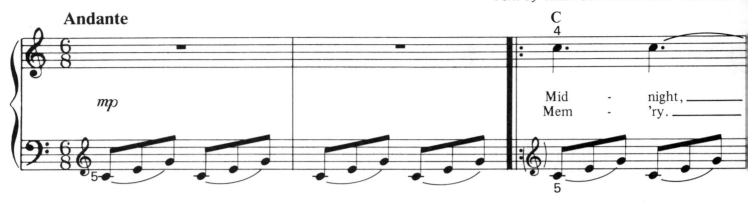

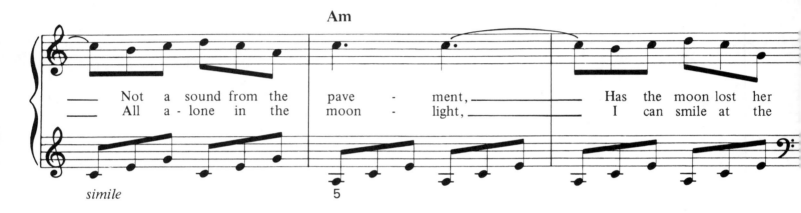

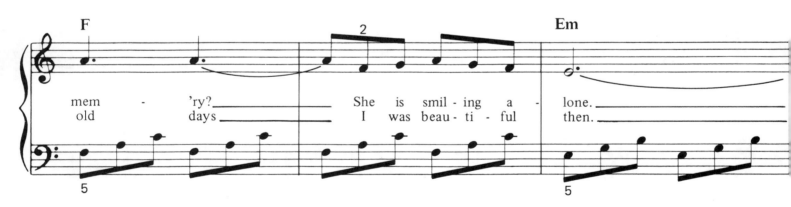

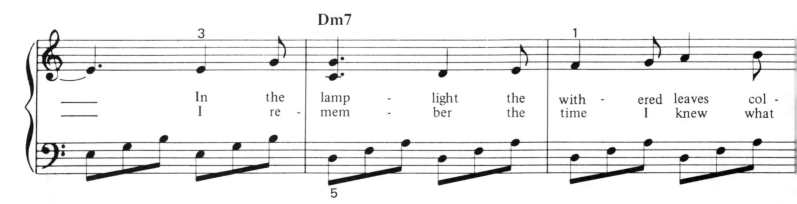

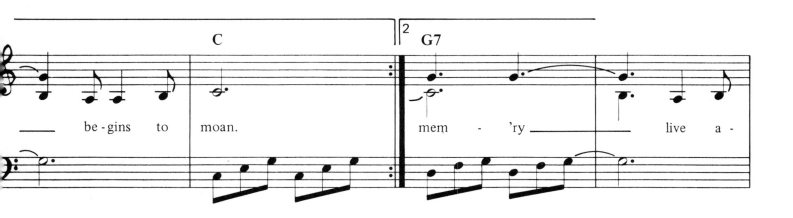

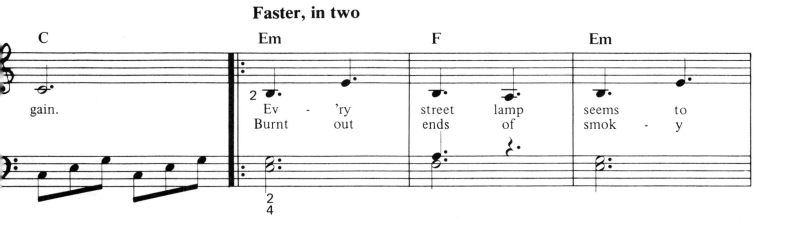

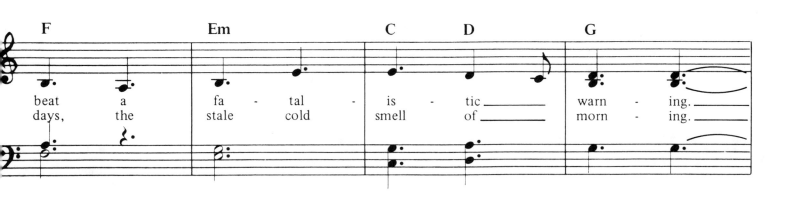

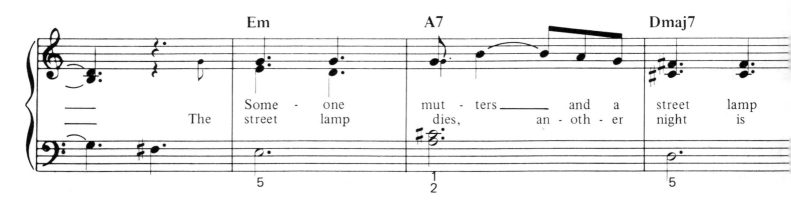

Em — A7 — Dmaj7

The Some - one mut - ters____ and a street lamp
street lamp dies, an - oth - er night is

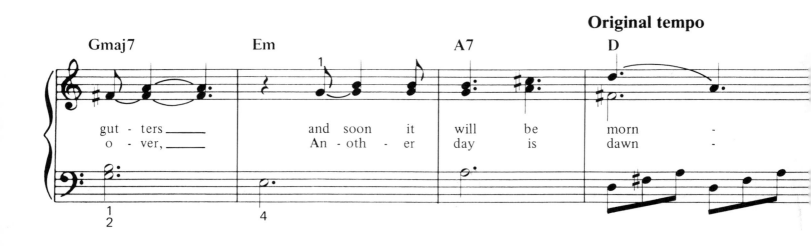

Original tempo

Gmaj7 — Em — A7 — D

gut - ters____ and soon it will be morn -
o - ver,____ An - oth - er day is dawn

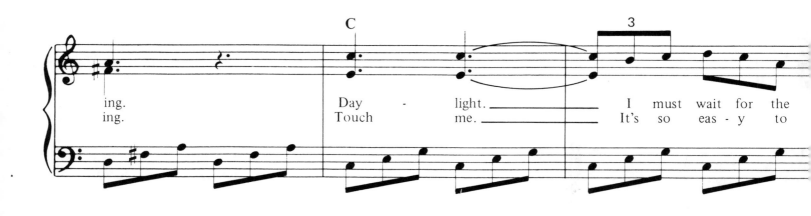

C

ing. Day - light.____ I must wait for the
ing. Touch me.____ It's so eas - y to

Am — F

sun - rise,____ I must think of a new life____
leave me____ all a - lone with the mem - 'ry____

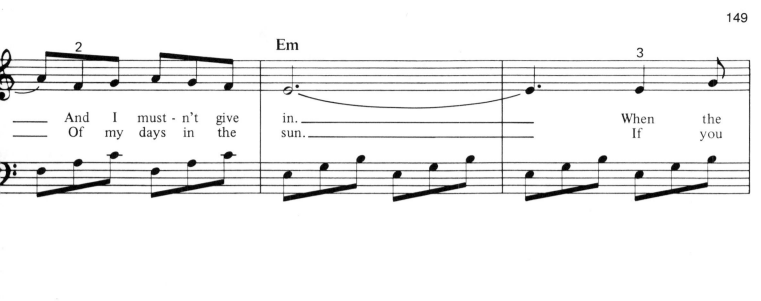

And I must-n't give in. When the
Of my days in the sun. If you

dawn comes to - night will be a mem - o - ry too
touch me you'll un - der - stand what hap - pi - ness is,

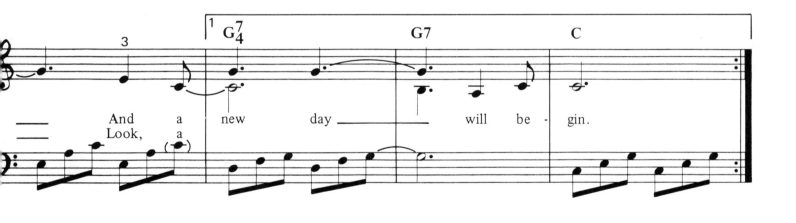

And a new day will be - gin.
Look, a

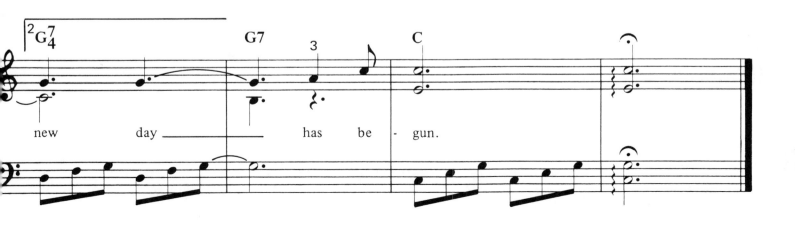

new day has be - gun.

LOOK TO THE RAINBOW
(From "FINIAN'S RAINBOW")

Words by E.Y. HARBURG
Music by BURTON LANE

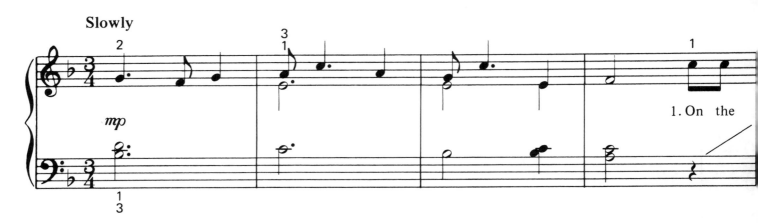

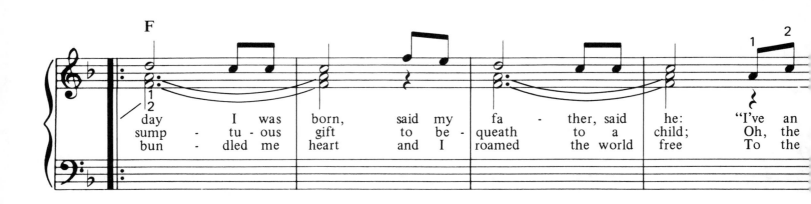

day ___ I was born, said my fa - ther, said he: "I've an
sump - tu - ous gift to be - queath to a child; Oh, the
bun - dled me heart and I roamed the world free To the

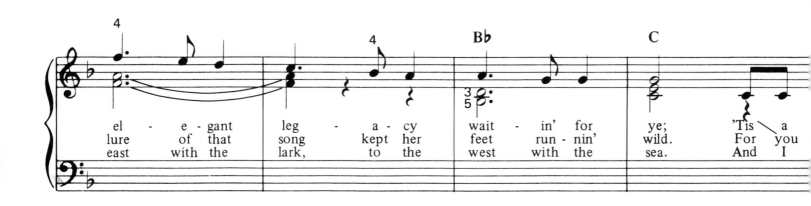

el - e - gant leg - a - cy wait - in' for ye; 'Tis a
lure of that song kept her feet run - nin' wild. For you
east with the lark, to the west with the sea. And I

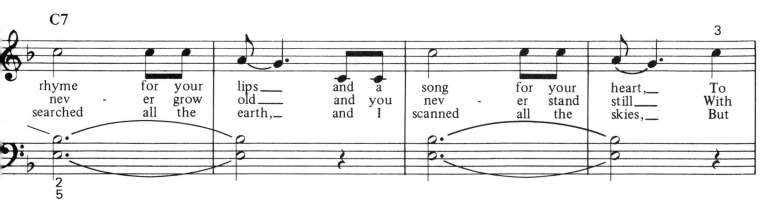

rhyme for your lips___ and a song for your heart,___ To
nev - er grow old___ and you nev - er stand still,___ With
searched all the earth,___ and I scanned all the skies,___ But

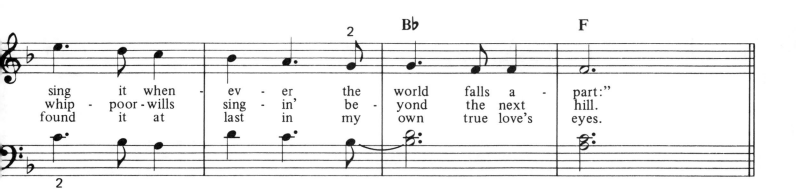

sing it when - ev - er the world falls a - part:"
whip - poor - wills sing - in' be - yond the next hill.
found it at last in my own true love's eyes.

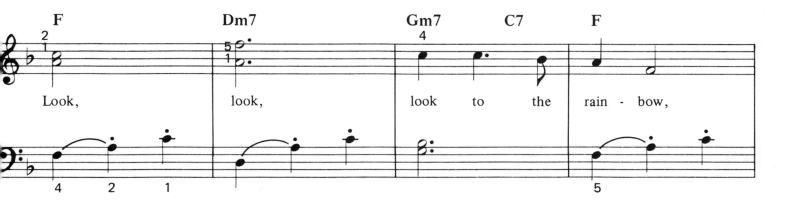

Look, look, look to the rain - bow,

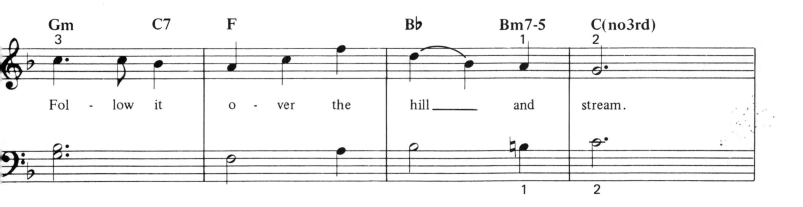

Fol - low it o - ver the hill___ and stream.

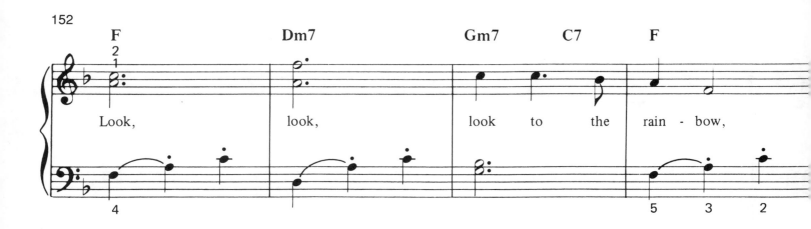

Look, look, look to the rain - bow,

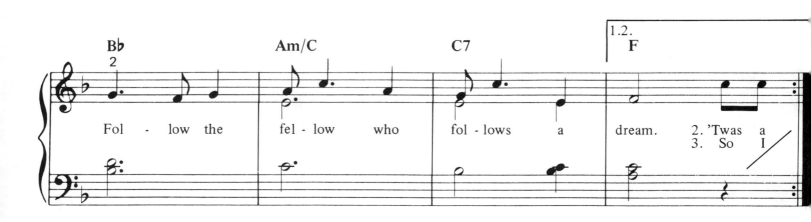

Fol - low the fel - low who fol - lows a dream. 2. 'Twas a
3. So I

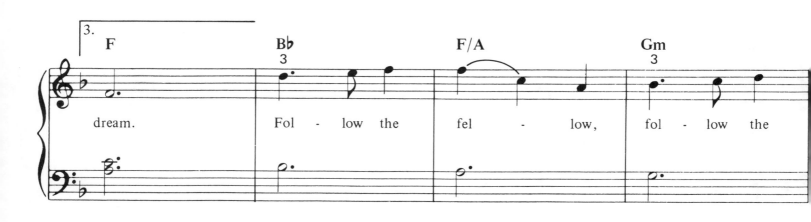

3.
dream. Fol - low the fel - low, fol - low the

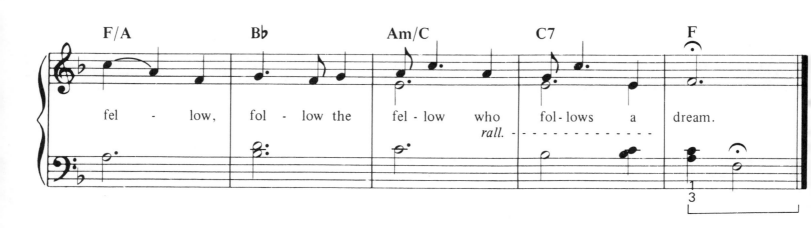

fel - low, fol - low the fel - low who fol - lows a dream.

MY CUP RUNNETH OVER
(FROM "I DO! I DO!")

Words by TOM JONES
Music by HARVEY SCHMIDT

cup run - neth o - ver with love.
cup run - neth o - ver with love.

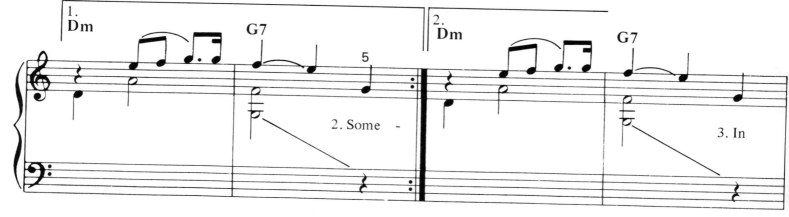

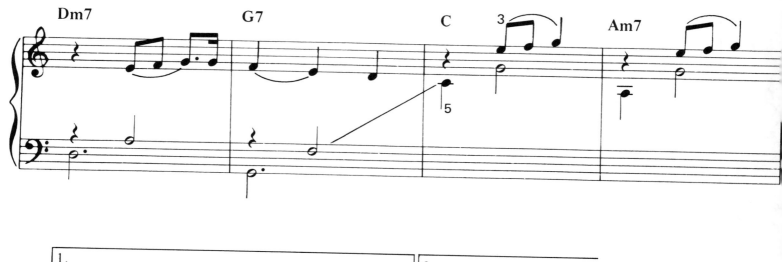

2. Some -

3. In

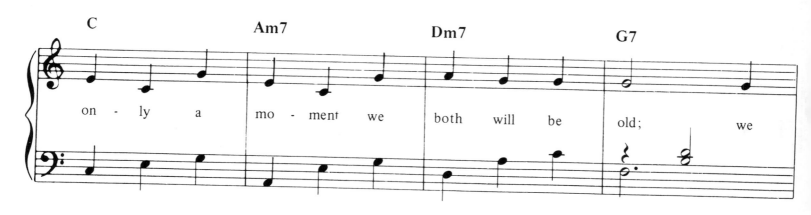

on - ly a mo - ment we both will be old; we

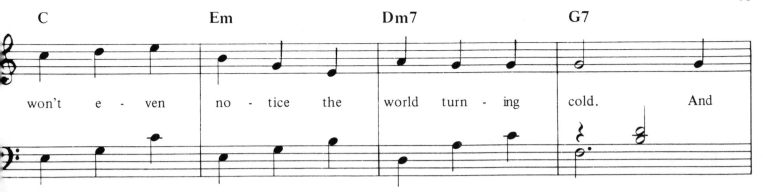

won't e - ven no - tice the world turn - ing cold. And

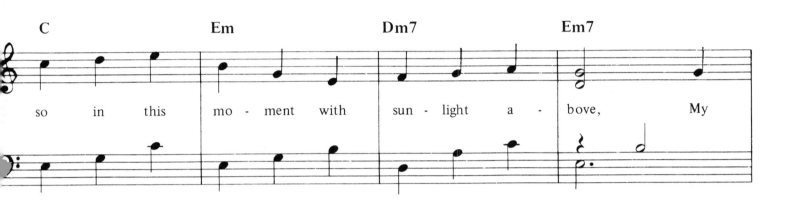

so in this mo - ment with sun - light a - bove, My

cup run - neth o - ver with love,

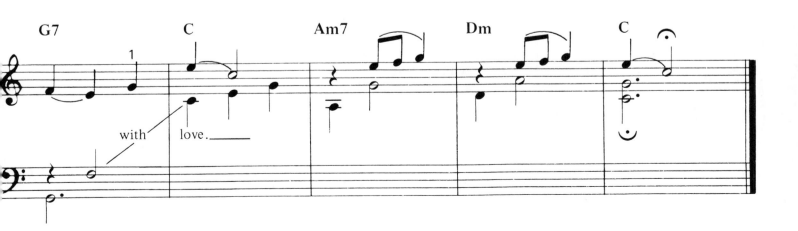

with love.

MY FAVORITE THINGS
(From "THE SOUND OF MUSIC")

Lyrics by OSCAR HAMMERSTEIN II
Music by RICHARD RODGERS

Lively, in one ($\lessgtr$. = 1 beat)

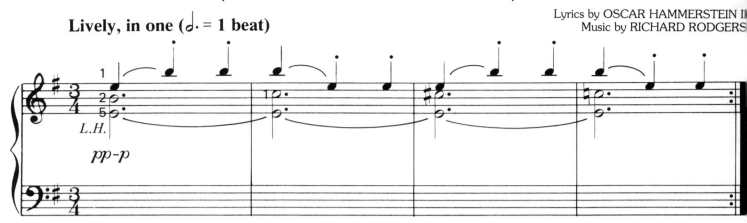

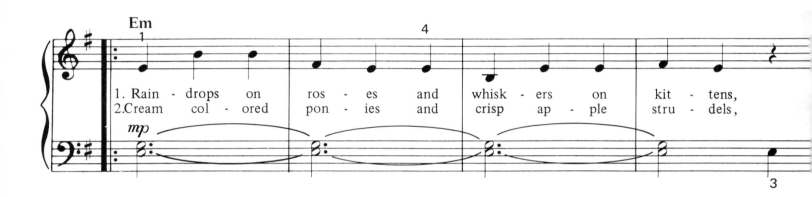

1. Rain - drops on ros - es and whisk - ers on kit - tens,
2. Cream col - ored pon - ies and crisp ap - ple stru - dels,

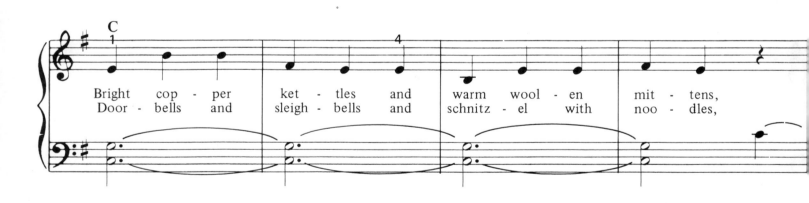

Bright cop - per ket - tles and warm wool - en mit - tens,
Door - bells and sleigh - bells and schnitz - el with noo - dles,

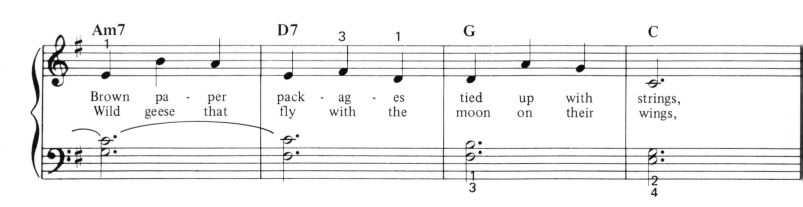

Brown pa - per pack - ag - es tied up with strings,
Wild geese that fly with the moon on their wings,

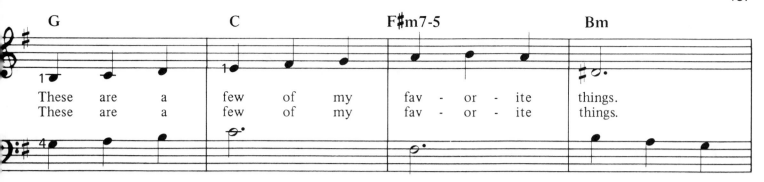

These are a few of my fav - or - ite things.
These are a few of my fav - or - ite things.

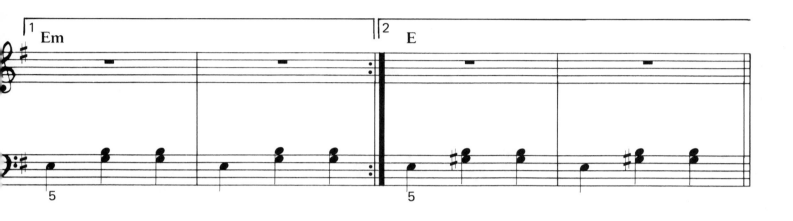

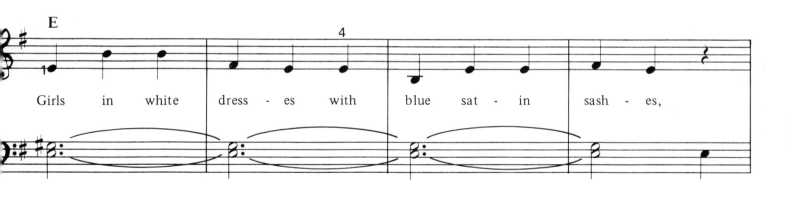

Girls in white dress - es with blue sat - in sash - es,

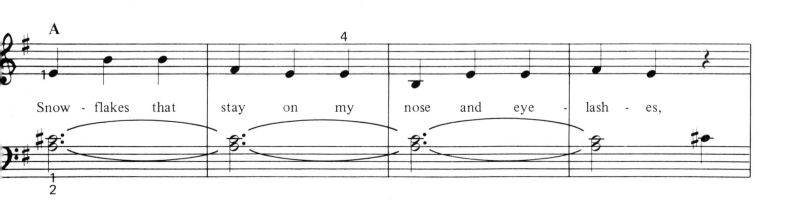

Snow - flakes that stay on my nose and eye - lash - es,

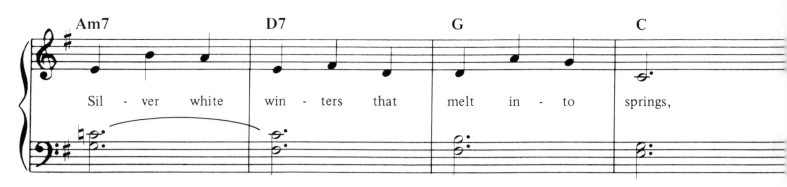

Silver white winters that melt into springs,

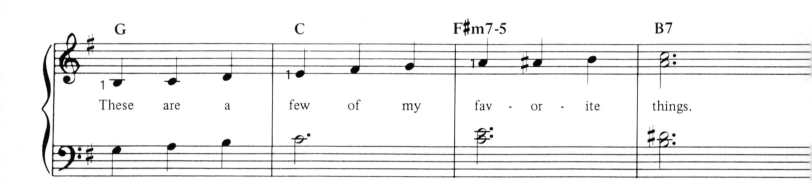

These are a few of my favorite things.

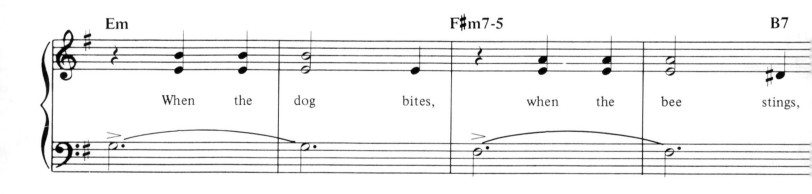

When the dog bites, when the bee stings,

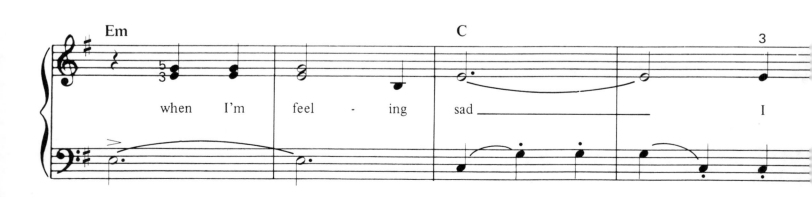

when I'm feeling sad I

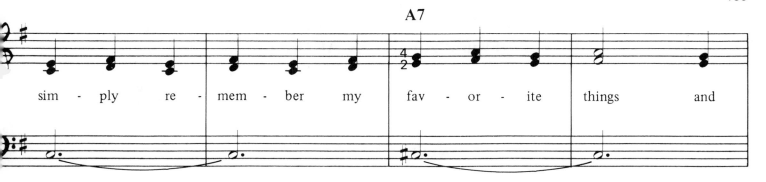

simp - ply   re - mem - ber   my   fav - or - ite   things   and

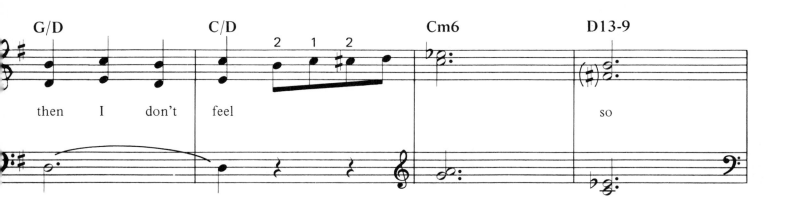

then   I   don't   feel   so

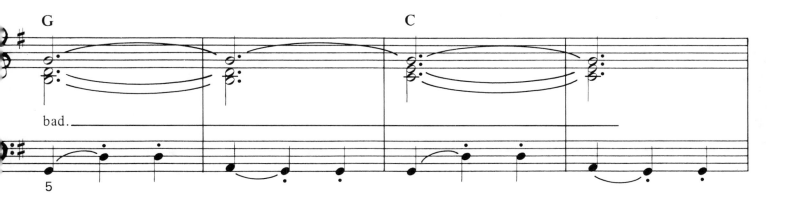

bad.

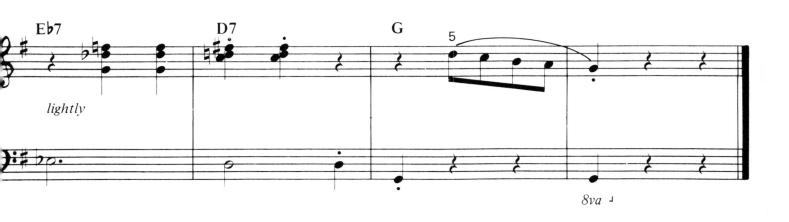

lightly

8va ♩

MY FUNNY VALENTINE
(From "BABES IN ARMS")

Words by LORENZ HART
Music by RICHARD RODGERS

161

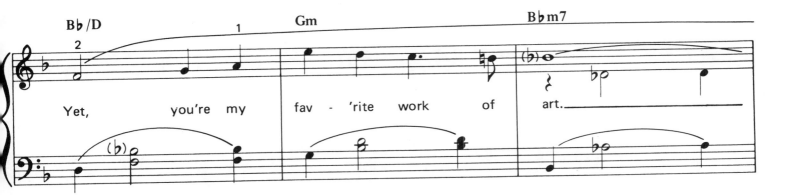

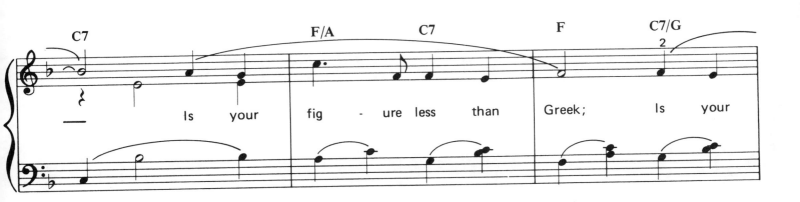

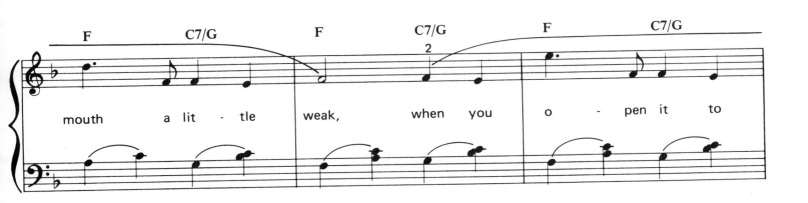

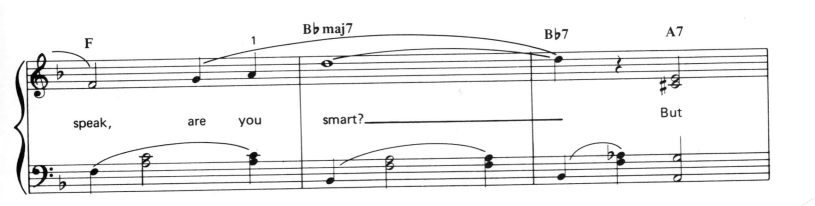

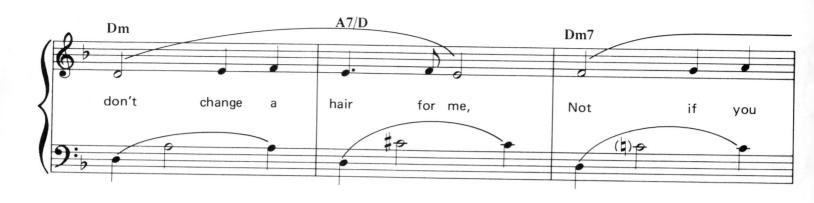

don't change a hair for me, Not if you

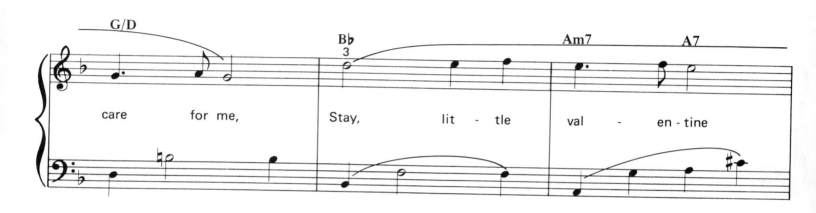

care for me, Stay, lit - tle val - en -tine

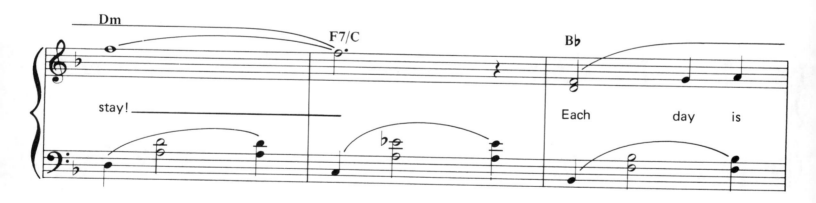

stay! _____ Each day is

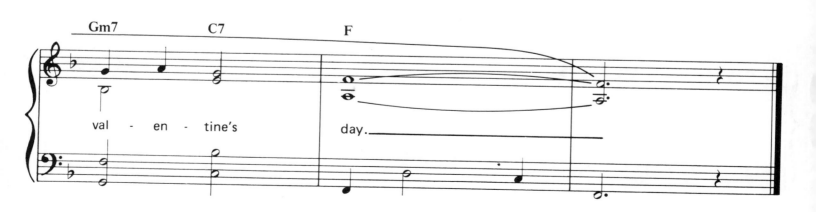

val - en - tine's day. _____

OKLAHOMA
(From "OKLAHOMA!")

Lyrics by OSCAR HAMMERSTEIN II
Music by RICHARD RODGERS

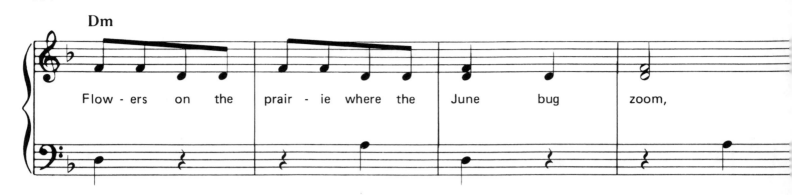

Flow - ers on the prair - ie where the June bug zoom,

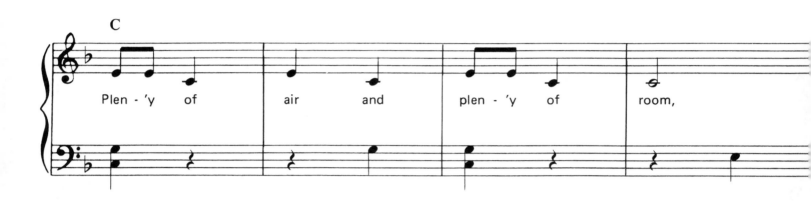

Plen - 'y of air and plen - 'y of room,

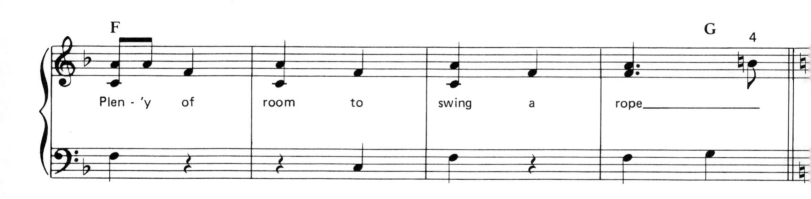

Plen - 'y of room to swing a rope____

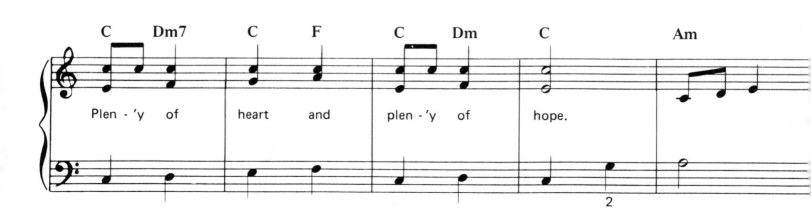

Plen - 'y of heart and plen - 'y of hope.

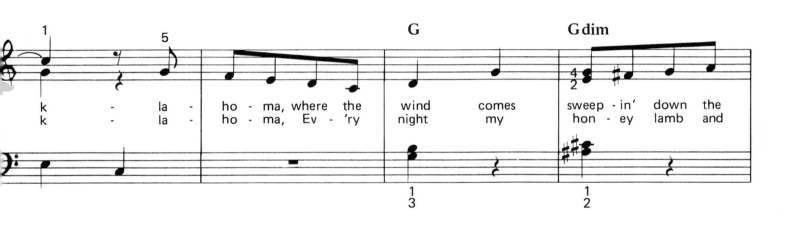

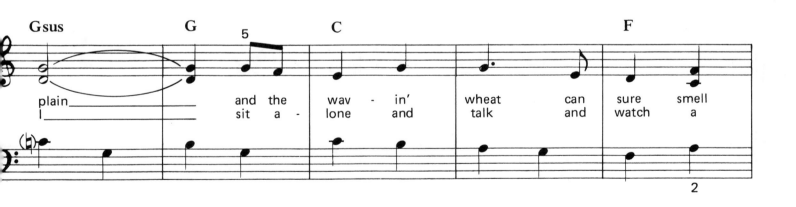

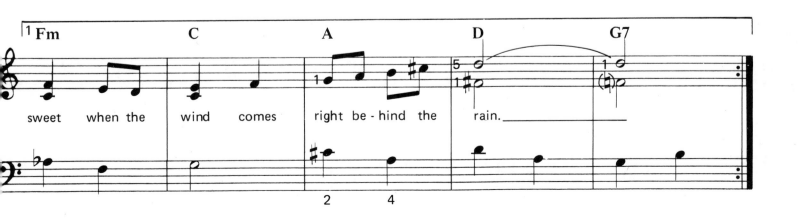

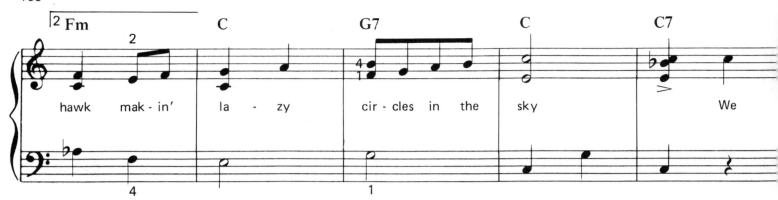

hawk mak-in' la - zy cir-cles in the sky We

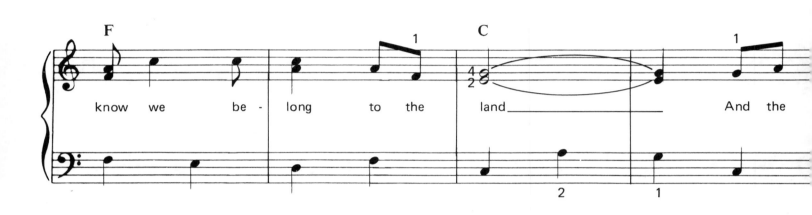

know we be - long to the land_____ And the

land we be - long to is grand! And when we

say_____ Yeeow! A - yip-i - o - ee

ay!_____ We're on - ly say - in'

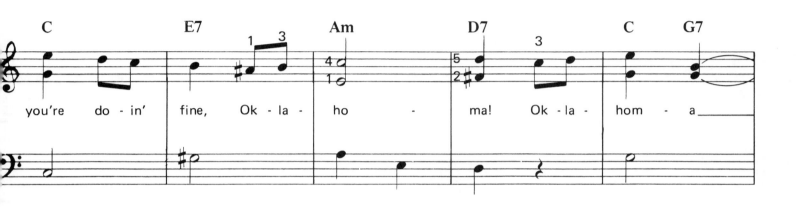

you're do - in' fine, Ok - la - ho - ma! Ok - la - hom - a____

To Coda ⊕   **D.S. al Coda**
(lyric 1)

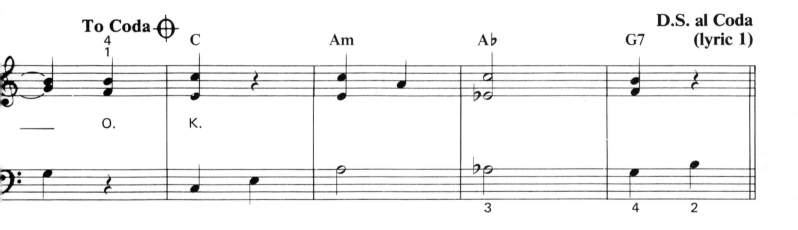

____ O. K.

CODA

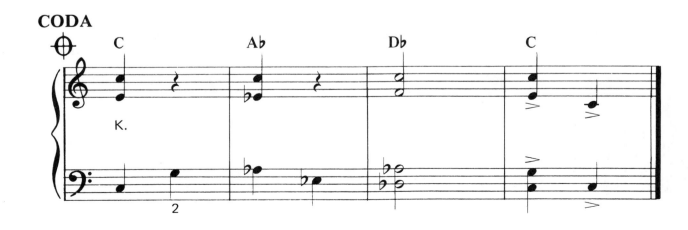

K.

OH, WHAT A BEAUTIFUL MORNIN'

(From "OKLAHOMA!")

Lyrics by OSCAR HAMMERSTEIN II
Music by RICHARD RODGERS

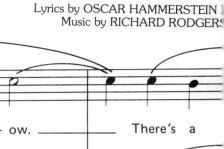

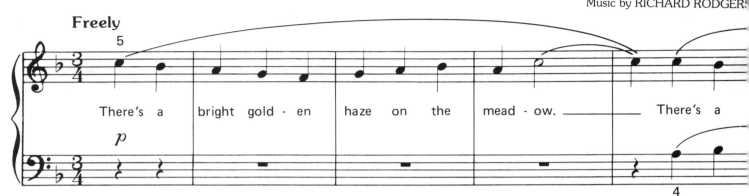

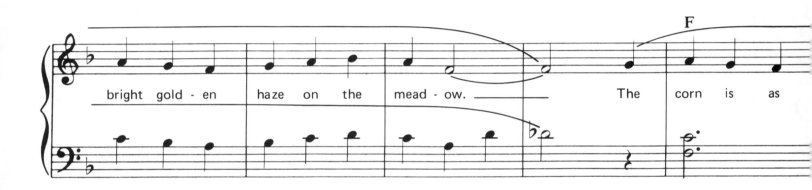

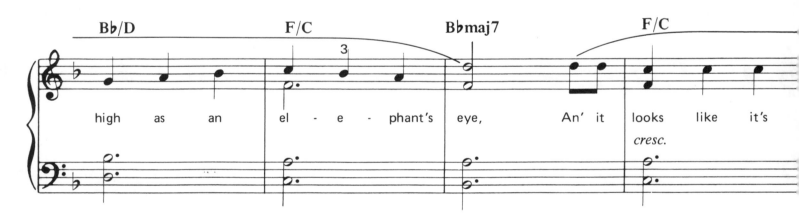

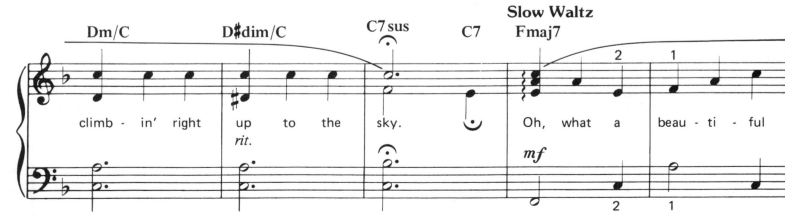

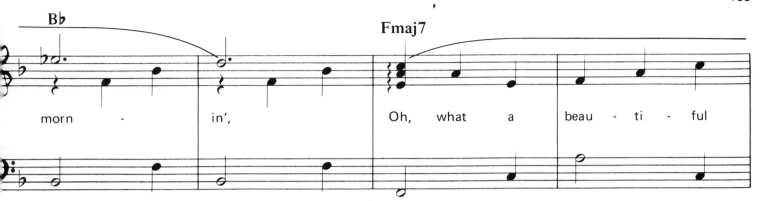

morn - in', Oh, what a beau - ti - ful

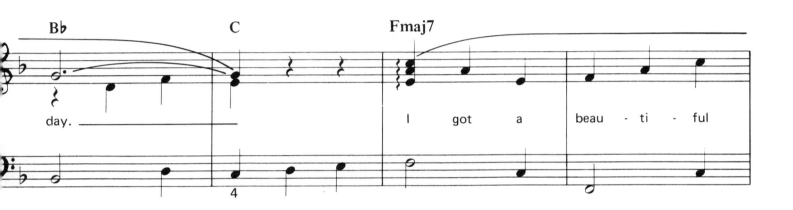

day. _____ I got a beau - ti - ful

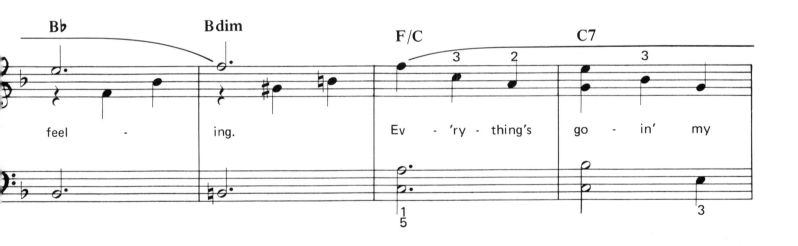

feel - ing. Ev - 'ry - thing's go - in' my

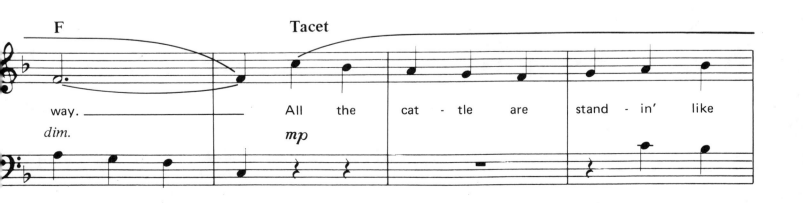

way. _____ All the cat - tle are stand - in' like

dim. _mp_

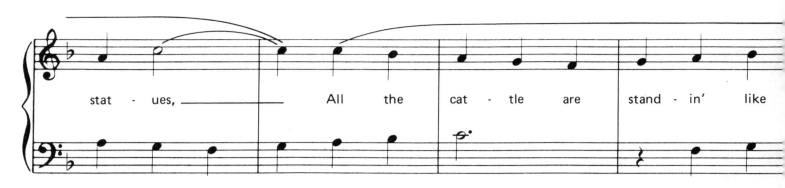

statues, _____ All the cat - tle are stand - in' like

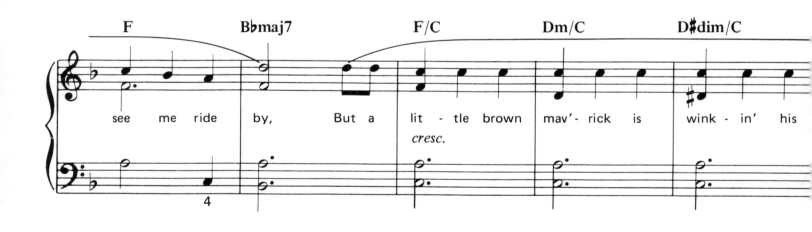

statues. _____ They don't turn their heads as they

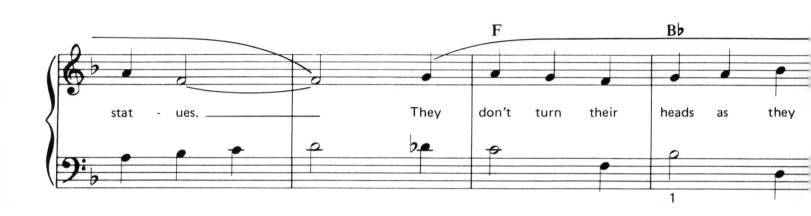

see me ride by, But a lit - tle brown mav' - rick is wink - in' his

cresc.

eye. Oh, what a beau - ti - ful morn -

poco rit. *a tempo*

OL' MAN RIVER

(From "SHOW BOAT")

Words by OSCAR HAMMERSTEIN II
Music by JEROME KERN

Slowly (♩ = 1 count)

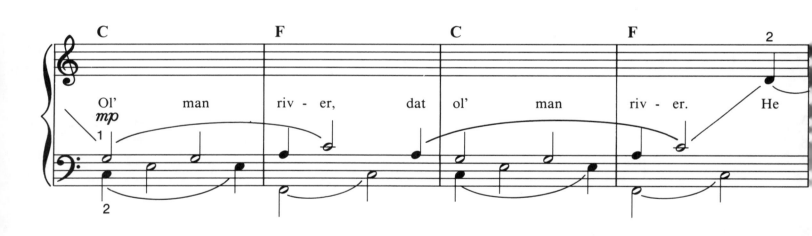

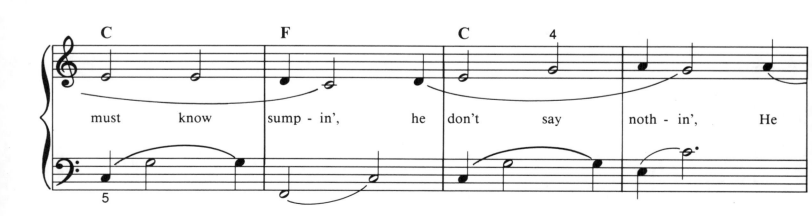

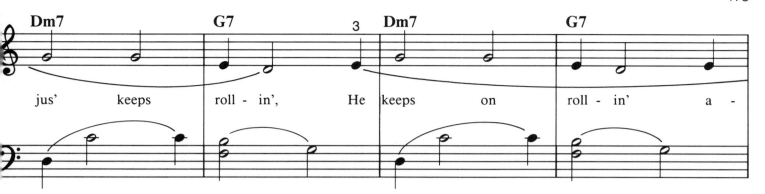

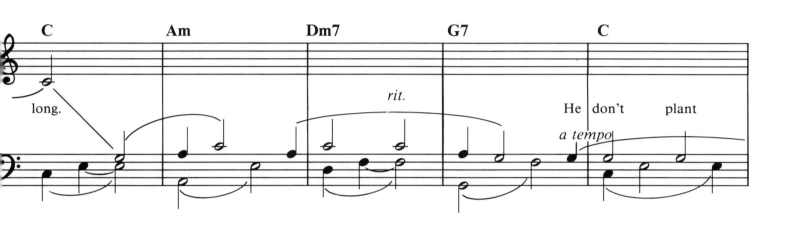

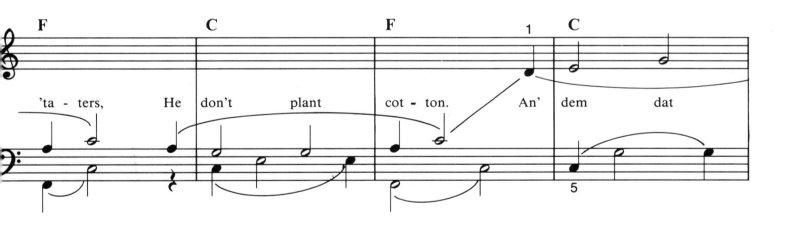

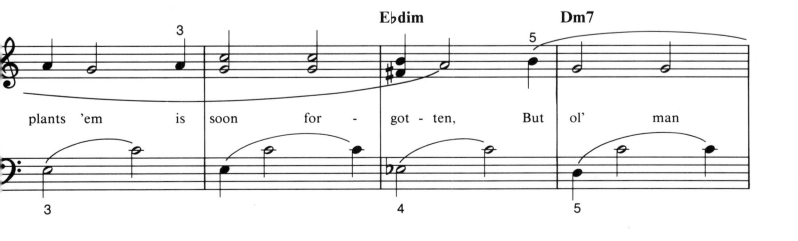

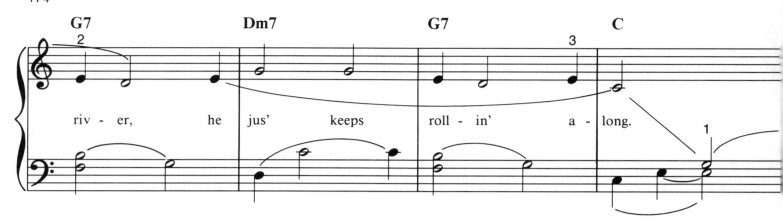

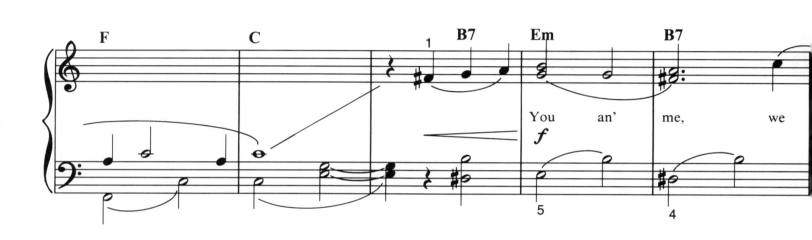

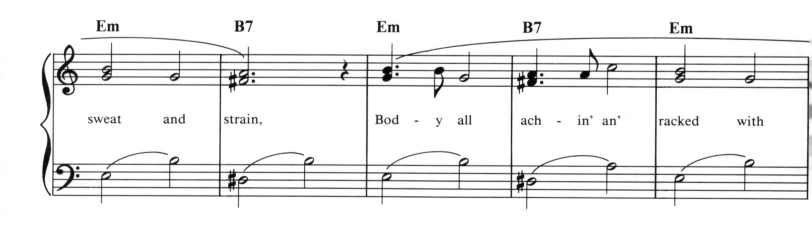

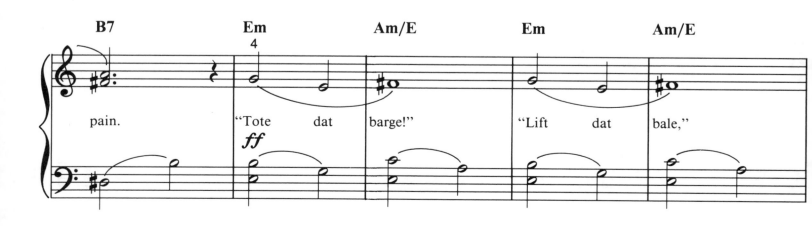

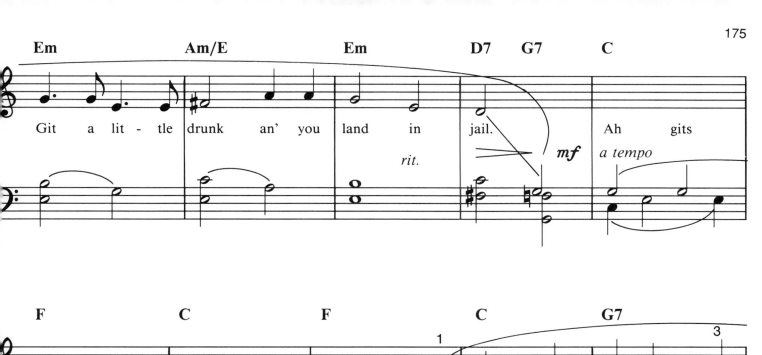

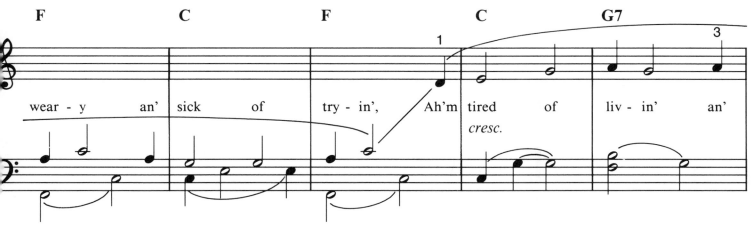

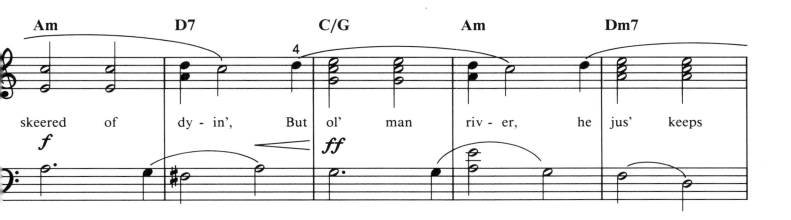

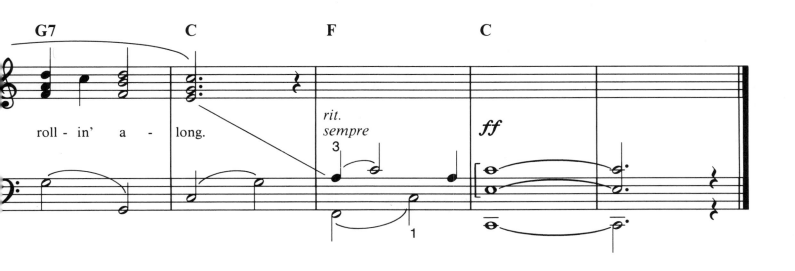

ON THE STREET WHERE YOU LIVE
(From "MY FAIR LADY")

Words by ALAN JAY LERNER
Music by FREDERICK LOEWE

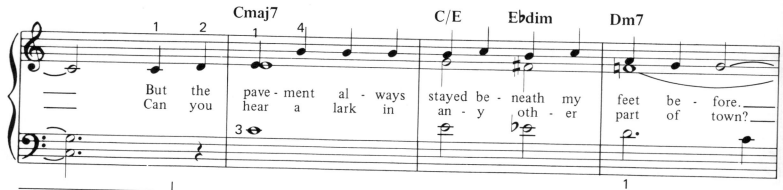

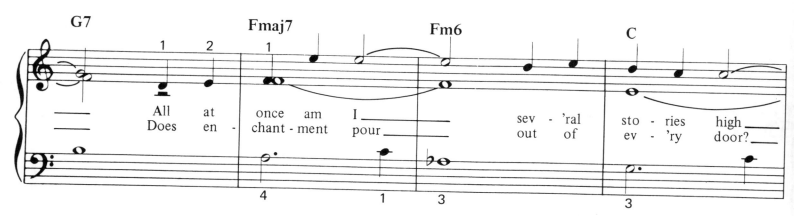

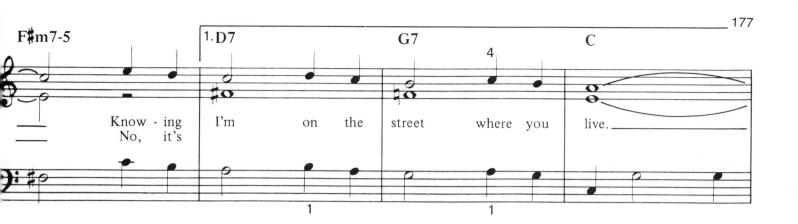

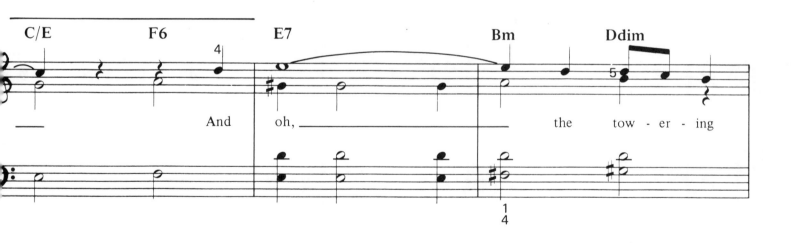

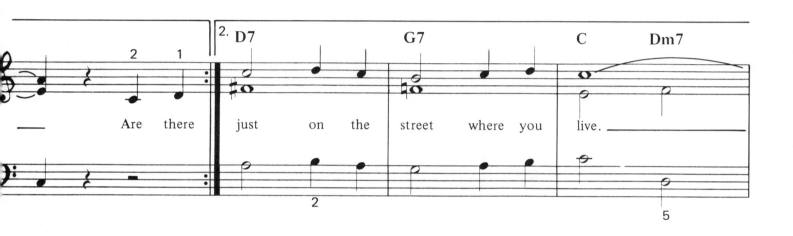

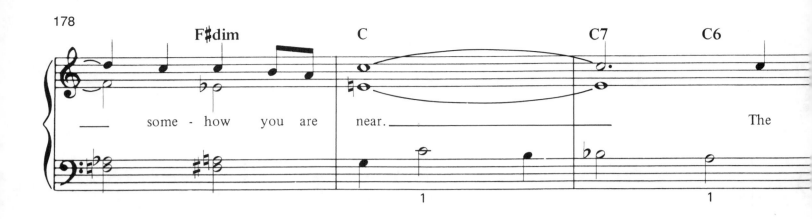

some - how you are near. The

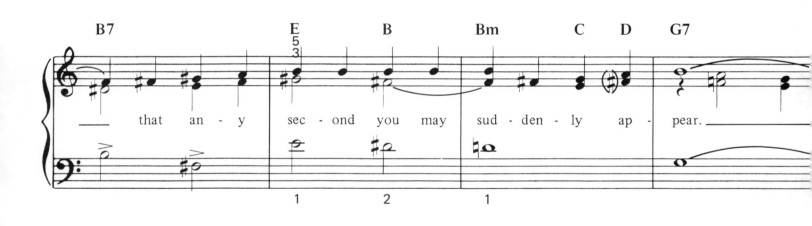

o - - ver - pow - er - ing feel - ing

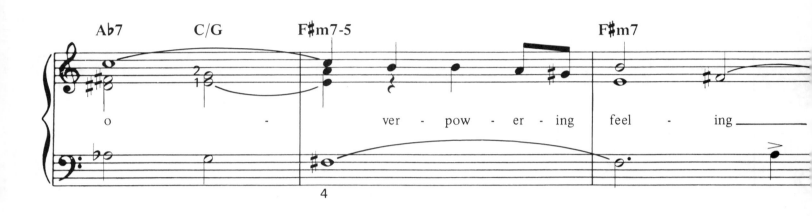

that an - y sec - ond you may sud - den - ly ap - pear.

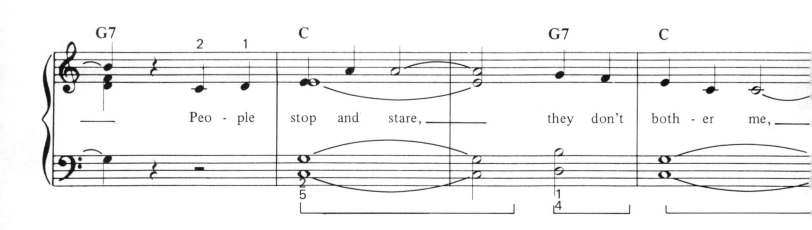

Peo - ple stop and stare, they don't both - er me,

For there's no - where else on earth that I would

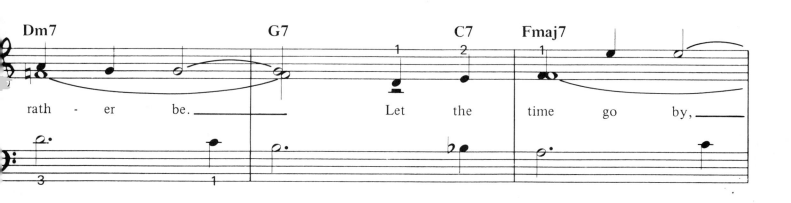

rath - er be. _____ Let the time go by, _____

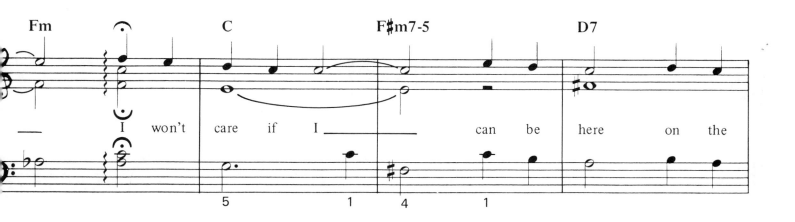

_____ I won't care if I _____ can be here on the

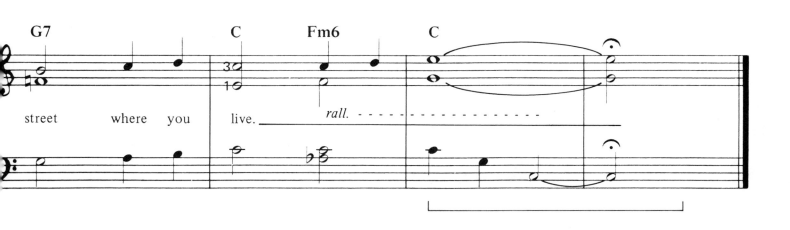

street where you live. _____ *rall.* - - - - - - - - - - - - - - -

ON A CLEAR DAY
(You Can See Forever)

Words by ALAN JAY LERNER
Music by BURTON LANE

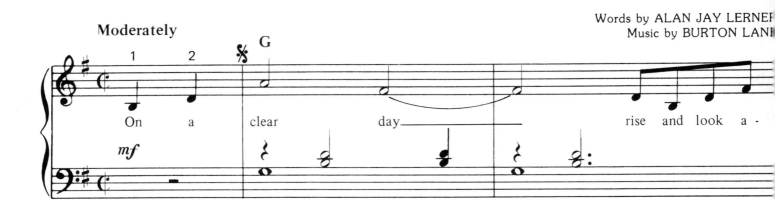

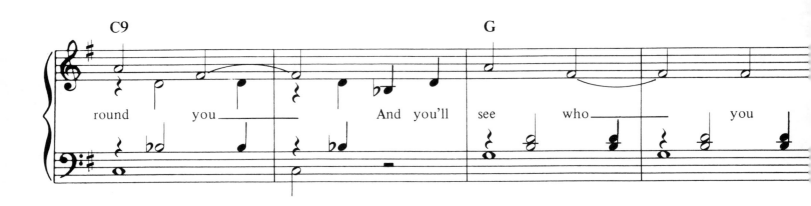

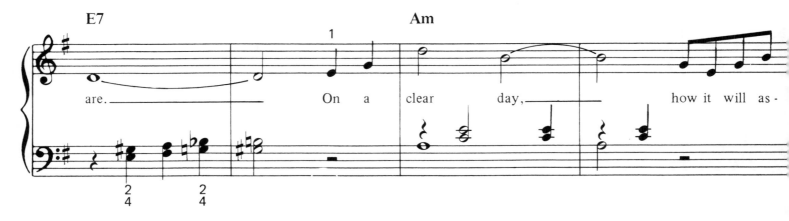

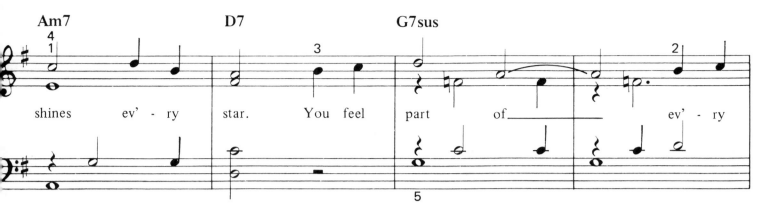

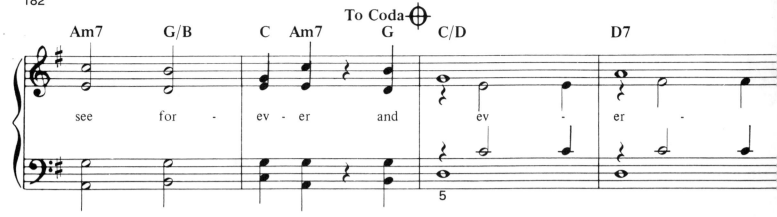

see for - ev - er and ev - er -

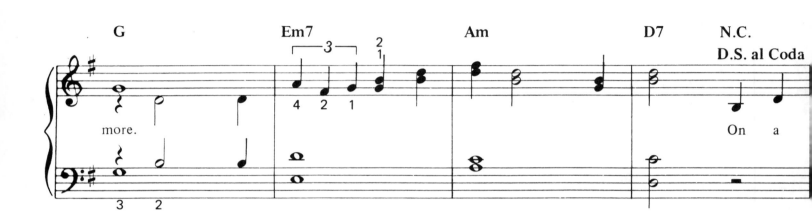

more.   On a

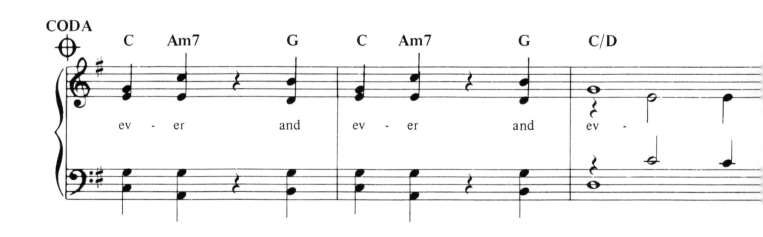

ev - er and ev - er and ev -

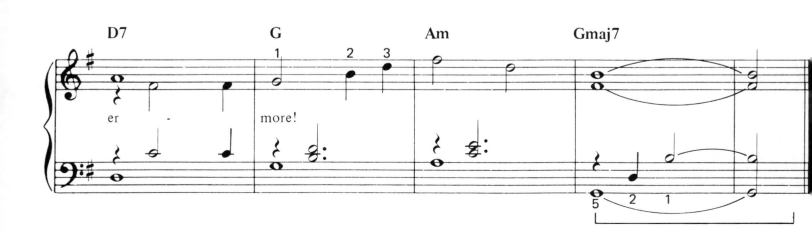

er - more!

PEOPLE
(From "FUNNY GIRL")

Words by BOB MERRILL
Music by JULE STYNE

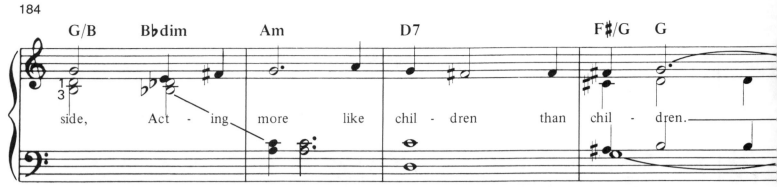

side, Act - ing more like chil - dren than chil - dren.

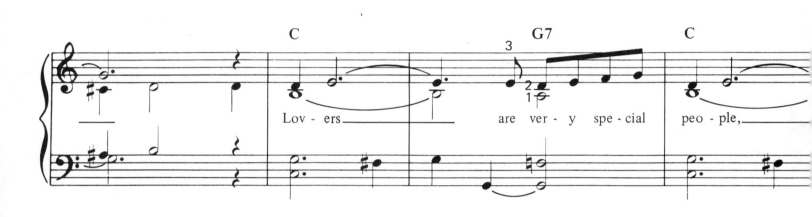

Lov - ers _____ are ver - y spe - cial peo - ple,

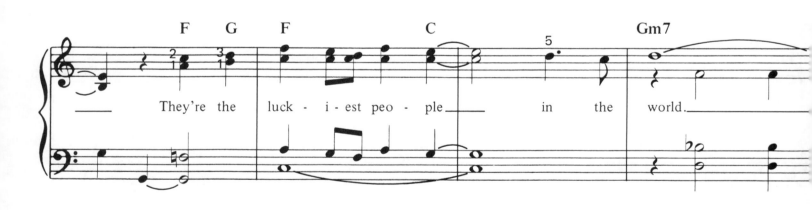

They're the luck - i - est peo - ple _____ in the world.

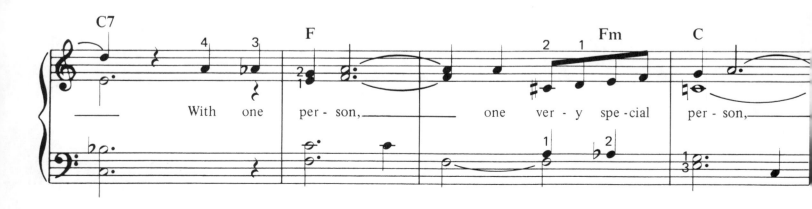

With one per - son, _____ one ver - y spe - cial per - son,

A feel - ing deep in your soul _____ says, "You were half, now you're whole."

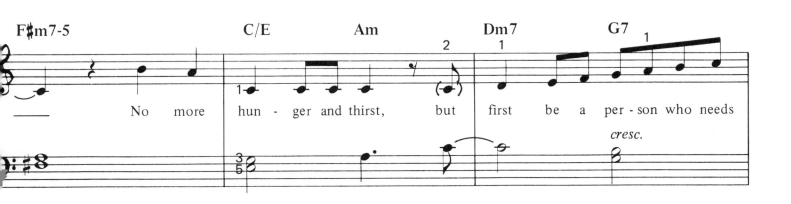

No more hun - ger and thirst, but first be a per - son who needs

cresc.

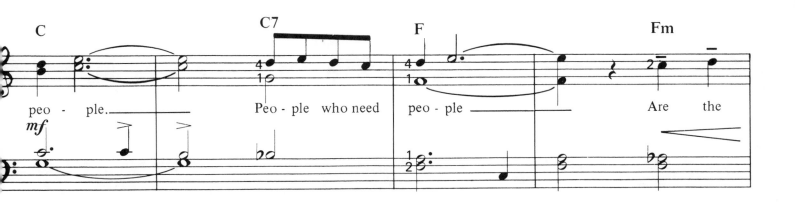

peo - ple. Peo - ple who need peo - ple _____ Are the

mf

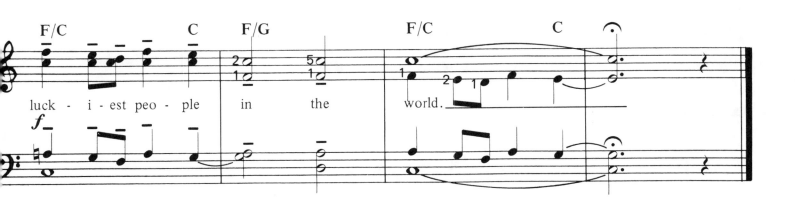

luck - i - est peo - ple in the world. _____

f

PEOPLE WILL SAY WE'RE IN LOVE

(From "OKLAHOMA!")

Lyrics by OSCAR HAMMERSTEIN
Music by RICHARD RODGERS

With a lilt

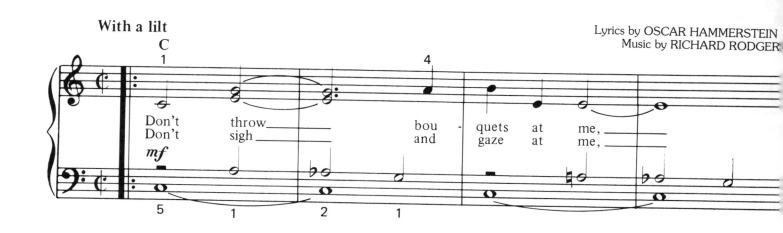

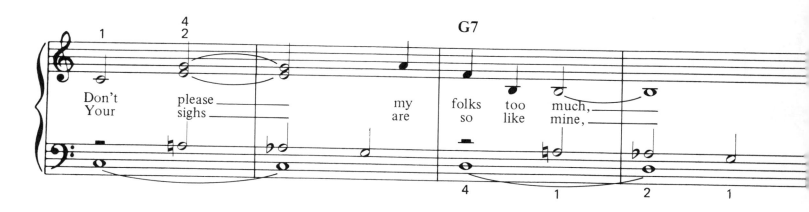

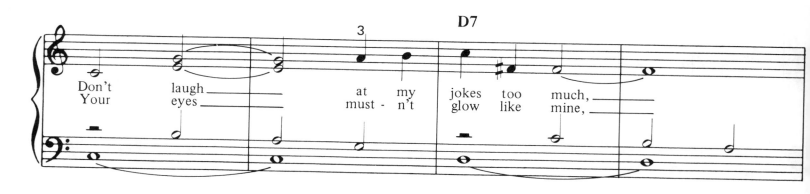

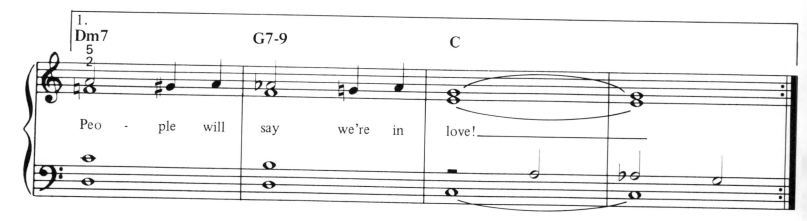

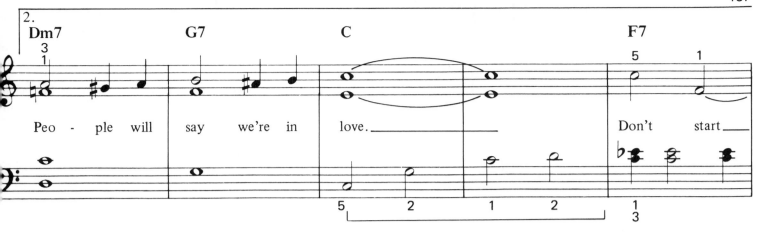

2.

Dm7　　　　G7　　　　C　　　　　　　　F7

Peo - ple will say we're in love.＿＿＿ Don't start＿＿＿

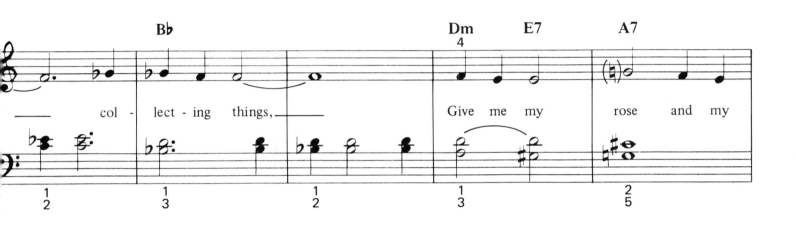

Bb　　　　　　　　Dm　E7　　A7

＿＿ col - lect - ing things,＿＿＿ Give me my rose and my

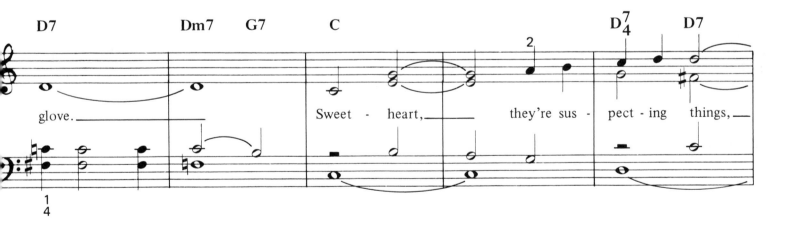

D7　　　　Dm7　G7　　　C　　　　　D7/4　D7

glove.＿＿＿ Sweet - heart,＿＿＿ they're sus - pect - ing things,＿＿＿

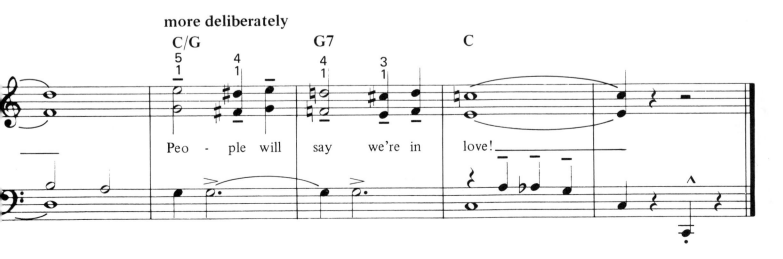

more deliberately

C/G　　　　G7　　　　C

Peo - ple will say we're in love!＿＿＿

SEND IN THE CLOWNS

(From "A LITTLE NIGHT MUSIC")

Music and Lyrics by
STEPHEN SONDHEIM

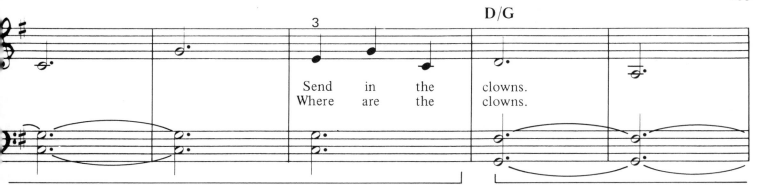

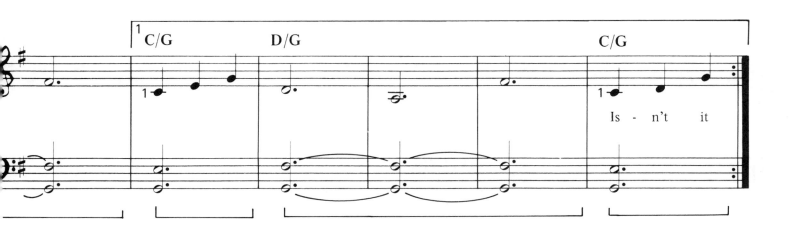

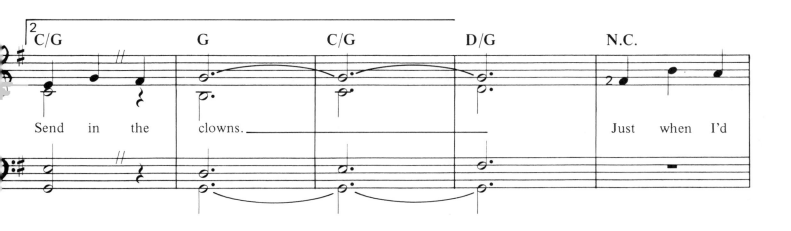

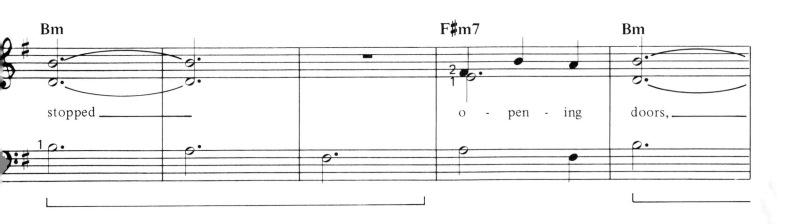

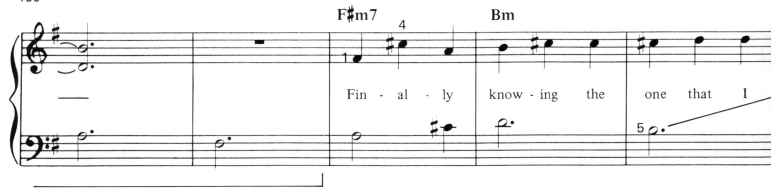

F♯m7 **Bm**

Fin - al - ly know - ing the one that I

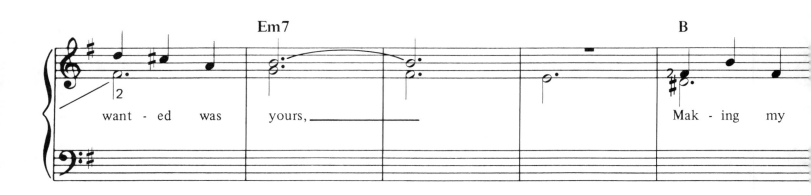

Em7 **B**

want - ed was yours, _____

Mak - ing my

G/D **A/C♯** **Cmaj7** **Bsus4**

en - trance a - gain with my u - su - al flair, _____

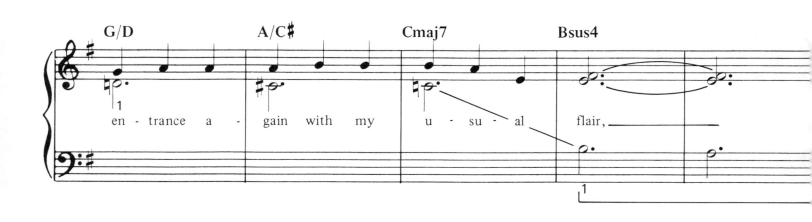

Cm6 **Bm**

Sure of my lines, _____

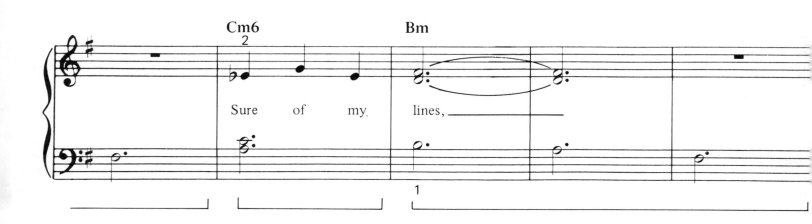

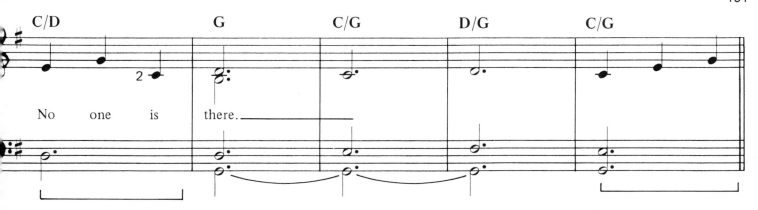

No one is there.

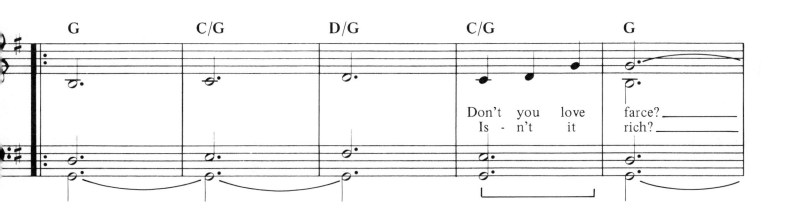

Don't you love farce?_____
Is - n't it rich?_____

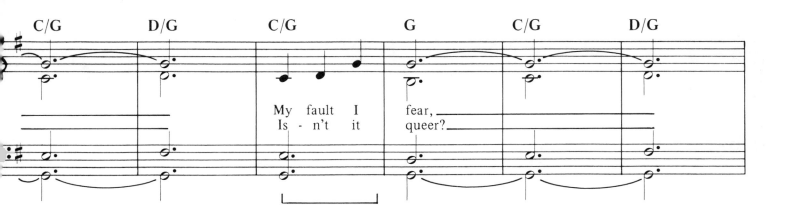

My fault I fear,_____
Is - n't it queer?_____

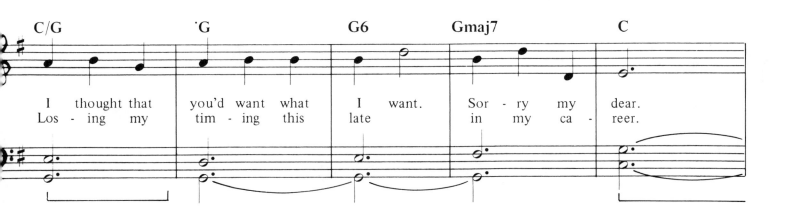

I thought that you'd want what I want. Sor - ry my dear.
Los - ing my tim - ing this late in my ca - reer.

But   where are   the   clowns?
And   where are   the   clowns?

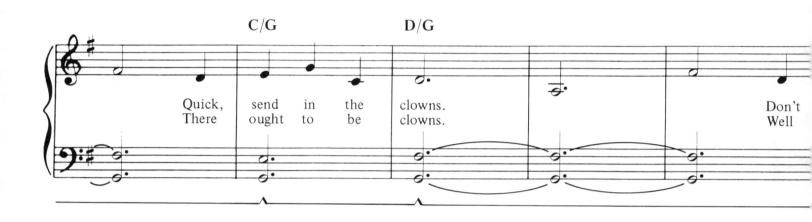

Quick,   send   in   the   clowns.
There   ought   to   be   clowns.

Don't
Well

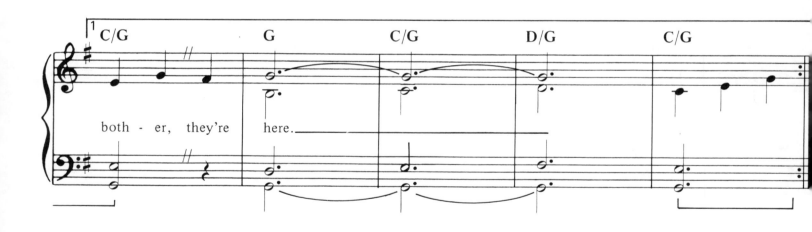

both - er, they're   here.

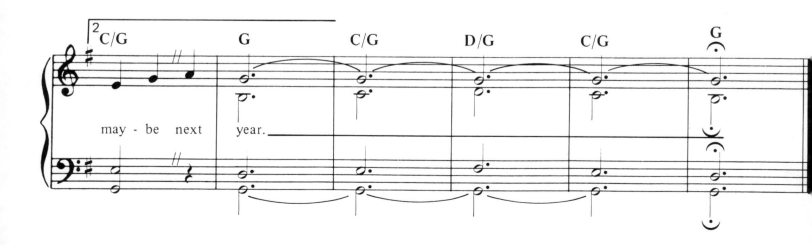

may - be next   year.

SMALL WORLD
(From "GYPSY")

Words by STEPHEN SONDHEIM
Music by JULE STYNE

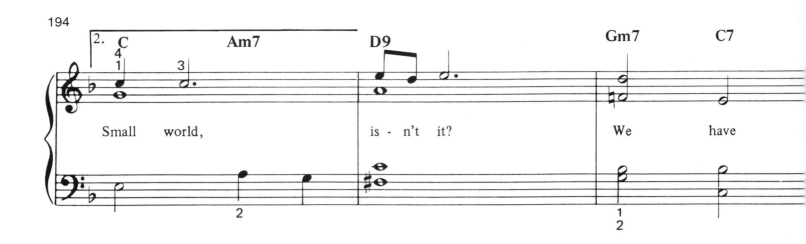

Small world, is - n't it? We have

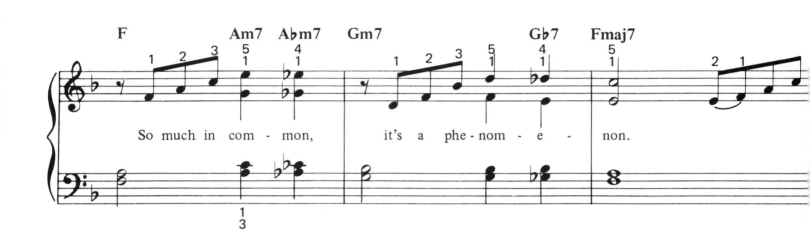

So much in com - mon, it's a phe - nom - e - non.

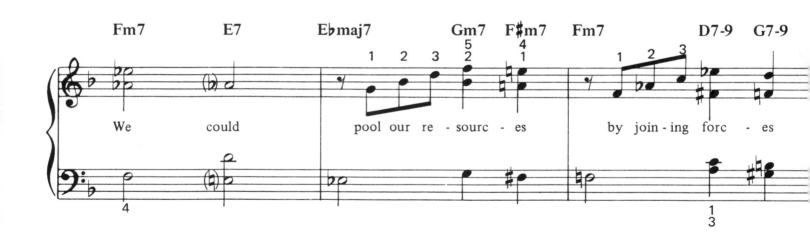

We could pool our re - sourc - es by join - ing forc - es

from now on. Luck - y you're a girl who likes chil - dren,

that's an im - port - ant sign; Luck - y, _____ 'cause I'd

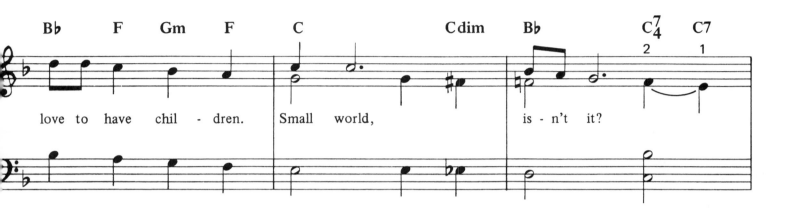

love to have chil - dren. Small world, is - n't it?

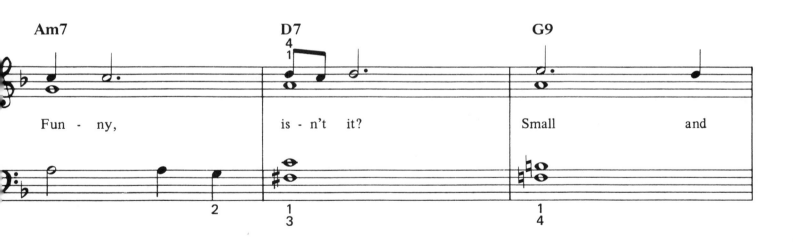

Fun - ny, is - n't it? Small and

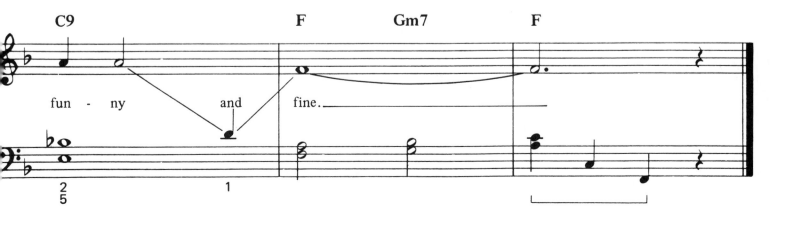

fun - ny and fine. _____

SEPTEMBER SONG

(From the Musical Play "KNICKERBOCKER HOLIDAY")

Words by MAXWELL ANDERSON
Music by KURT WEILL

Moderately Slow

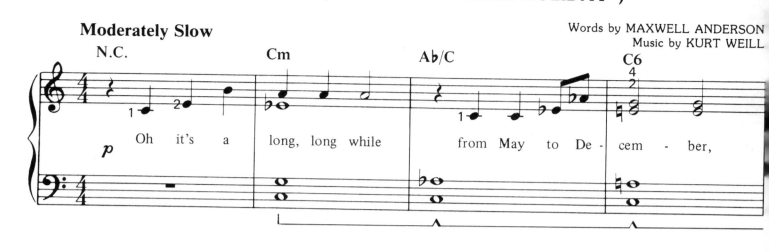

Oh it's a long, long while from May to De- cem -ber,

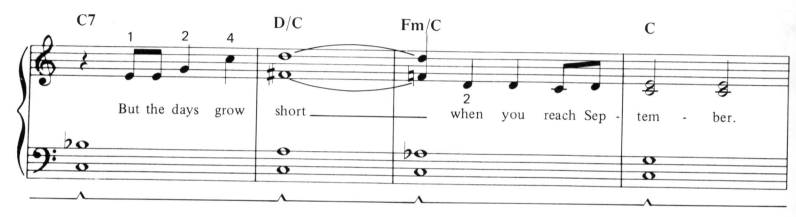

But the days grow short _____ when you reach Sep - tem - ber.

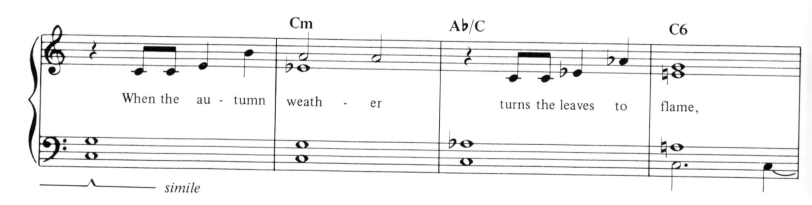

When the au -tumn weath - er turns the leaves to flame,

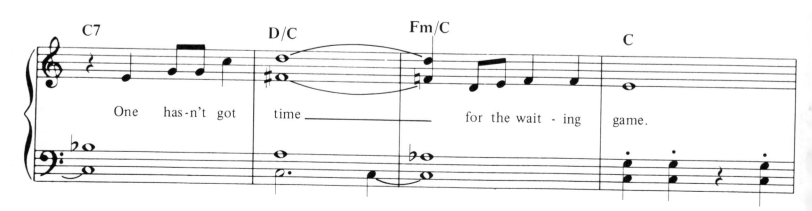

One has -n't got time _____ for the wait - ing game.

Oh, the days dwin-dle down to a pre-cious few,

Sep-tem-ber, No-vem-ber!

And these few pre-cious days I'll spend with you,

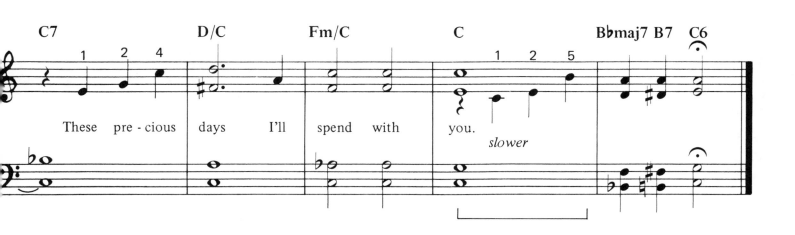

These pre-cious days I'll spend with you. *slower*

SEVENTY SIX TROMBONES

(From "THE MUSIC MAN")

By MEREDITH WILLSON

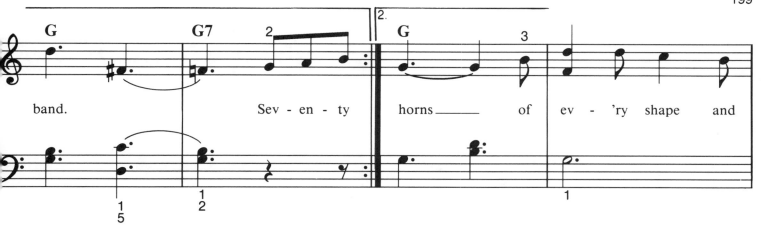

band. Sev - en - ty horns_____ of ev - 'ry shape and

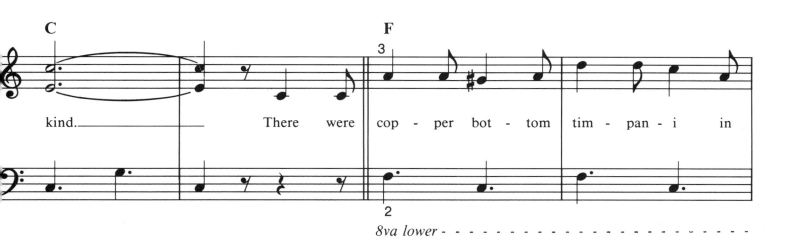

kind._____ There were cop - per bot - tom tim - pan - i in

8va lower - - - - - - - - - - - - - - - -

horse pla - toons_____ Thun - der - ing, thun - der - ing

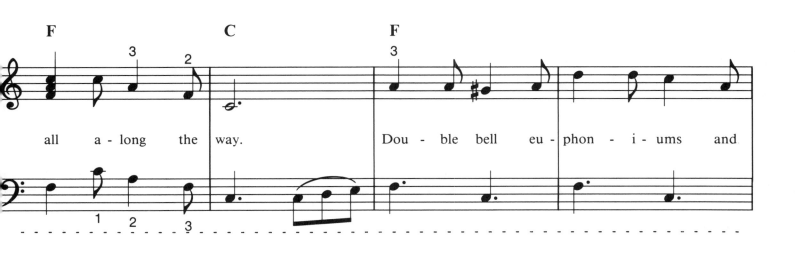

all a - long the way. Dou - ble bell eu - phon - i - ums and

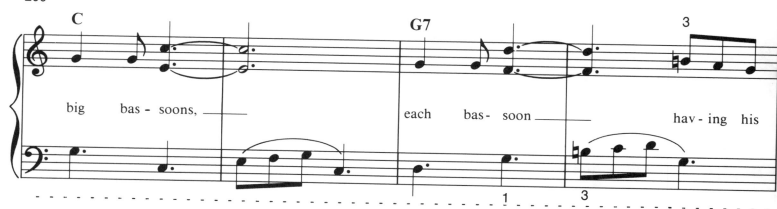

big bas - soons, _____ each bas- soon _____ hav - ing his

big fat say. There were fif - ty mount - ed can - on in the

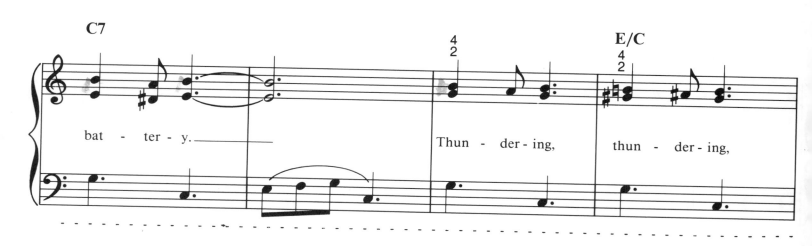

bat - ter - y. _____ Thun - der - ing, thun - der - ing,

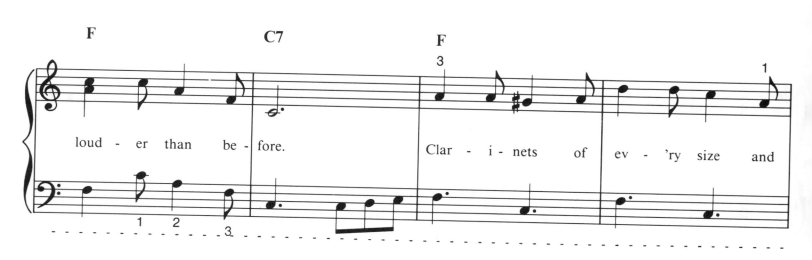

loud - er than be - fore. Clar - i - nets of ev - 'ry size and

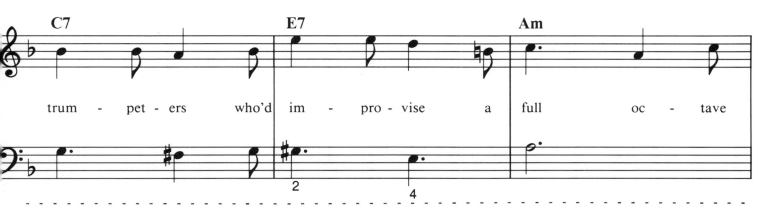

trum - pet - ers who'd im - pro - vise a full oc - tave

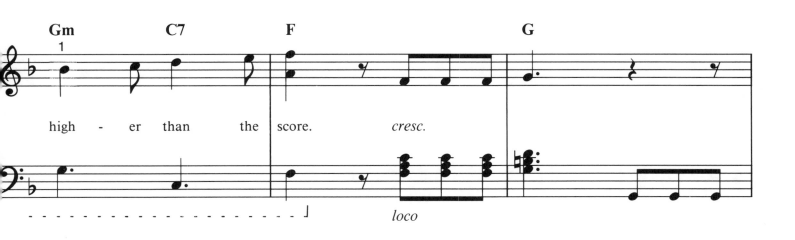

high - er than the score. *cresc.*

loco

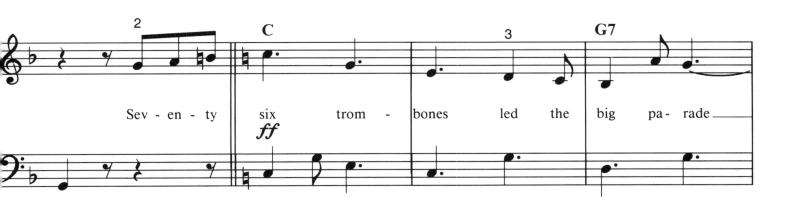

Sev - en - ty six trom - bones led the big pa - rade

ff

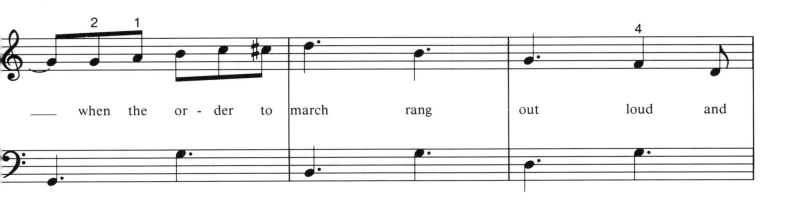

when the or - der to march rang out loud and

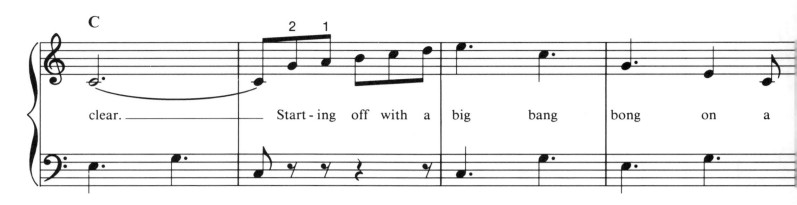

clear. Start-ing off with a big bang bong on a

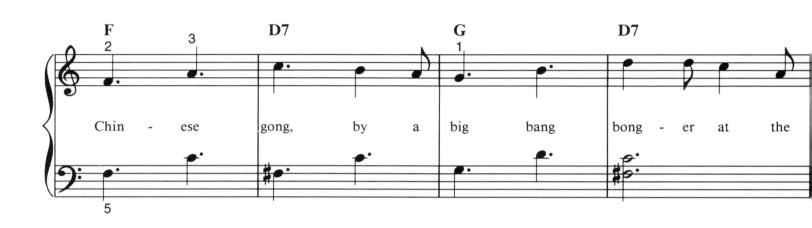

Chin - ese gong, by a big bang bong - er at the

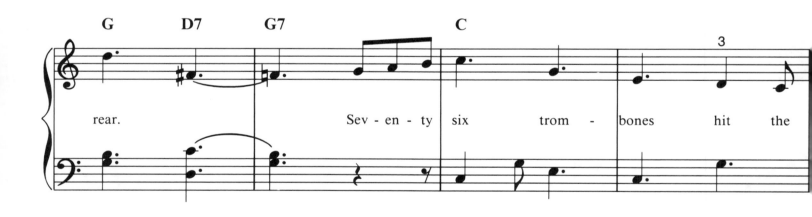

rear. Sev - en - ty six trom - bones hit the

coun - ter - point while a hun - dred and ten cor -

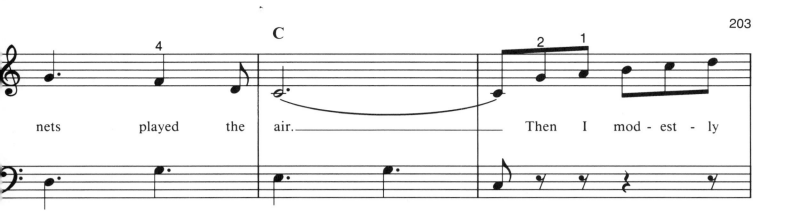

nets played the air.———— Then I mod - est - ly

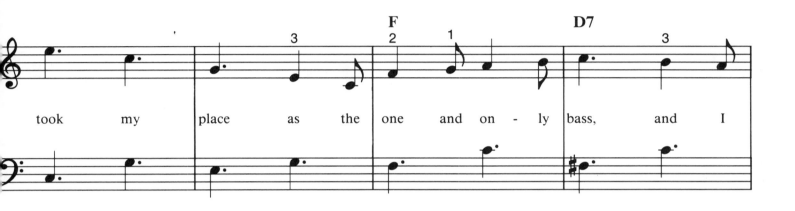

took my place as the one and on - ly bass, and I

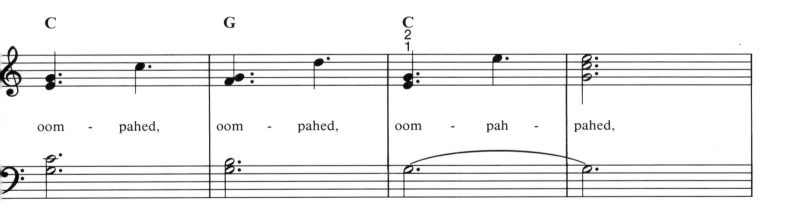

oom - pahed, oom - pahed, oom - pah - pahed,

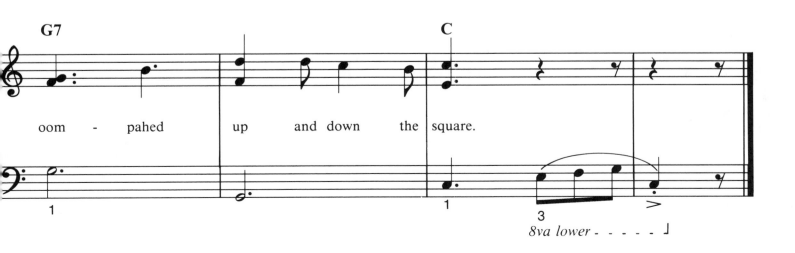

oom - pahed up and down the square.

8va lower - - - - - ⌐

SMOKE GETS IN YOUR EYES

(From "ROBERTA")

Words by OTTO HARBACH
Music by JEROME KERN

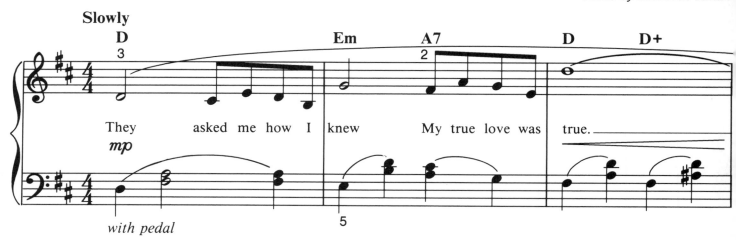

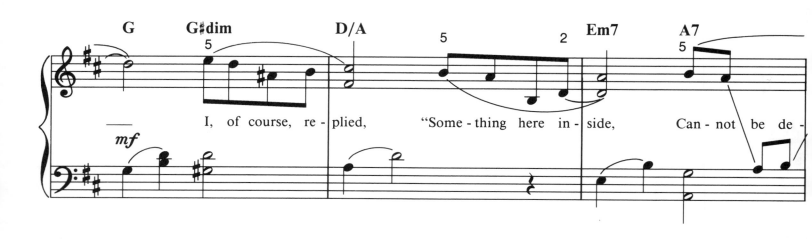

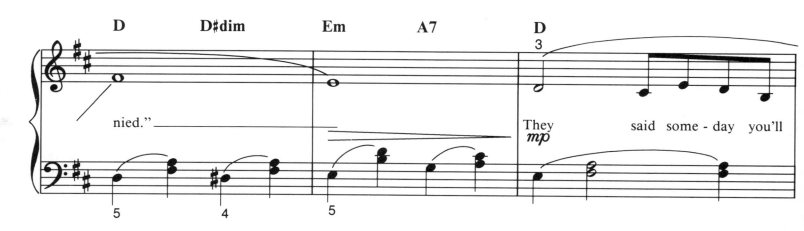

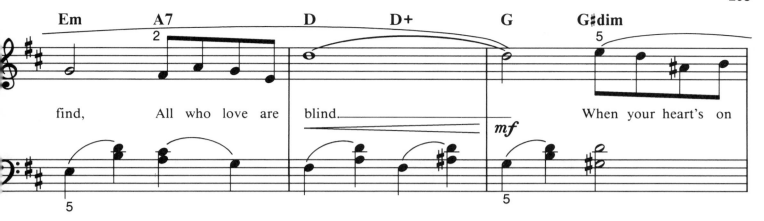

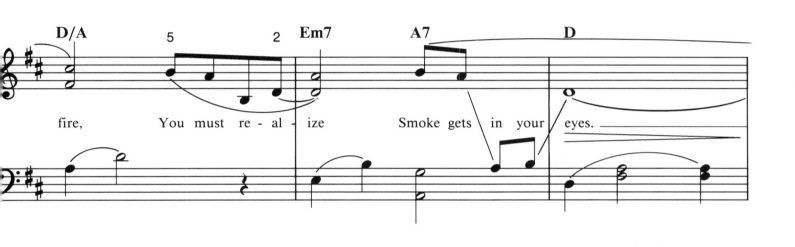

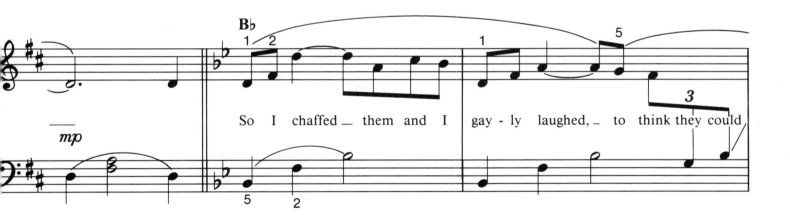

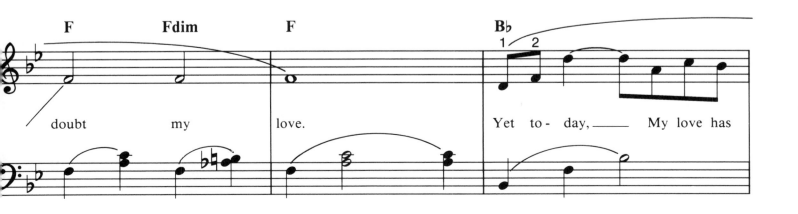

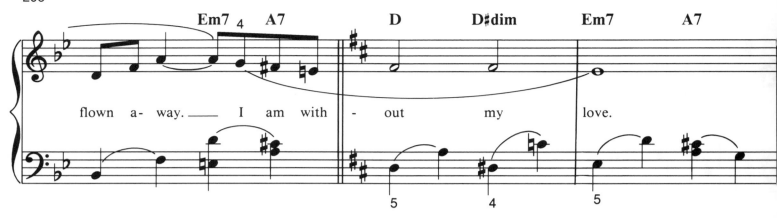

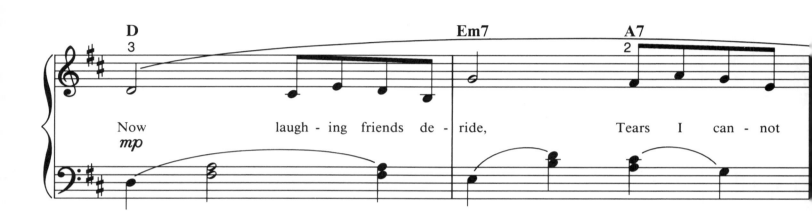

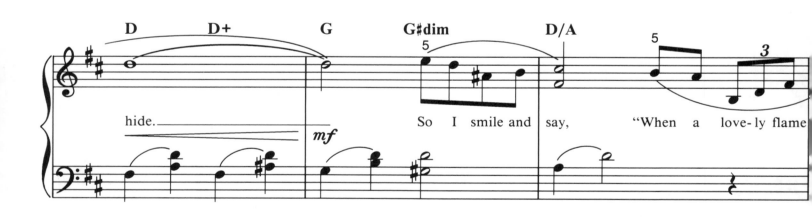

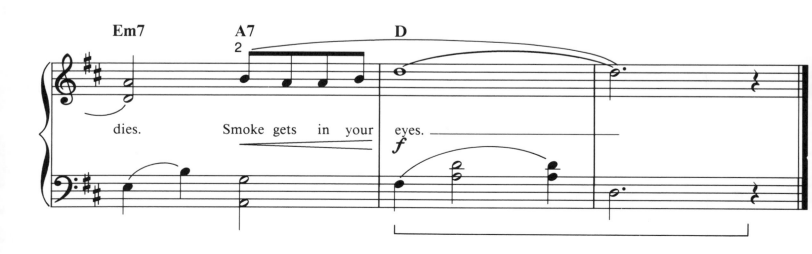

THE SOUND OF MUSIC
(From "THE SOUND OF MUSIC")

Lyrics by OSCAR HAMMERSTEIN II
Music by RICHARD RODGERS

song it hears._____ My heart wants to beat like the wings of the

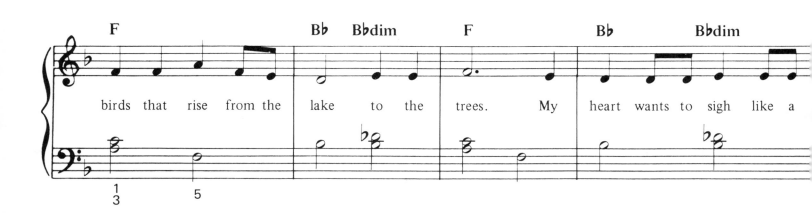

birds that rise from the lake to the trees. My heart wants to sigh like a

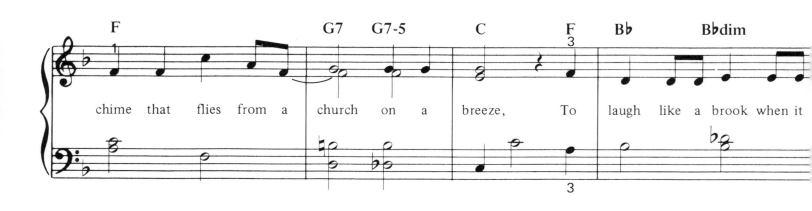

chime that flies from a church on a breeze, To laugh like a brook when it

trips and falls o-ver stones on its way, To sing through the night like a

lark who is learn-ing to pray. I go to the hills when my heart is

lone - ly, _____ I know I will hear what I've heard be -

fore. _____ My heart will be blessed with the sound of mu - sic,

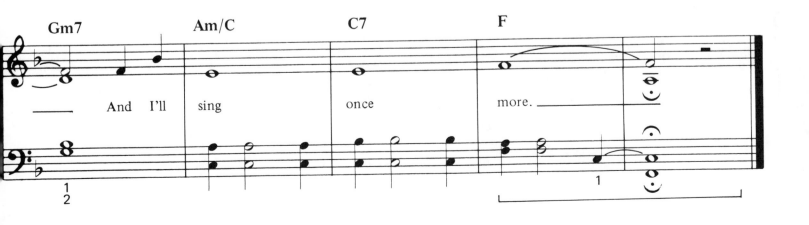

_____ And I'll sing once more. _____

SOME ENCHANTED EVENING
(From "SOUTH PACIFIC")

Lyrics by OSCAR HAMMERSTEIN II
Music by RICHARD RODGERS

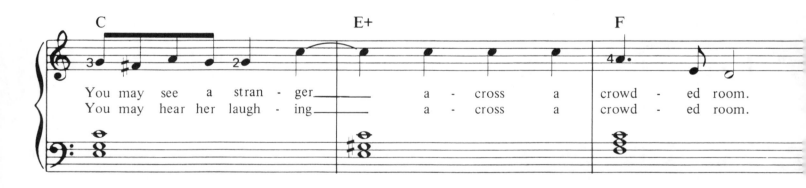

then____ that some - where you'll see her a -
seems____ the sound of her laugh - her will

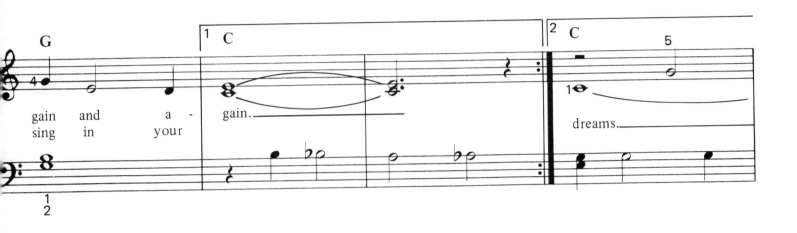

gain and a - gain.____
sing in your

dreams.____

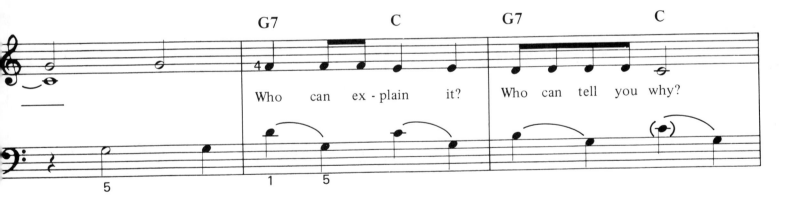

Who can ex - plain it? Who can tell you why?

Fools give you rea - sons, wise men nev - er try.____

Some en-chant-ed eve - ning

when you find your true love,— when you feel her call you—

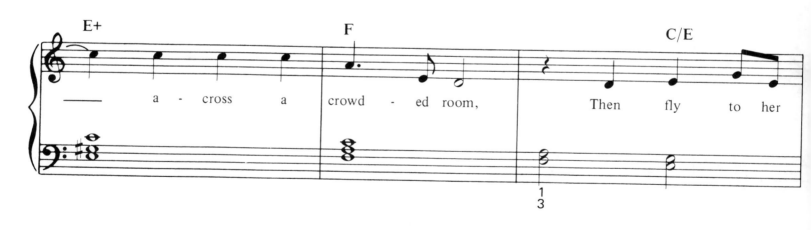

a - cross a crowd - ed room, Then fly to her

side and make her your own—

or all through your life you may dream all a -

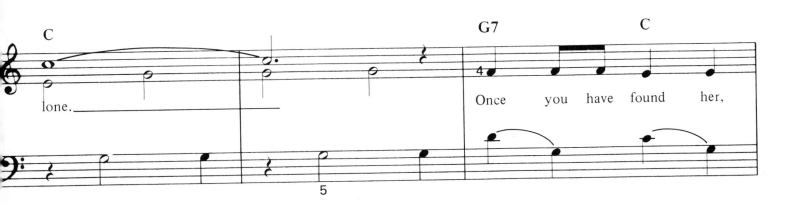

lone._____ Once you have found her,

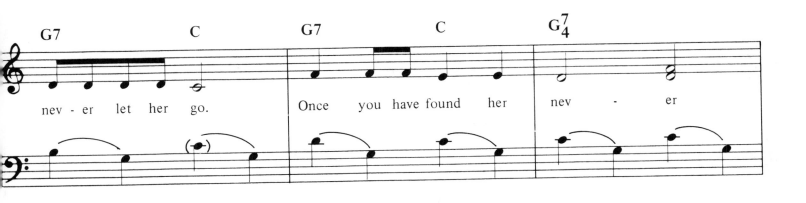

nev - er let her go. Once you have found her nev - er

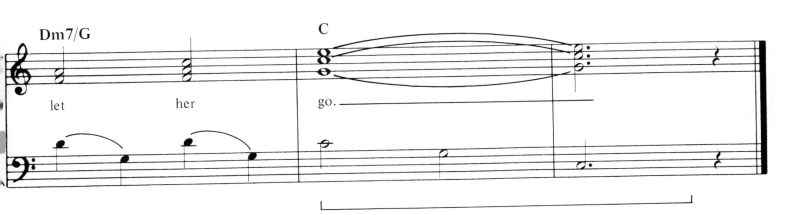

let her go. _____

SUNRISE, SUNSET
(From the Musical "FIDDLER ON THE ROOF")

Words by SHELDON HARNICK
Music by JERRY BOCK

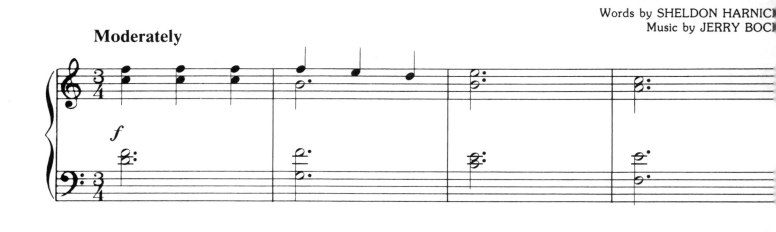

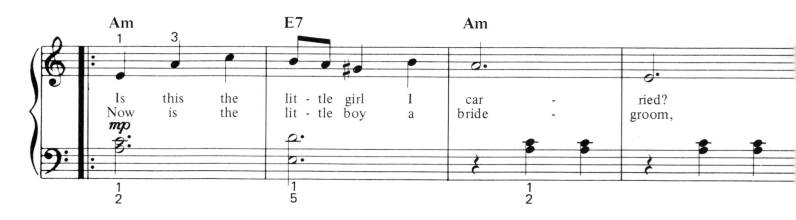

- mem-ber grow - ing
- can - o - py I

old see - er, them

When Side did by

they?____
side.____

When did she
Place the gold

get to be a
ring a - round her

beau -
fin -

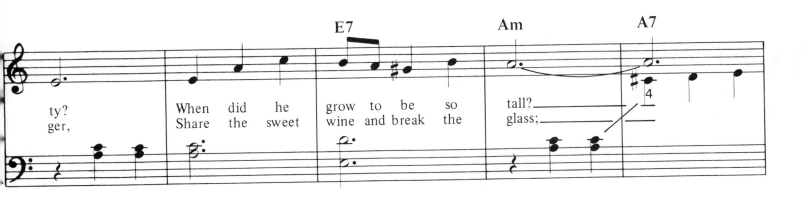

ty?
ger,

When did he
Share the sweet

grow to be so
wine and break the

tall?____
glass;____

Was - n't it
Soon the full

yes - ter - day when
cir - cle will when have

they
come

were
to

small?____
pass.____

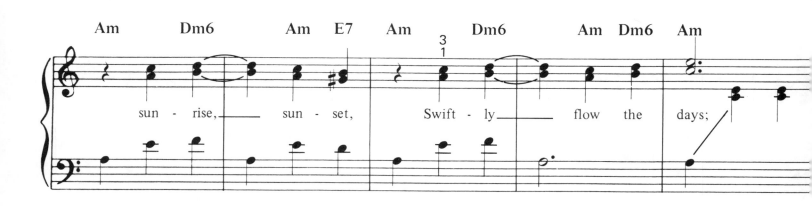

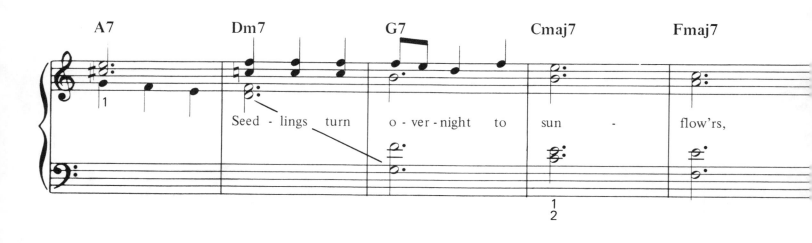

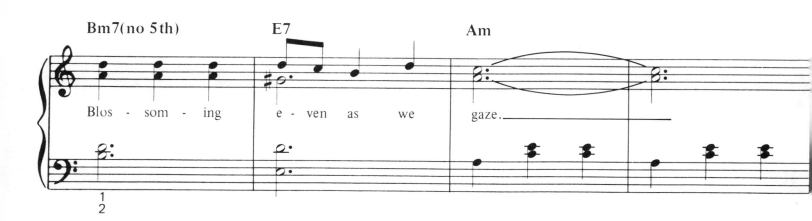

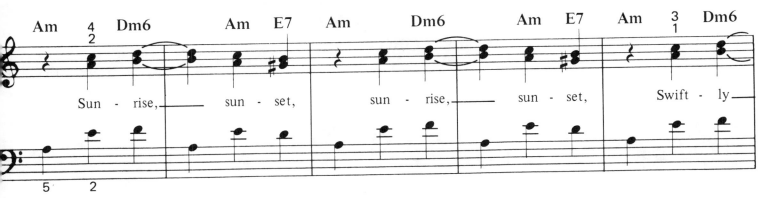

Sun - rise,___ sun - set, sun - rise,___ sun - set, Swift - ly

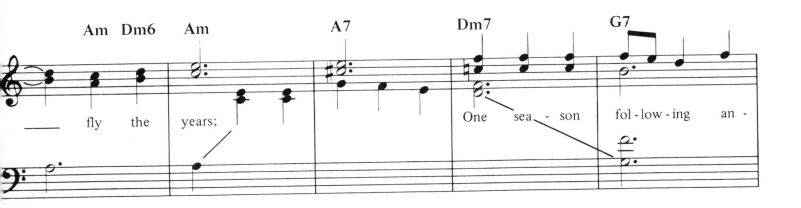

___ fly the years; One sea - son fol - low - ing an -

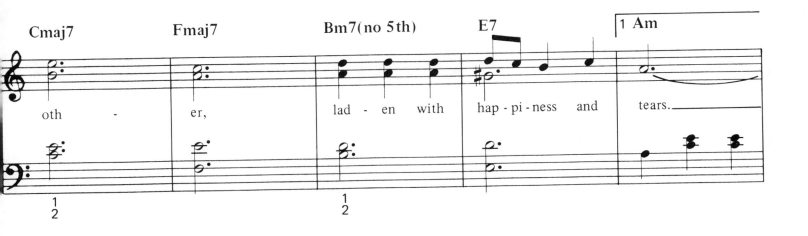

oth - er, lad - en with hap - pi - ness and tears.___

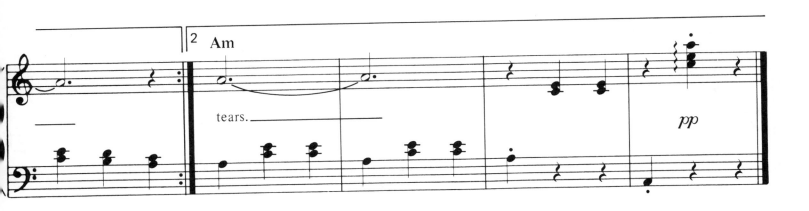

tears.___

SUMMERTIME

(From "PORGY AND BESS")

Words by DuBOSE HEYWARD
Music by GEORGE GERSHWIN

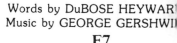

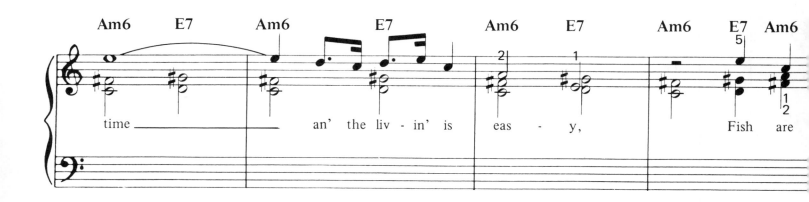

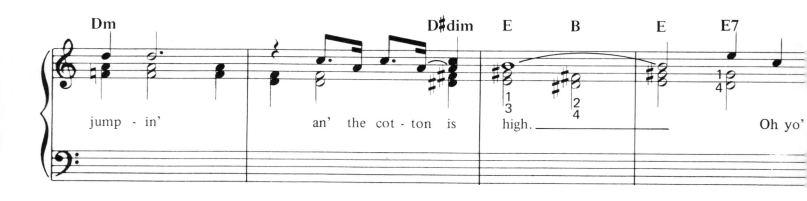

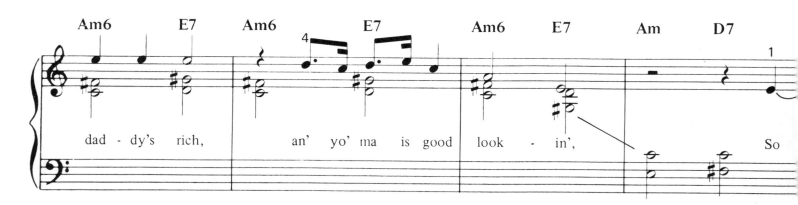

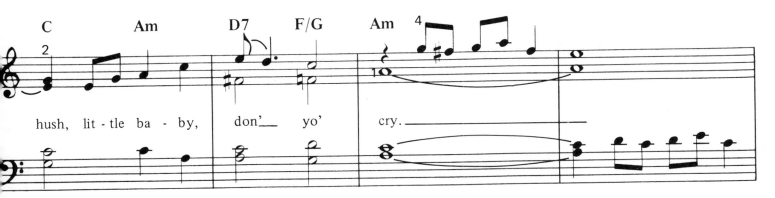

hush, lit - tle ba - by, don'___ yo' cry. _____

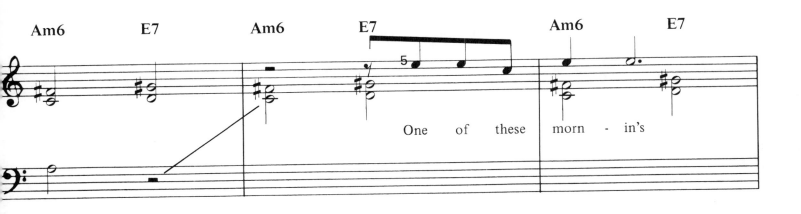

One of these morn - in's

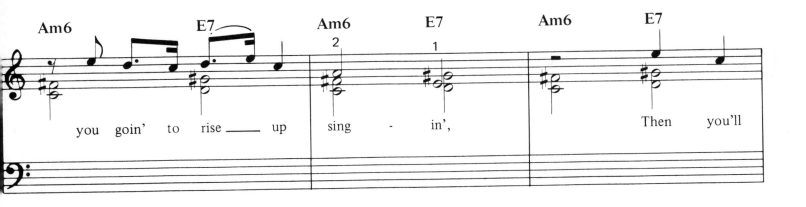

you goin' to rise ___ up sing - in', Then you'll

spread yo' wings an' you'll take ___ the sky. _____

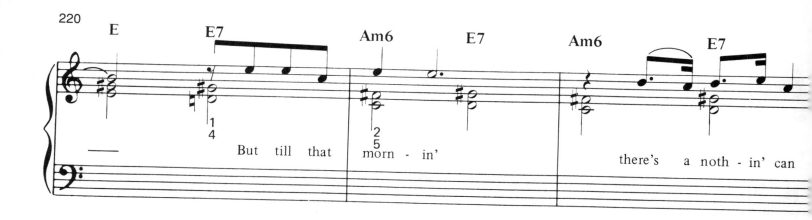

But till that morn - in'

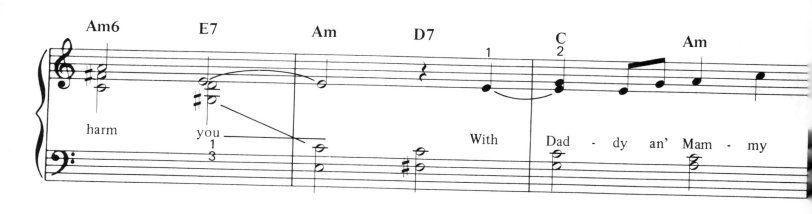

harm you   With Dad - dy an' Mam - my

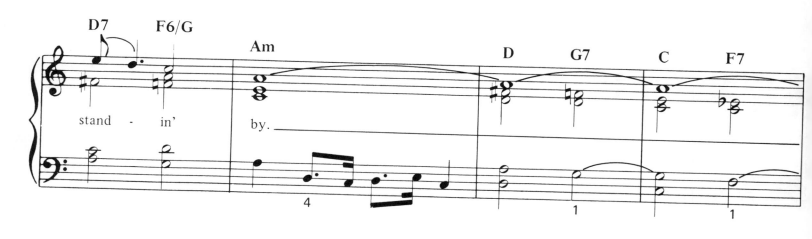

stand - in'   by.

THIS NEARLY WAS MINE

(From "SOUTH PACIFIC")

Lyrics by OSCAR HAMMERSTEIN II
Music by RICHARD RODGERS

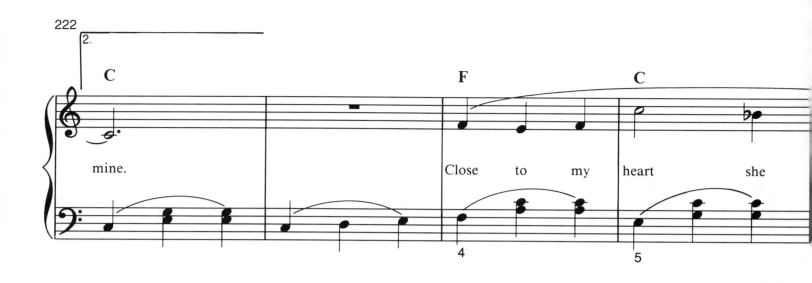

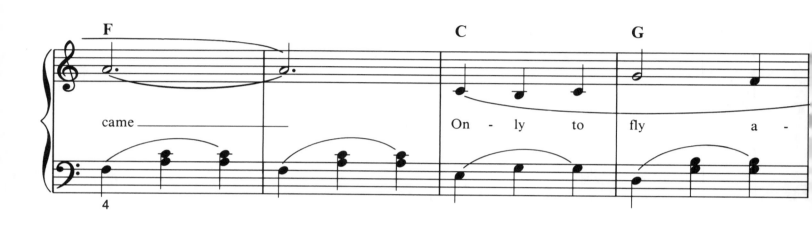

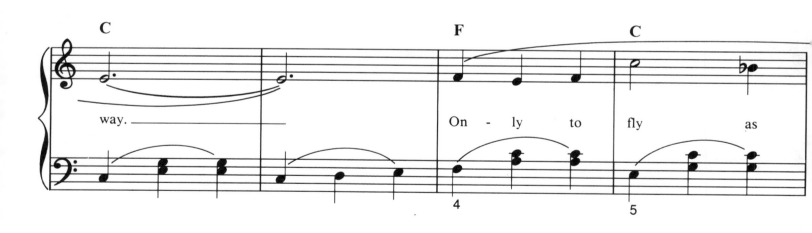

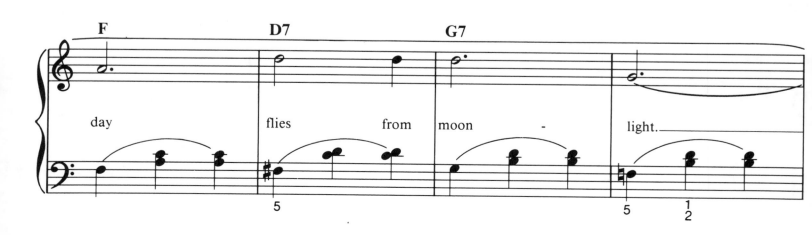

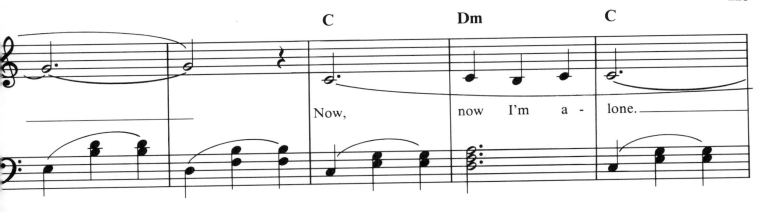

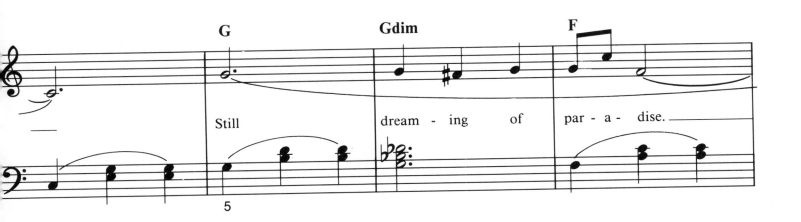

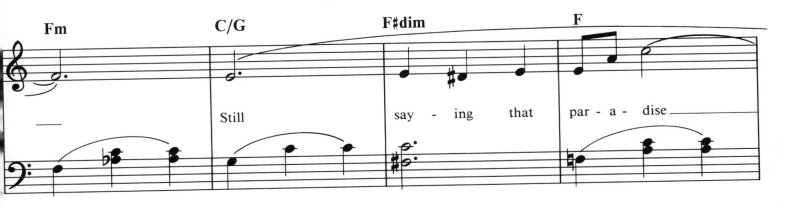

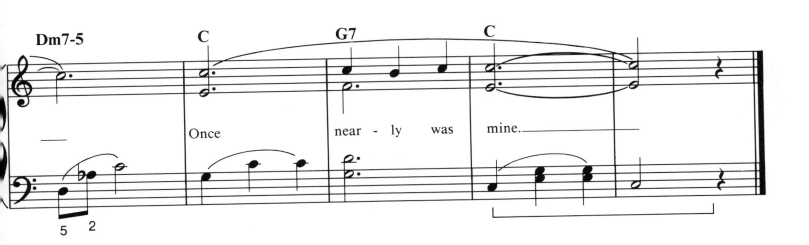

TRY TO REMEMBER
(From "THE FANTASTICKS")

Words by TOM JONES
Music by HARVEY SCHMIDT

Slowly, with tenderness

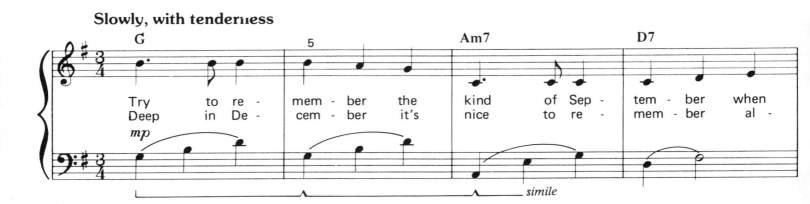

Try to re- | member the | kind of Sep- | tem- ber when
Deep in De- | cem- ber it's | nice to re- | mem- ber al-

life | was | slow and | oh, so | mel-low.___ | Try to re-
tho' | was you | know the | snow will | fol-low.___ | Deep in De-

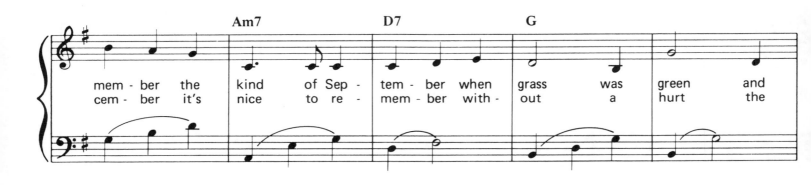

mem- ber the | kind of Sep- | tem- ber when | grass was a | green and
cem- ber it's | nice to re- | mem- ber with- | out a | hurt the

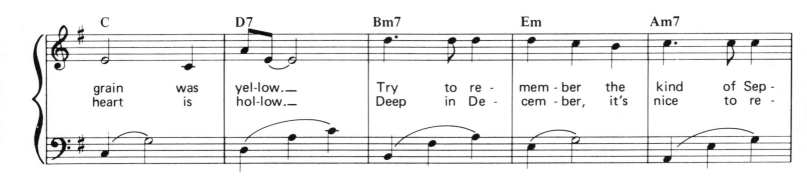

grain | was yel-low.___ | Try to re- | mem- ber the | kind of Sep-
heart | is hol-low.___ | Deep in De- | cem- ber, it's | nice to re-

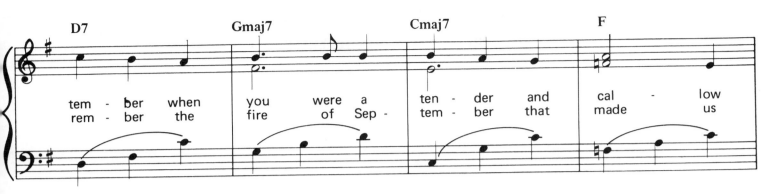

D7   **Gmaj7**   **Cmaj7**   **F**

tem - ber when / you were a / ten - der and / cal - low
rem - ber the / fire of Sep - / tem - ber that / made us

D7   **G**   **Am7**

fel-low.__ / Try to re - / mem - ber and / if you re -
mel-low.__ / Deep in De - / cem - ber our / hearts should re -

D7   **G**   **C**

mem - ber, then / fol-low.__ } / Fol- low, fol - low, / fol - low, fol - low, fol - low,
mem - ber and / fol-low.__ }

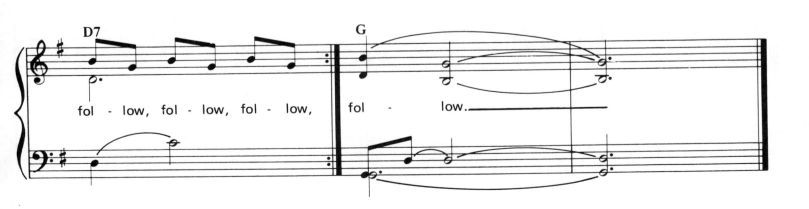

D7   **G**

fol - low, fol - low, fol - low, / fol - low._____

TILL THERE WAS YOU

(From "THE MUSIC MAN")

By MEREDITH WILLSON

Moderately

p

Cmaj7

There were bells   on the
mp

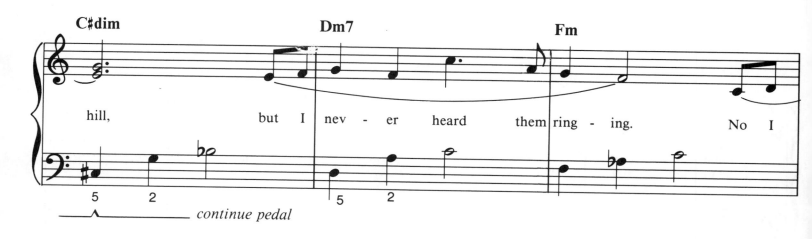

C#dim   **Dm7**   **Fm**

hill,   but I nev - er heard them ring - ing.   No I

continue pedal

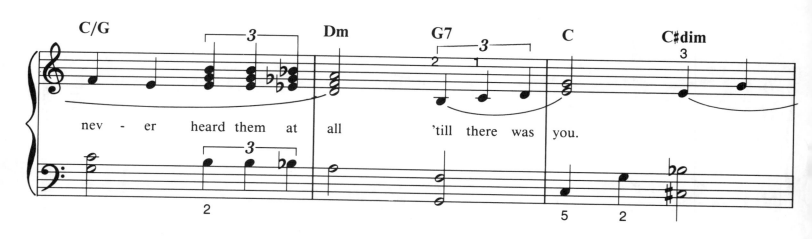

C/G   **Dm**   **G7**   **C**   **C#dim**

nev - er heard them at all   'till there was you.

There were birds in the sky, but I

nev - er saw them wing - ing, No, I nev - er saw them at

all, till there was you. And there was
cresc.

mu - sic and there were won - der - ful ro - ses, they

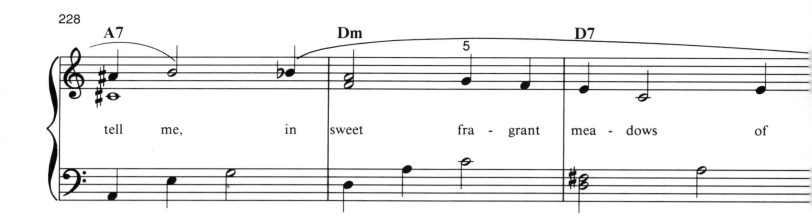

tell me, in sweet fra - grant mea - dows of

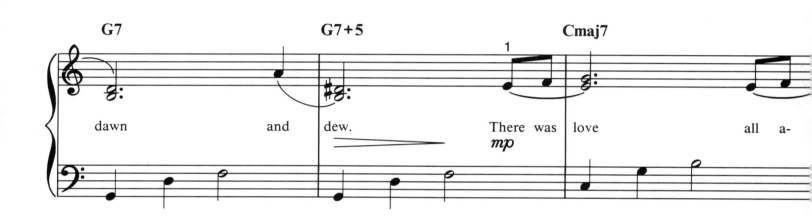

dawn and dew. There was love all a-

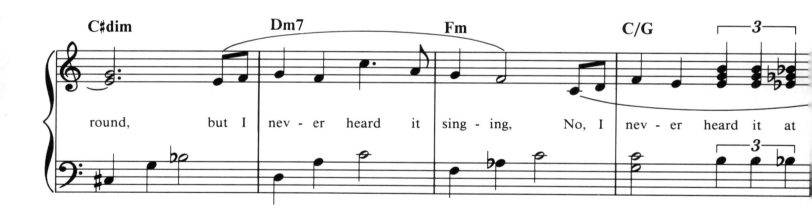

round, but I nev - er heard it sing - ing, No, I nev - er heard it at

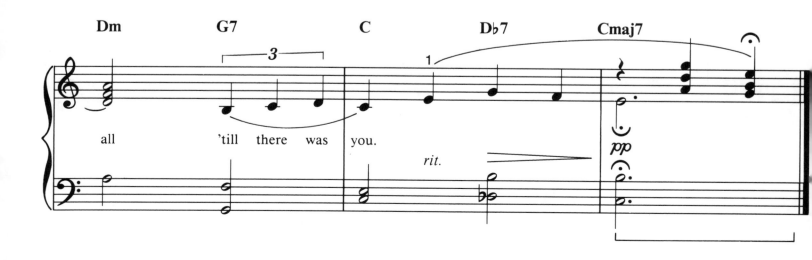

all 'till there was you.

UNEXPECTED SONG
(From "SONG AND DANCE")

Music by ANDREW LLOYD WEBBER
Lyrics by DON BLACK

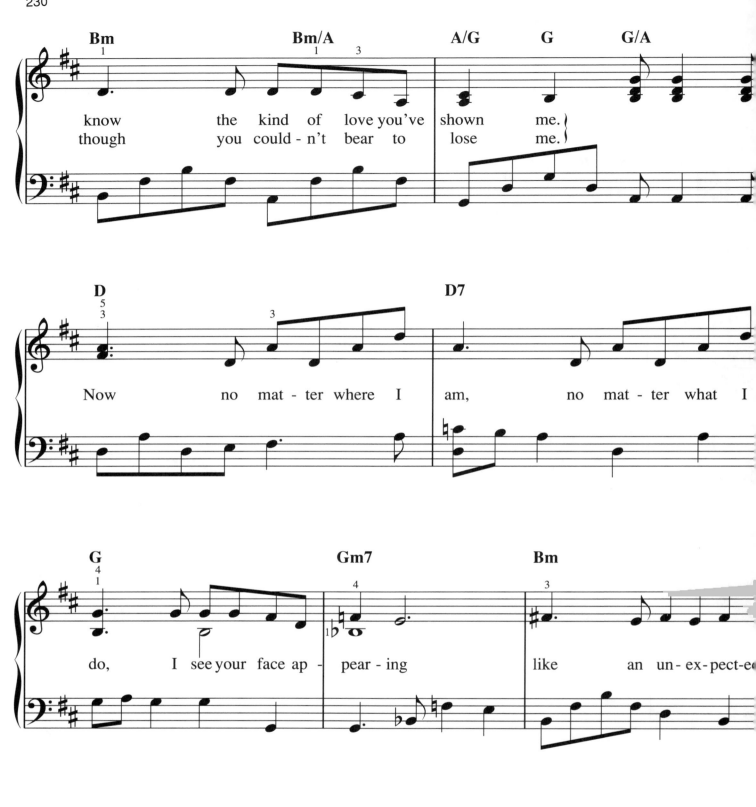

WHAT KIND OF FOOL AM I?

(From the Musical Production "STOP THE WORLD - I WANT TO GET OFF")

Words and Music by LESLIE BRICUSSE
and ANTHONY NEWLEY

Moderately slow

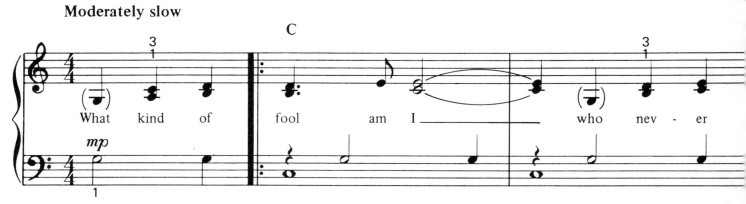

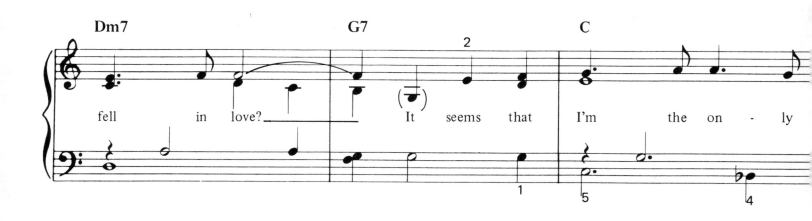

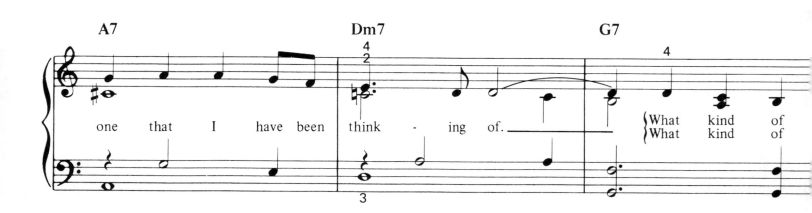

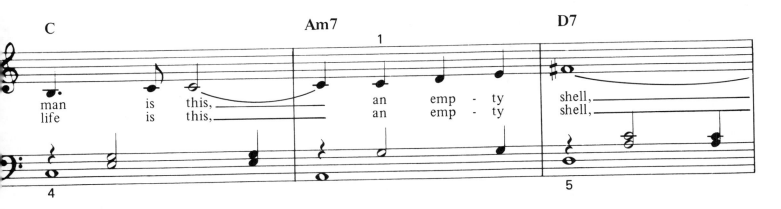

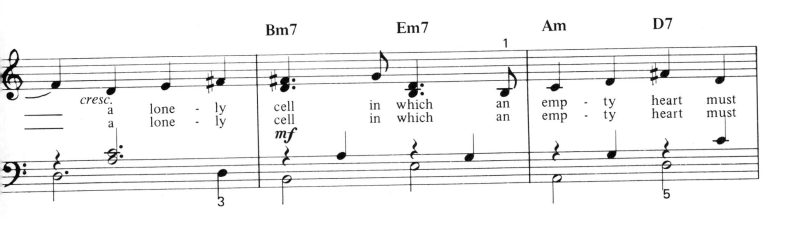

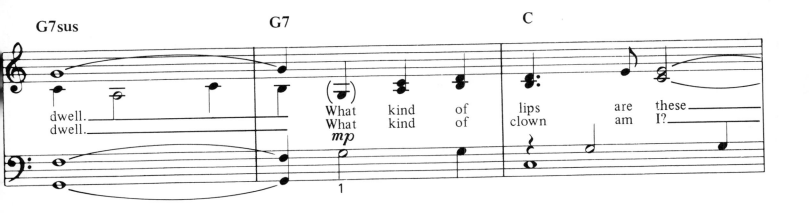

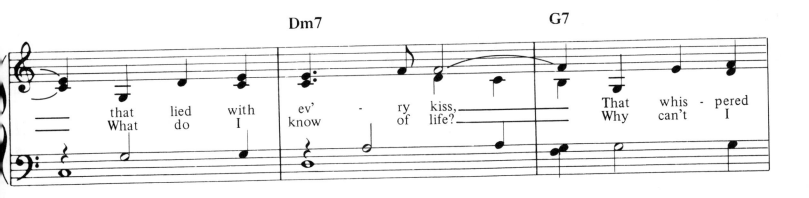

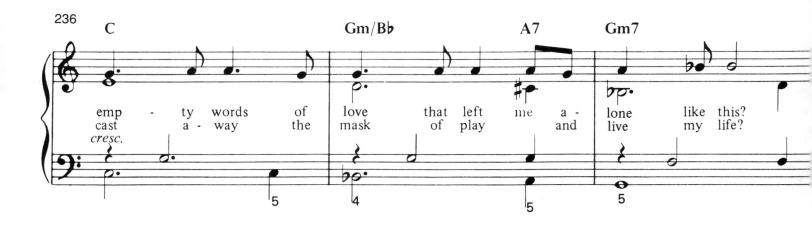

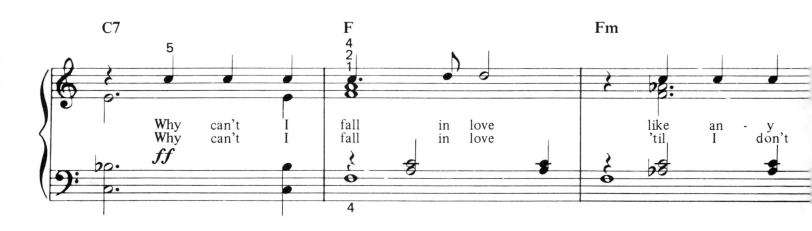

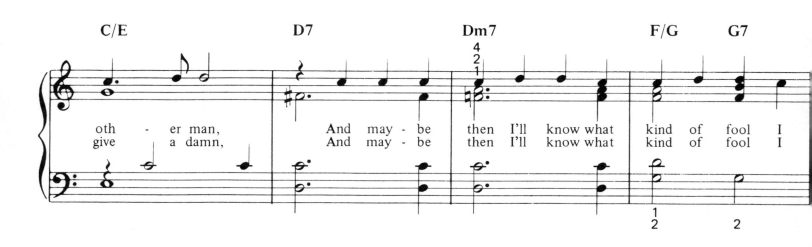

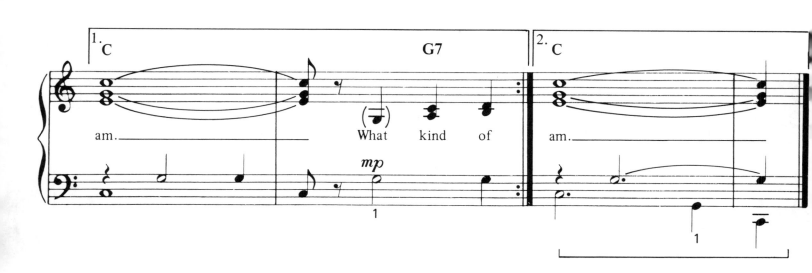

WHERE OR WHEN

(From "BABES IN ARMS")

Words by LORENZ HART
Music by RICHARD RODGERS

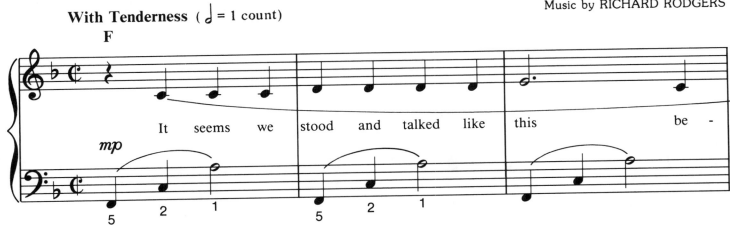

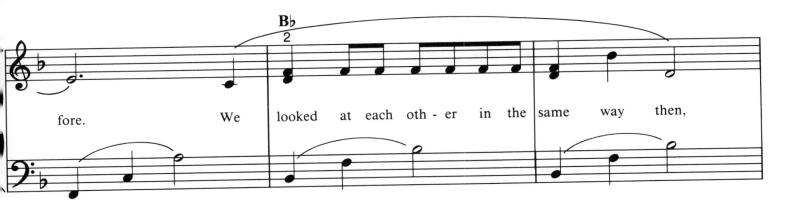

The clothes you're wear-ing are the clothes you

wore. The smile you are smil-ing you were smil-ing then,

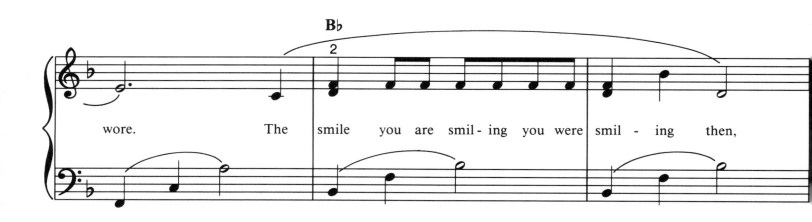

But I can't re-mem-ber where or when.

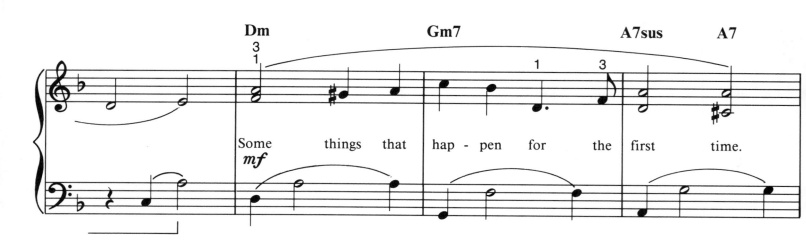

Some things that hap-pen for the first time.

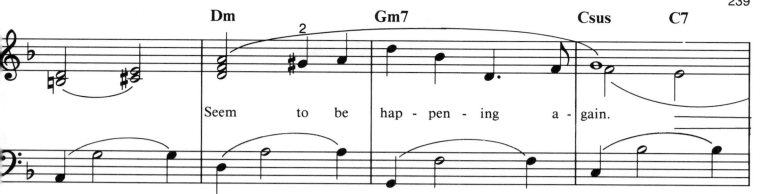

Seem   to   be   hap - pen - ing   a - gain.

mp And   so   it   seems that   we   have   met   be -

fore,   and   laughed   be - fore,   and   loved   be - fore,   But
cresc.   *sempre cresc.*

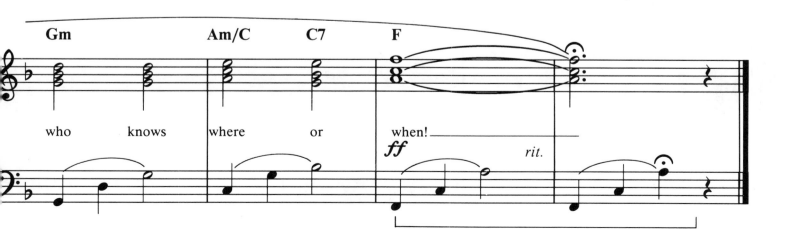

who   knows   where   or   when!
ff   *rit.*

WOULDN'T IT BE LOVERLY

(From "MY FAIR LADY")

Words by ALAN JAY LERNER
Music by FREDERICK LOEWE

With a Graceful Lilt

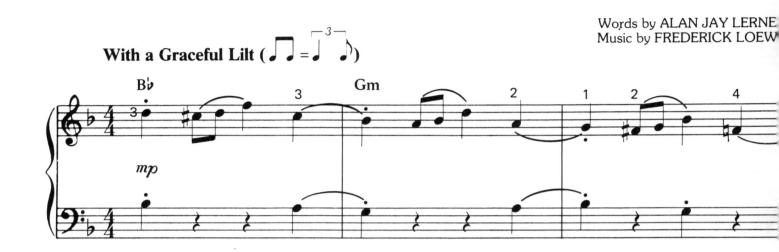

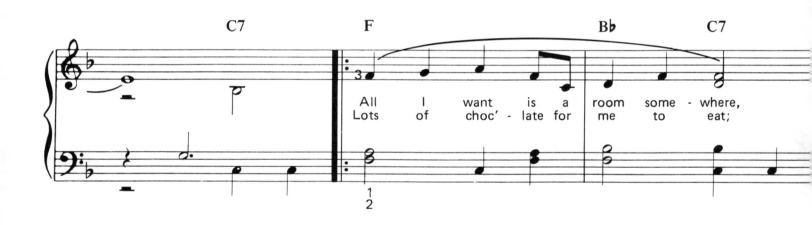

All I want is a room some - where,
Lots of choc' - late for me to eat;

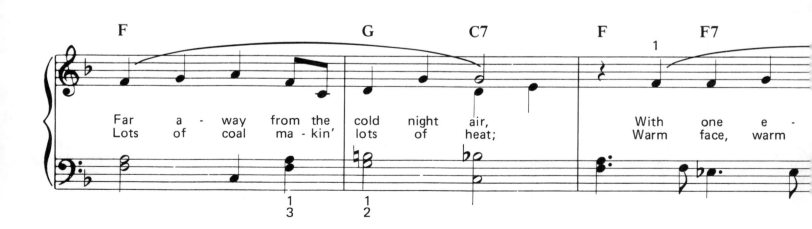

Far a - way from the cold night air,
Lots of coal ma - kin' lots of heat;

With one e -
Warm face, warm

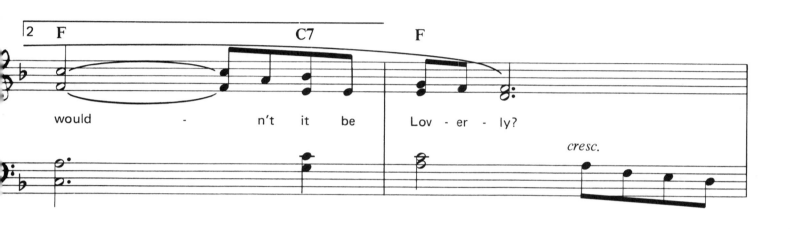

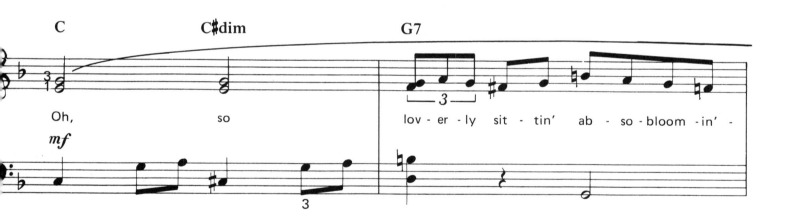

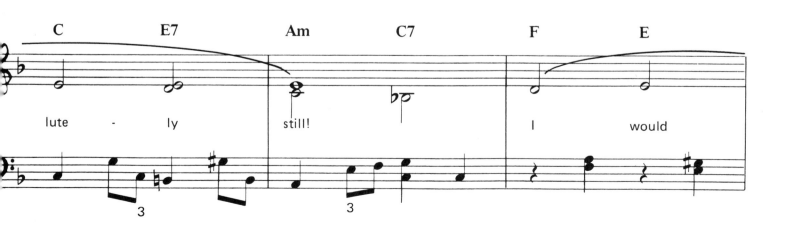

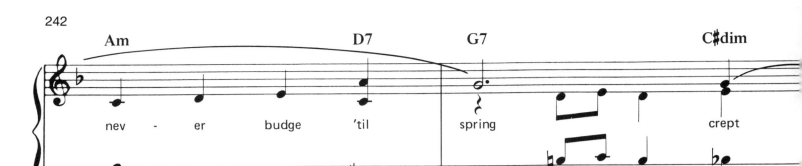

nev - er budge 'til spring crept

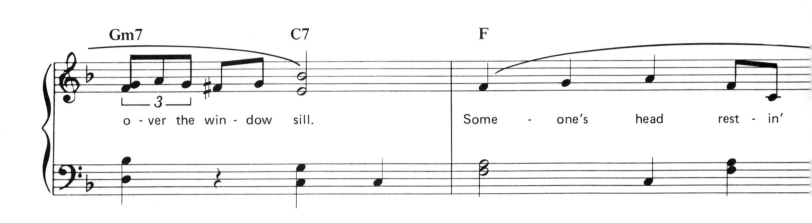

o - ver the win - dow sill. Some - one's head rest - in'

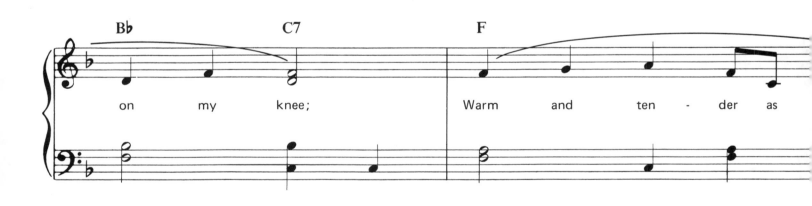

on my knee; Warm and ten - der as

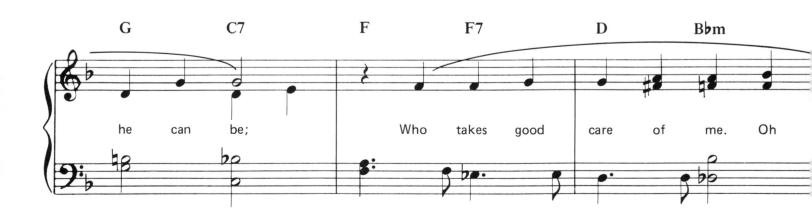

he can be; Who takes good care of me. Oh

would - n't   it   be

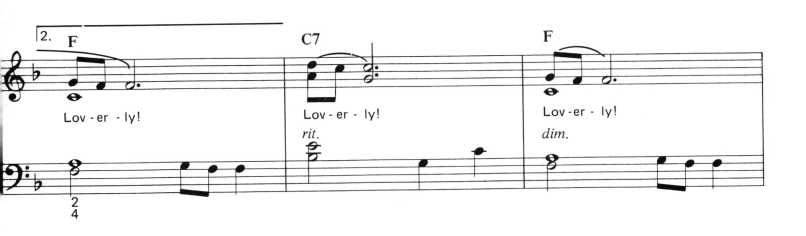

1. Lov - er - ly?

2. Lov - er - ly!   Lov - er - ly!   Lov - er - ly!

rit.   *dim.*

Lov - er - ly!   Lov - er - ly!

p

8va

WHO CAN I TURN TO

(When Nobody Needs Me)

(From the Musical Production "THE ROAR OF THE GREASEPAINT — The Smell Of The Crowd")

Words and Music by LESLIE BRICUSSE
and ANTHONY NEWLEY

Slowly with expression

Who can I turn to when no-bod-y needs me? My heart wants to know and so I must go where des-ti-ny leads me. With no star to guide me and

no one be-side me,_____ I'll go on my way and

af - ter the day the dark - ness will hide me._____ And

may - be to-mor - row_____ I'll find what I'm af - ter,_____

I'll throw off my sor - row, beg steal or bor - row

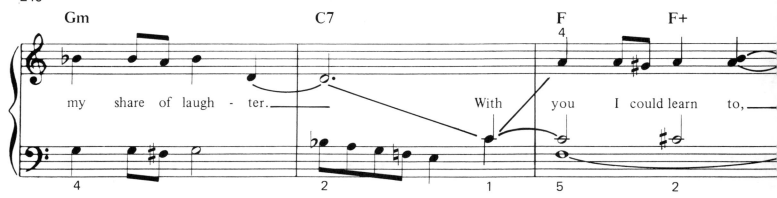

my share of laugh - ter.____ With you I could learn to,____

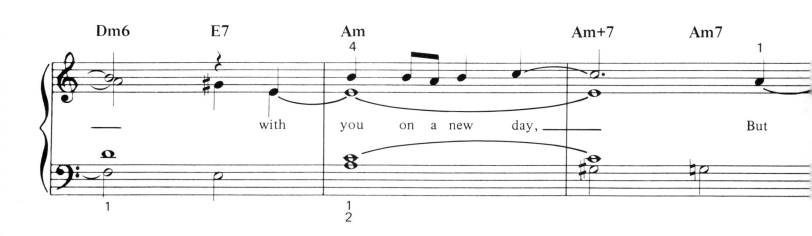

____ with you on a new day,____ But

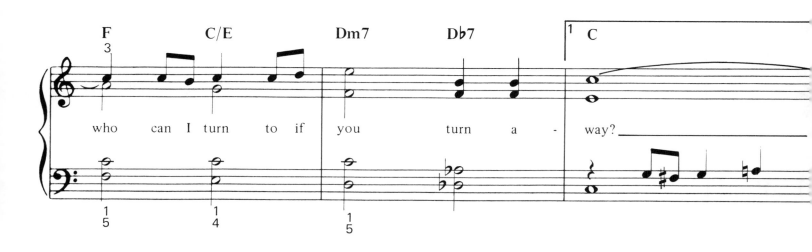

who can I turn to if you turn a - way?____

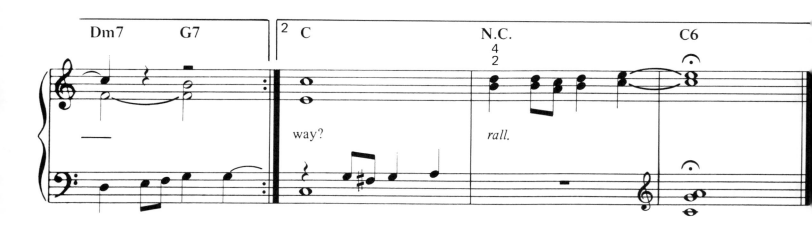

____ way? rall.

YOU'LL NEVER WALK ALONE

(From "CAROUSEL")

Lyrics by OSCAR HAMMERSTEIN II
Music by RICHARD RODGERS

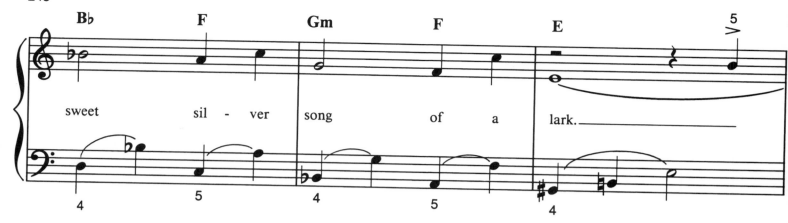

Bb … **F** … **Gm** … **F** … **E**

sweet sil - ver song of a lark.

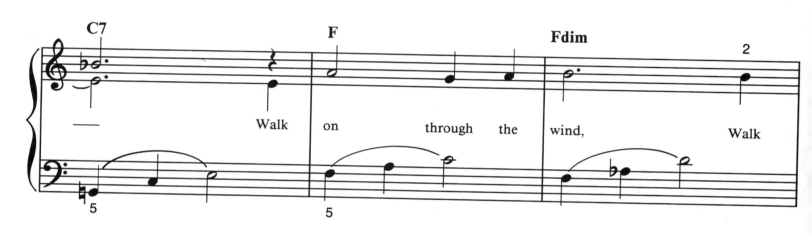

C7 … **F** … **Fdim**

Walk on through the wind, Walk

C/E … **Fm6** … **C**

on through the rain, Tho' your dreams be

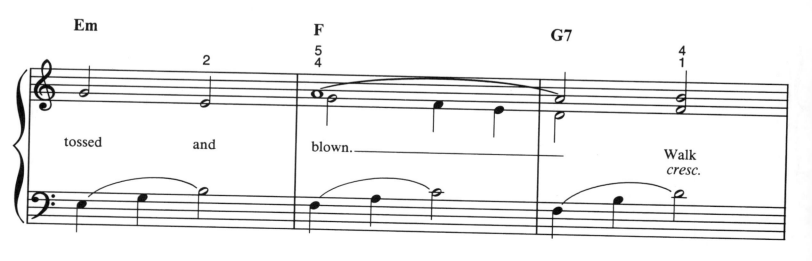

Em … **F** … **G7**

tossed and blown. Walk
cresc.

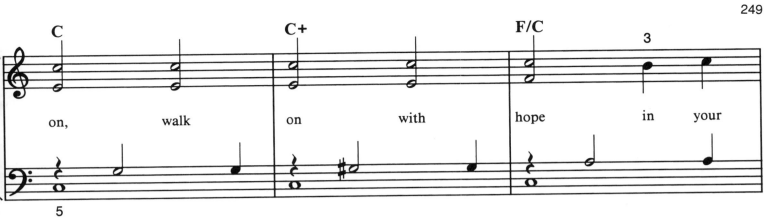

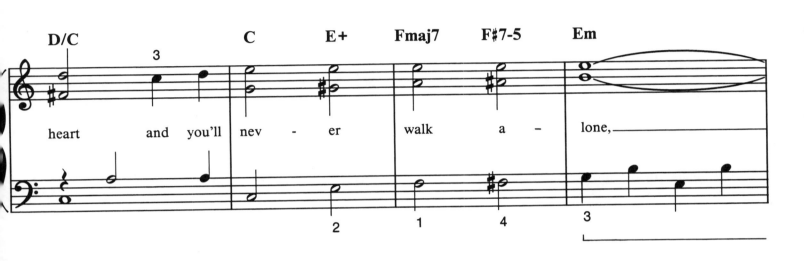

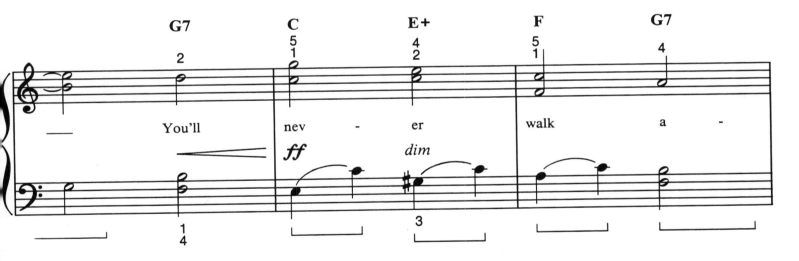

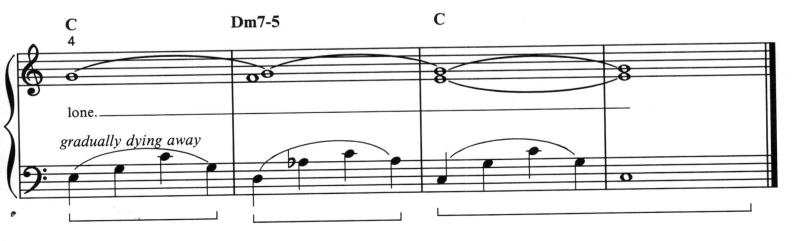

YOUNGER THAN SPRINGTIME

(From "SOUTH PACIFIC")

Lyrics by OSCAR HAMMERSTEIN
Music by RICHARD RODGER

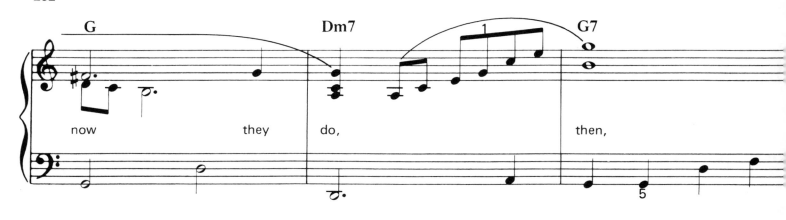

now   they   do,   then,

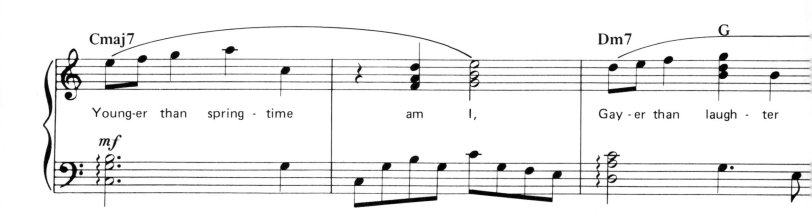

Young-er than spring - time   am I,   Gay -er than laugh - ter

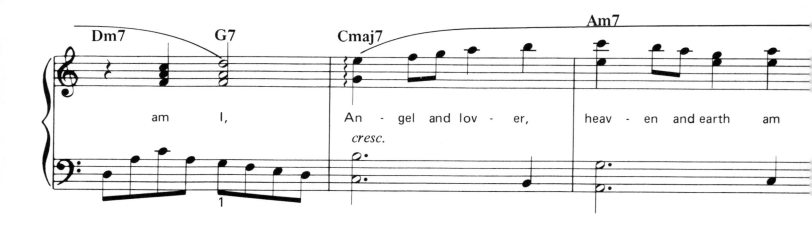

am I,   An - gel and lov - er,   heav - en and earth   am

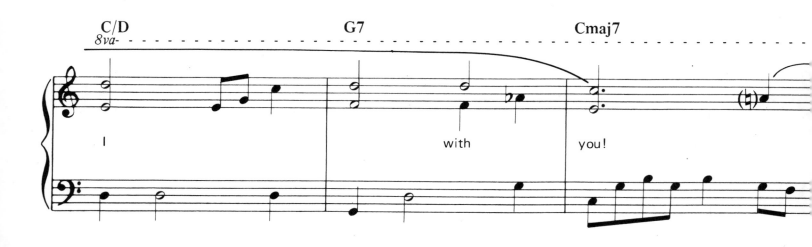

I   with   you!

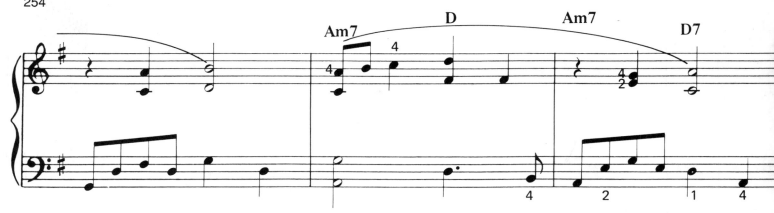

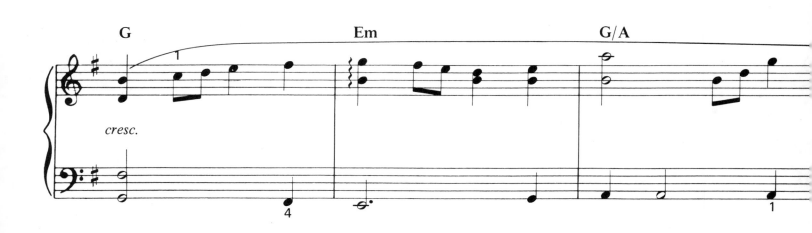

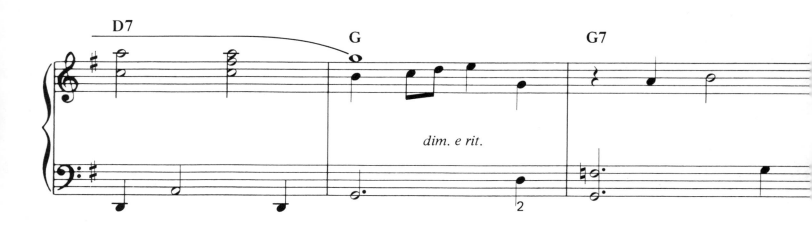

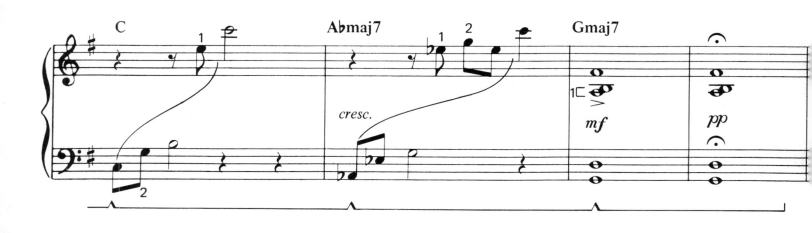